CRIME AND INVESTIGATIVE REPORTING IN THE UK

Marianne Colbran

First published in Great Britain in 2022 by

Policy Press, an imprint of
Bristol University Press
University of Bristol
1–9 Old Park Hill
Bristol
BS2 8BB
UK
t: +44 (0)117 374 6645
e: bup-info@bristol.ac.uk

Details of international sales and distribution partners are available at
policy.bristoluniversitypress.co.uk

ISBN 978-1-4473-5890-9 hardcover
ISBN 978-1-4473-5892-3 ePub
ISBN 978-1-4473-5893-0 ePdf

Cover design: Hayes Design and Advertising
Front cover image: Shutterstock/Claudio Rozante
Bristol University Press and Policy Press use environmentally responsible
print partners.
Printed in Great Britain by CPI Group (UK) Ltd, Croydon, CR0 4YY

To Melony and Rupert

Contents

List of figures

Acknowledgements

First and foremost, many thanks to the journalists, the press officers and senior police officers who very kindly agreed to be interviewed and who, in very many cases, gave up several hours of their time to speak with me. For obvious reasons, I cannot name any of you but without your help and insights, this book would never have been written.

Many thanks to the Mannheim Centre at the London School of Economics and Political Science and to Dr Leonidas Cheliotis for continuing to support my visiting fellowship at the School. Many thanks as well to friends and colleagues at the Centre for their support, particularly Professor Paul Rock, Professor Frances Heidensohn and Dr Janet Foster. Special thanks go to Professor Paul Rock for numerous readings of my drafts and for his wisdom and insight, and also to Dr Justin Ellis at the University of Newcastle for his invaluable comments and help in steering me towards a final draft.

Many thanks to the three anonymous peer reviewers for my publisher, Bristol University Press, who provided detailed comments on my initial outline and on an earlier draft and whose kind and thoughtful insights were of great assistance. Many thanks to Helen Davis and Rebecca Tomlinson at Bristol University Press for championing the project and showing such enthusiasm right from the outset. A version of Chapter 5 was originally published in 2020 as 'Policing, social media and the new media landscape: Can the police and the traditional media ever successfully bypass each other?', *Policing and Society*, 30(3): 295–309.

Many thanks are due to my very dear friend, Maria Spirova, who was instrumental in getting the whole project off the ground and setting up some initial interviews. Finally, huge thanks to my husband, Phil, for his support throughout the project, and for proofreading and editing multiple drafts of the chapters that follow.

1

Why study crime news?

Introduction

On 5 July 2011, I was working flat out to finalise my PhD on how production processes affected storytelling on British crime dramas. At the same time, I was putting the finishing touches to an application for a postdoctoral fellowship at Oxford, exploring much of the same territory but this time looking at crime reporting. In the middle of this, a friend texted me to ask if I'd heard about the phone-hacking scandal and told me to check the news.

I checked *The Guardian*'s website to see that the lead headline read 'Missing Milly Dowler's voicemail hacked by *News of the World*'. The report by Nick Davies and Amelia Hill revealed that when 13-year-old Milly, who was later found murdered, had gone missing in 2002, the *News of the World* had hacked or gained illicit access to her phone. The story was followed by further revelations that bereaved relatives of victims of the 2005 bombings in Central London had also had their mobile phones hacked; and that payments had been made by News International, then the publisher of the *News of the World*, to a number of Metropolitan Police officers. The Metropolitan Police Commissioner, Sir Paul Stephenson, and the assistant commissioner, John Yates, resigned. Days later, the *News of the World* closed down. There could not have been a more auspicious time for submitting a proposal to research police/news media relations in the United Kingdom.

I started my research at Oxford in the autumn of 2011. At the same time, three reviews of police/news media relations (HMIC, 2011; Filkin, 2012; Leveson, 2012a, 2012b) and three major police investigations – Operation Elveden (into phone hacking), Operation Weeting (into illegal payments by the press) and Operation Tuleta (into computer hacking) – were being carried out. Although evidence was still being heard daily as part of the Leveson Inquiry, there had already been a swift clampdown on all contact between the press and police, both official and unofficial.

Among the crime reporters I spoke to at this time, there was anger at the way in which many of their colleagues had been arrested, with respondents describing dawn raids, the breaking down of doors and what they suggested was overzealousness on the part of the Metropolitan Police. As one respondent commented, "It's not South America, it's not mass murder, it's about a few officers being bunged a few quid to talk about things that the Met refuse to talk about". At the same time, press officers at

Scotland Yard described their frustration at the new restrictions and how, in a climate where colleagues had been investigated for having a coffee with a press contact, using discretion to decide what could or could not be given as background to a journalist was a luxury they could no longer afford. But most respondents, both police and press, argued that this could only be a temporary state of affairs.

A period of severe ill-health brought my research to a halt for two years; but when I went back into the field in 2015, to review my initial findings with contacts, I discovered that relations between the police and the national press had become significantly more problematic. The riots in the United Kingdom in August 2011, triggered by the shooting of a young man, Mark Duggan, by police in Tottenham, had been a turning point for police interest in social media. Before the advent of the internet, police organisations could only appeal for help with investigations or appeal for witnesses through the traditional media. During the riots, however, police forces realised that platforms such as YouTube and Facebook allowed them to communicate directly with the public; they could ask for help directly with finding and charging rioters through posting photographs or closed-circuit television (CCTV) footage on social media.

My reporter contacts had a more cynical view of the police's newfound interest in social media, arguing that it allowed the police to control the flow of information more tightly than ever before. They told me that, although crime incidents were being reported daily on the Metropolitan Police's Twitter feed and news website, when they rang the Press Bureau for background information or to speak to investigating officers, they were invariably fobbed off.

It was clear that this was only part of an increasingly complex landscape. In 2009, during the G20 Summit Protests in London, mobile phone footage of the death of newspaper vendor, Ian Tomlinson, was produced by a bystander and subsequently handed to a reporter at *The Guardian*. It showed that Tomlinson's death was not due to a heart attack, as the Metropolitan Police had initially claimed, but was instead due to police violence – challenging the official version of events.

Over the next ten years, all round the world, more and more bystanders would record instances of police violence, often uploading them to YouTube immediately as first-hand documentation, before the police could take control of the situation and release their version of events. In 2020, several bystanders recorded the murder of George Floyd by a police officer in Minneapolis, who pressed on Floyd's neck with his knee for more than nine minutes until Floyd lost consciousness. In less than 24 hours, the videos went viral, triggering protests globally and calls for the trial of the officers involved. The police as an organisation have never been more visible – yet seemingly, in the United Kingdom, less accountable.

I went on to write two articles on the impasse in relations between the Metropolitan Police and the national press for the *British Journal of Criminology* and *Policing and Society*, and was subsequently approached to expand my research into a full-length monograph. While I was preparing my proposal for a book exploring the effect of the Leveson and Filkin Reports on police/news media relations, I attended an event called 'Conspiracy', hosted at the Centre for Investigative Journalism at Goldsmiths University. It brought together a community of investigative journalists, whistleblowers, hackers and experts to discuss ways of challenging power and reinvigorating the field of investigative journalism. It was a conference that was to change the whole direction of my research.

During the conference, I heard about the significant changes in investigative journalism around the world and, in particular, the emergence of investigative journalism start-ups, sometimes referred to as 'non-profits'. Speakers talked about working collaboratively across borders rather than in competition with other outlets – on stories such as the Paradise Papers, a global investigation into the offshore activities of some of the world's most powerful people and companies, or on national and local levels with a variety of non-journalists. They discussed how new models of funding, including philanthropic grants and collective ownership, allowed start-up journalists the time and freedom to conduct 'slow journalism'. Other contributors talked about new ways of researching stories through open-source intelligence (OSINT) – such as the investigative start-up *Bellingcat*'s[1] work on the shooting down of Malaysia Airlines Flight 17 (MH17) in 2014, using Google Earth and videos uploaded to Facebook to prove that the Russian military had initiated the attack. Above all, they talked about giving voice to communities that would often be voiceless or stigmatised in legacy media and expanding the traditional remit of crime news by covering the kinds of stories not often tackled by legacy media reporters, such as crimes of social harm, crimes within the family, white-collar crime and corporate corruption.

Before the conference, I had intended to send in a proposal on the current crisis in crime reporting and the inability of crime reporters to carry out their Fourth Estate role. Now I realised there was an extra beat to the story: the rebirth and reinvigoration of the investigative journalism tradition in the United Kingdom and, in particular, the reversing of representational harm to marginalised and stigmatised communities.

The murder of George Floyd triggered massive demonstrations, in cities throughout the United States and across the globe, against police brutality and the victimisation of people of colour. But along with the worldwide criticism of the police actions in Minneapolis, there was an increasing criticism of crime journalism. In an article published by *NiemanLab* in 2020, the journalists Tauhid Chappell and Mike Rispoli argued that crime journalism was 'racist, classist, fear-based clickbait masking as journalism' and that it 'creates lasting harm for the communities that newsrooms are supposed to serve' (Chappell and Rispoli, 2020). In the United Kingdom, journalists – and members of the public – were expressing similar concerns over existing crime coverage, particularly of people of colour and other stigmatised, vulnerable or marginalised communities. In an interview for *Byline Times*, the Labour MP Dawn Butler asked why the murder of two women of colour, Bibaa Henry and Nicole Smallman, in London's Fryent Park in June 2020, had received so little coverage in comparison to the coverage of the abduction and murder of a young White woman, Sarah Everard, who was killed by Wayne Couzens, a serving Metropolitan Police officer, in March 2020. As Ms Butler commented in the article: 'The fact is Bibaa and Nicole were black women and they were ... murdered, stabbed to death. ... And this hardly made the news. And you think to yourself: how can this not have made the news?' (Butler, quoted in Matharu, 2021).

This book explores the development of crime and investigative journalism in the United Kingdom over the last 40 years – from the symbiotic relations between the police and the press in the 1980s and 1990s, through the complete breakdown of that relationship in the 2010s and the reimagining of crime news by the new non-profits in the 2020s.

Why study crime news?

According to Campbell (2016), the origins of crime reporting lie in the accounts written by the Ordinary of Newgate, the chaplain of the prison where condemned men and women spent their last days. The Ordinary would interview the condemned about their lives and their wrong-doing, and then publish those accounts to be bought in their thousands by the growing number of literate Londoners. Charles Dickens started his career as a court reporter, often reporting on his visits to prisons for the *Daily News*, which he subsequently edited. On the subject of the death penalty, he wrote:

> there is about it a horrible fascination, which, in the minds ... of good and virtuous and well-conducted people, supersedes the horror legitimately attracting to crime itself, and causes every word and action of a criminal under sentence of death to be the subject of a morbid interest and curiosity. (Dickens, published in the *Daily News*, 28 February 1846, cited in Campbell, 2016, p x)

Dickens argues that such reports were popular because 'it is in the secret nature of those of whom society is made up, to have a dark and dreadful interest in the punishment at issue' (Dickens, published in the *Daily News*, 28 February 1846, cited in Campbell, 2016, p x). But, according to Chibnall

(1977), it is that same morbid interest and curiosity that has led researchers to dismiss crime news as 'essentially apolitical', 'an example of the worst excesses of journalistic superficiality and sensationalism' and 'a curiosity of no more than marginal importance to the understanding of mass communications' (Chibnall, 1977, p 1).

Yet, as many scholars have noted, knowledge and preferences about policing and crime are, for most people, shaped by the mass media rather than through personal experience. As Reiner notes:

> Police activity bears most heavily upon a relatively restricted group of people at the base of the social hierarchy, who are disproportionately the complainants, victims or offenders processed by the police. Politically, though, the most crucial sectors for determining police prestige, power, and resources are the majority higher up the social scale, whose contacts with the police (and certainly adversarial encounters) are confined mainly to the police's traffic-control functions. For these strata the mass media are the main source of perceptions and preferences about policing. (Reiner, 2010, p 177)

Such media representations are also important to the police, in terms of the 'attainment of "consent"' (Reiner, 2010, p 178). As Reiner argues, policing, 'especially in Britain, has always been a matter of symbolism as much as substance' (Reiner, 2003, p 259). Most of the time the police do not use criminal law to restore order, and they relatively rarely make arrests. Reiner concludes that 'most police work is neither social service nor law-enforcement but order maintenance – the settlement of conflicts by means other than formal policing' (Reiner, 2010, p 144). However, as Reiner (2010) argues, the symbolic significance of the police is profound (Walker, 1996; Loader, 1997; Manning, 1997, 2001, 2003; Wilson, 2000; Loader and Mulcahy, 2003). He suggests that, as an organisation, the police 'signify that there exists an agency charged with apprehending offenders, so that there is always some prospect (however small statistically) of penal sanctions' (Reiner, 2010, p 177). As a result, ever since the first days of modern-day policing, 'there has been a continuing concern with constructing and maintaining a favourable image of policing as a benign, honourable, and helpful service' (Reiner, 2010, p 177) – which, in today's mediated world, has become an increasingly professionalised public relations operation (Mawby, 1999, 2002a, 2002b).

There are other reasons, less obvious but just as important in many ways, for studying crime news – and, even more importantly, its production. Campbell argues that crime 'is in many ways, the prism through which we see society and its anxieties and phobias' (Campbell, 2016, p xi). In 1910, as a young Home Secretary, Winston Churchill explained that 'the mood and temper of the public in regard to the treatment of crime and criminals is one of the most unfailing tests of the civilisation of any country' (cited in Campbell, 2016, p xi). In the same vein, Chibnall (1977) makes a case for the importance of crime news, arguing how it illustrates most effectively, above all other news genres:

> the system of beliefs, values, and understandings which underlies newspaper representations of reality. There is, perhaps, no other domain of news interest in which latent press ideology becomes more explicit than in what we may term 'law-and-order news'. Nowhere else is it made quite so clear what it is that newspapers value as healthy and praiseworthy or deplore as evil and degenerate in society. (Chibnall, 1977, p x)

Crime news – and indeed all news – is thus not a simple reporting of events or a gathering of facts. As Berger and Luckmann note:

> To understand the state of the socially constructed universe (of meaning) at any given time, or its change over time, one must understand the social organisation that permits the definers to do their defining. Put a little crudely, it is essential to keep pushing questions about the historically available conceptualisations of reality from the abstract 'what?' to the sociologically concrete 'says who?'. (Berger and Luckmann, 1967, p 134)

For many years, media criminology has focused rather more on the 'what?' than on the 'sociologically concrete "says who?"'. Since the 1990s, there has been a considerable body of news media criminology that has developed in the United Kingdom (Greer, 2010a) exploring how stories about crime and justice are constructed according to particular cultural assumptions and ideologies. However, as Greer (2010a) argues, there has been a dearth of media ethnography. This state continues with a few notable exceptions, namely Lee and McGovern (2014) and Ellis (2021). Greer argues for the importance of research into media production thus:

> The study of media content can provide important insights into the role of expressive cultural forms in interpreting our social world and constructing particular versions of reality. But this research is at its richest, and surely has the greatest explanatory potential, when the *process* of production is considered as well as the *product* that results. (Greer, 2010a, p 3, emphasis in original)

This book aims to fill that knowledge gap, through an in-depth exploration of the social processes of the production of crime news in the United Kingdom over the last 40 years. This is the first book in the United Kingdom on police/ news media relations since Mawby's seminal work *Policing Images* in 2002; and the first book to be written on crime reporting in the United Kingdom in over a quarter of a century. It sets out, in Berger and Luckmann's words, to answer the question 'says who?' – to explore who has a voice to make legitimate knowledge claims in crime news reporting, who defines what matters, and whose voices are left out of the discourse.

Police, public and news media relations in context

Studies on police and the media pre-Leveson

Greer argues that two theoretical paradigms shaped news media research in the 20th century – the liberal pluralist paradigm and what he terms 'the control paradigm' (Greer, 2010b, p 491). Liberal pluralist approaches are, according to Greer, 'underpinned by the ideals of classical liberal theory, and emphasize the principles of freedom, choice and democracy' (Greer, 2010b, p 491). This paradigm stresses the autonomy of media professionals and the role of the news media to accurately inform audiences, protect democracy and serve the interests of the social majority. The 'control paradigm' is influenced by Marxist and critical theory and stresses the unequal distribution of economic and cultural power in society. In this paradigm, news selection is shaped by elite interests and the demands of capitalist enterprise; and a key focus is on the extent to which media professionals, knowingly or unknowingly, engage in the reproduction of dominant ideologies or ideas that are favourable to the politically and economically powerful in society.

One of the earliest studies of the production of crime news was *Policing the Crisis* (Hall et al, 1978). Taking a Marxist approach, Hall et al argue that time pressures and the need for media statements to be grounded in 'authoritative' and 'objective' statements from 'accredited sources' lead to 'a systematically structured over-accessing to the media of those in powerful and privileged institutional positions' (Hall et al, 1978, p 58). They suggest that this structured preference given to the opinions of the powerful or 'primary definers' (Hall et al, 1978, p 59) leads to interpretations of events or subjects that set the terms of reference for subsequent debate and discussions. According to Leishman and Mason (2003), this in turn shapes a particular news agenda, but also leads to what they term ' "mutually reinforcing" relations between those experts who initially "define" the parameters of a discourse and the media (the "secondary definers") who reproduce and transform controversial topics into issues of major public and thus political concern' (Leishman and Mason, 2003, p 43). Hall et al conclude that 'the prevailing tendency in the media is towards the reproduction, amidst all their contradictions, of the definitions of the powerful' (Hall et al, 1978, p 65). A further early study by Chibnall (1977), while arguing that output is 'not a product of editorial conspiracy, but a reflection of the social organization of reporting' (Chibnall, 1977, pp 115–16), nevertheless concluded that power in the relationship was asymmetrically skewed in favour of the police.

Later studies in the 1990s and early 2000s suggested that the relationship between the police and the news media was rather more complex than these early studies had suggested. In a Canadian study from this period, Ericson et al (1987, 1989, 1991) argue that 'police-reporter transactions entail controls from both sides, and interdependency' (Ericson et al, 1989, p 125); and that from police perspectives, the media 'have some fundamental assets that put them in a powerful position: the power to deny a source any access; the power to sustain coverage that contextualizes the source negatively' and 'the power of the last word' (Ericson et al, 1989, p 378). Schlesinger and Tumber (1994) examine both the practice of special crime reporters and news sources such as the police. They suggest that Hall et al's analysis (1978) is problematic in that, even among the privileged elite, there are inequalities of access to the media and competition for space and time by privileged sources.

Mawby (1999) examines media coverage of stories of police corruption and leakage of information by key witnesses in the Fred and Rosemary West murder trials; he argues that, far from being able to control information for their organisational advantage, police control of the media was not as 'complete as upholders of the orthodox view would suggest' (Mawby, 1999, p 278). Freckelton (1988) argued that the relationship between the police and the media is essentially symbiotic, a relationship which he suggests is not conducive to investigative journalism, depending too much on unnamed police sources and an unwillingness to seek out more independent or alternative voices.

Since these studies, a number of social, political, cultural and technological changes in the United Kingdom have had an impact on the relationship between the police and the news media. In July 2011, the House of Commons Home Affairs Committee recorded concerns over senior Metropolitan Police officers accepting hospitality from senior employees of News International, the parent company of the *News of the World* and other national British newspapers (Mawby, 2012). This was followed by three separate reviews by Her Majesty's Inspectorate of Constabulary (HMIC, 2011), Elizabeth Filkin (Filkin, 2012) and Lord Leveson (Leveson, 2012a, 2012b) of the relationship between the press and the police. One of the key recommendations of the Filkin Report was the recording of all contact between the police and the press, which was immediately implemented across all British police forces, leading Mawby to comment that the balance of police–press power was now completely in 'favour of the police, who have subsequently used … the recommendations for the recording of police–press contacts to further control the flow of police news and information' (Mawby, 2014, p 253).

The impact of digital communication technologies on police/ media/public relations

Another key change of the last decade has been the increasing use of new digital communication technologies by the police and by the news media, and the ways in which these have transformed relations between the police, the press and the public. Two early studies (Greer and McLaughlin, 2010; Mawby, 2010) explored the impact of digital communications technologies on the police/media/public relationships in the United Kingdom. In a study of relations between regional and national crime reporters and eight regional police forces, including heads of communications within those forces, Mawby (2010) argued that an expansion in police corporate communications had coincided with a worldwide crisis in the news media and, as a result, suggested that the asymmetric police/news media relationship identified by Hall et al (1978) and Chibnall (1977) endured. In a case study exploring coverage of the 2009 G20 Summit Protests in London, Greer and McLaughlin (2010) explored the news-making process from another angle, arguing that new technologies could, on occasion, enable members of the public to produce information challenging the 'official' version of events. They discuss how mobile phone footage produced by a bystander showed that the death of a newspaper vendor, Ian Tomlinson, was due to police brutality and not natural causes – the version of events given to the press by the Metropolitan Police – and how, as a result, the 'news media focus at G20' changed 'from "protestor violence" to "police violence"' (Greer and McLaughlin, 2010, p 1041). Thus, at the end of the 2000s, while justifiable concern was noted in the United Kingdom over 'the future ability of crime reporters to provide independent critical reporting on policing and crime' (Mawby, 2010, p 1073), in a rapidly changing media and cultural landscape, new technologies appeared to offer new opportunities for the public and the press to monitor the police and for the press to continue to carry out its Fourth Estate role.

Over the last ten years, studies have explored how smartphones have enabled bystanders to film and share footage of violent police encounters with citizens (Schneider, 2016; Sandhu and Haggerty, 2017; Ellis, 2020). While the use of technology to 'police the police' dates back at least to George Holliday's camcorder footage of the 1991 beating of Rodney King (Lawrence, 2000), its prevalence and impact are new, and attributable to social media (Doyle, 2011; Bock, 2016; Simonson, 2016; Hockin and Brunson, 2018). The use of social media allows citizens to bypass the traditional media, to upload and share footage instantaneously, thereby making it difficult for police organisations to confiscate or control footage (Schneider, 2016; Ellis, 2020). Accordingly, multimedia platforms can be seen as contributing to the development of a 'monitory democracy' (Keane, 2013), allowing publics to directly act as watchdog and ombudsman, rather than relying on journalists and other mediating institutions.

However, more recent studies in Australia and the United States have suggested that the use of social media has allowed the police to increase their control over the flow of communication to the public and has weakened the legacy media's traditional 'bridging position between two worlds that are structurally unconnected: the sources of news and the members of the audience' (Boczkowski and Mitchelstein, 2017, p 22). Lee and McGovern argue that the use of social media enables the police to communicate more directly with the public than ever before and also has opened up 'a range of possibilities for both image work and operational policing' (Lee and McGovern, 2014, p 60). While, in the past, police organisations would have achieved many of these objectives through the legacy media, Lee and McGovern argue that these new technologies are increasingly enabling the police to 'bypass the traditional media altogether' (Lee and McGovern, 2014, p 114).

In the United Kingdom, however, these seismic changes in how the police, the media and the public communicate with each other have taken place in the wake of one of the biggest policing and media scandals in recent memory. Even now, over ten years after the initial inquiries (HMIC, 2011; Filkin, 2012; Leveson, 2012a, 2012b) into police/news media relations, severe constraints on police/press contact remain in place (Colbran, 2017, 2020), leaving many mainstream crime journalists believing that they are no longer able to carry out their Fourth Estate role. For this reason, a study on contemporary police/news media relations in the United Kingdom is not only timely but crucial.

The contributions of this book

This book examines four decades of crime and investigative reporting in the UK, drawing on empirical research and applying novel theoretical and conceptual frameworks to the police/media/public nexus. It seeks to make three primary contributions to the field of police/news media relations and to research on the production of crime news, by:

- re-evaluating classic criminological texts from the 1970s, 1980s and 1990s, suggesting that police/media/public relations might be even more complex than previously imagined, and expanding the discussion to explore police/news media relations in the first decade of the 2000s;
- exploring the subsequent impact of the Leveson and Filkin Reports and the advent of social media on police/media/public relations; and
- advancing understanding of the role that digital start-ups are playing in expanding the remit of crime news.

This book builds on the existing body of knowledge by problematising the police/media/public relationship with more recent case studies. The research draws on over 60 interviews with a hard-to-access sample (especially given the current restrictions on police/press contact in the United Kingdom) of senior police officers, press officers, editors and national crime news reporters, as well as journalists and managing editors on the new journalism start-ups.

The book concentrates on relations between the MPS, the national press and the new journalism start-ups for three reasons. First, the focus of all three of the inquiries into police/news media relations was on relations between senior MPS officers and the press. Second, the economic crisis affecting the news industry hit regional papers and outlets hardest, whereas all the national news outlets contacted in the course of this study still maintained at least one, and in most cases two or three, members of staff involved in crime reporting. Finally, the MPS's media relations are more complex than those of other forces for a number of reasons: the MPS's operational territory is the capital city, a focus for national media attention, and it is by far the largest force in England and Wales, with national policing responsibilities, such as for counter-terrorism, that attract media attention.

Revisiting classic texts on police/news media relations

Although the bulk of the analysis deals with the effect of new communication technologies on the police/media/public relationship, and how such technologies are facilitating new and alternate voices in crime reportage, the study begins in 1980, for two reasons. First, the experience of journalists, press officers and senior MPS officers interviewed for this study ranged between eight years and over 30 years. Starting in 1980 allows the study to revisit canonical works by Chibnall (1977), Hall et al (1978), Ericson et al (1987, 1989, 1991) and Schlesinger and Tumber (1994), and to explore convergences and divergences in findings. It also permits the changes in police/media/public relationships to be considered in a broader social, cultural and economic context from those days through to the advent of the new journalism start-ups. The study empirically refines the understanding of police/media/public relations in the pre-digital years of the late 1970s and into the early 1990s, through in-depth interviews with police. In doing so, it adds nuance to the understanding of previous police/media/public relations research and suggests that the complexities of current police/media/public relations have continuities from those decades that may not have been fully articulated.

The impact of production processes on crime news content

The book makes a further key contribution in terms of expanding the understanding of how production processes and working practices, as well as social and cultural relations between news sources such as the police and the news media, shape the content of crime news. Since the 1990s, there has been a considerable body of news media criminology that has developed in the United Kingdom (Greer, 2010a), exploring how stories about crime and justice are constructed according to particular cultural assumptions and ideologies. Feminist criminological researchers (Gelsthorpe and Morris, 1990; Jewkes, 2011) have examined the treatment of women offenders and victims in the press and argue that crime is a gendered concept in news discourse. Greer and Jewkes (2005) and Jewkes (2011) have introduced the concept of the 'stigmatized other' in legacy media or the 'marked intolerance toward anyone or anything that transgresses an essentially conservative agenda' (Greer and Jewkes, 2005, pp 20–1). Scholars have also explored how mainstream media crime news coverage often concentrates on spectacular or unusual crimes. Conversely, crimes of social harm such as accidents at work, white-collar crime, corporate corruption, state violence and governments' denial of human rights and crimes of the environment such as pollution are under-reported; the same is true for crimes that do not occur within the public sphere, such as domestic violence, child or elder abuse, 'despite their arguably greater cost to individuals and society' (Jewkes, 2011, p 59). Finally, scholarship on race in the British media (Alibhai-Brown, 1998; Ross, 1998; McLaughlin, 2005; Saeed, 2007; Peplow and West, 2019; Elliott-Cooper, 2021) has explored representations of people of colour in crime news and, in particular, the ways in which journalists have failed to challenge racialised stereotypes.

In order to understand why journalists tell the stories they do, we need also to understand crime journalism's epistemological foundations: how do crime and investigative journalists know what they know; what makes good crime journalism; whose voices are heard in crime journalism and whose voices are omitted; and what role should crime and investigative journalists play in society? Central to all these questions is an understanding of the part played by production processes, journalistic 'norms' – or ways in which journalists decide on whether or not a story is newsworthy and how to frame it – and the social and cultural relations that underpin the creation of crime news. This book aims to provide at least some answers to these very pressing questions.

The role of digital start-ups in reducing representational harms

This book aims to advance empirically the understanding of the role digital start-ups might play in expanding the traditional remit of crime and investigative reporting and reducing representational harms through widening the media frame on reporting of vulnerable communities. This is a development that has been well documented in the field of journalism studies but not yet explored in criminology.

Over the last 40 years, there have been dramatic changes in the way crime, justice and policing have been reported. There are more news platforms, sites and formats than ever before. Sources of all kinds, including police organisations globally, have become more professional in their dealings with the media and with the public. Audiences have become more 'media-savvy' (Greer, 2010b, p 507) and also part of the news-making process, being encouraged to send tip-offs, further information and footage to journalists and, as this book will explore, being trained to take part in major investigations on a local and national scale. All these processes have been facilitated by new technological developments that increase the capacity of sources to control the flow of information to the media and the public but also the capacity for counter-definers to find a voice in the media.

While new technologies have radically transformed the police/public/media relationship, huge changes have also taken place in the field of journalism and, in particular, crime and investigative journalism. One of the biggest changes is the rise of the new investigative journalism start-ups, or non-profits, their impact on crime and investigative reporting and their impact on the content of crime news. These non-profits operate, as the name suggests, by creating journalism on a not-for-profit basis as opposed to the mainstream for-profit model.

In identifying characteristics of the start-up, Deuze and Witschge suggest that these are organisations built primarily around a web presence; they argue that workers on the start-ups in their study 'expressed a profound engagement with society, a critical attitude toward traditional newswork, as well as a commitment to the ideals of journalism' (Deuze and Witschge, 2020, p vii). Criticisms of legacy media include 'focusing too much on quantity over quality and caring more about producing to quota' (Deuze and Witschge, 2020, p 50), concentrating on short-form stories over long, investigative pieces, not engaging with audiences and lack of diversity both in newsrooms and in the stories being told. Conversely, start-ups are characterised by collaborative rather than competitive working practices, often sharing stories with legacy media to reach wider audiences, but also working with a wide variety of partners to investigate those stories, including local news media and members of the public (Alfter, 2016; Stonbely, 2017).

This study focuses on three British non-profits and projects, *The Bureau for Investigative Journalism*, the *Bureau Local* (a project set up by *The Bureau for Investigative Journalism*) and *The Bristol Cable*, and explores how these start-ups have transformed the field of investigative journalism in two other significant ways. First, the study explores how journalism is no longer practised just in newsrooms but 'increasingly takes place and shape elsewhere: at the edges and outside of traditional institutions, in new organizational settings, and also in alternative places inside of legacy media' (Deuze and Witschge, 2020, p 22). The study also investigates how, increasingly, both data specialists and members of the public are becoming directly involved with the process of journalism. I argue, drawing on these case studies, that at a time when legacy media crime journalism is fulfilling its Fourth Estate with less vigour and agency than ever before, start-ups are stepping in to fill that breach.

The study also explores the ways in which start-ups have expanded the remit of crime news. Although none of the non-profits featured in this study set out to cover 'traditional' crime news, I argue that, through very different working practices and as a result of very different business models to those of legacy media outlets, they are nevertheless changing the scope of crime news – by reporting on what they term systemic harms, rather than crimes as specific events. Although the content of news stories on start-ups remains under-researched in the United Kingdom, the websites of *The Bristol Cable*, the *Bureau Local* and *The Bureau for Investigative Journalism* all detail investigations of the crimes that legacy media have traditionally under-reported – crimes like domestic violence, child abuse, elder abuse, accidents at work or crimes of social harm such as pollution of the environment, much white-collar crime, corporate corruption, state violence and governments' denial or abuse of human rights (Jewkes, 2011). Studies (Callison and Young, 2020; Deuze and Witschge, 2020; Usher, 2021) have also noted that another key aspect of those working on non-profits is the desire to challenge what they perceive to be 'the overwhelming whiteness of mainstream media' (Callison and Young, 2020, p 7) and to give a voice to those traditionally under-represented in mainstream media. I explore how the new start-ups are attempting to reduce what they perceive as this representational harm through the widening of the media frame on the reporting of vulnerable and stigmatised communities.

New theoretical and conceptual frameworks

Finally, I provide new theoretical and conceptual approaches to the study of the relationship between policing and crime and investigative reporting and its representation through and in the media. Greer (2010b) argues that in order 'to apprehend the massive transformations across the news media environment' and 'the increasingly interactive manner in which [crime news] is created and consumed', it is necessary to develop 'new theoretical ... tools that permit the sustained and in depth engagement with the contemporary media environment' (Greer, 2010b, p 509). Such an approach, Greer argues, 'requires a renewed focus on interdisciplinarity' (Greer, 2010b, p 509).

In this study, I use three theoretical frameworks to capture the complexities of crime and investigative reporting in traditional newsroom settings and in the more contemporary setting of the new non-profits.

First, in order to explore power relations between the police and the media in both a traditional and contemporary setting, I draw from the field of cultural studies, as do Lee and McGovern (2014), to use the work of De Certeau (1984), which explores power relations between producers and users of social representations and how people reappropriate rituals, laws and representations imposed upon them by organisations or institutions. Lee and McGovern (2014) use this structure to explore how the police use social media and digital platforms to control the flow of information to the press and to the public; and how the press and public poach 'on the property of others' (De Certeau, 1984, p xii) by using the same platforms and new technologies as the police to enact 'tactics' of resistance (De Certeau, 1984, p xix) to monitor the police or to challenge the police version of events. This study uses this framework to understand the complex power relations between the police and the press and the impact of digital platforms on that relationship in the United Kingdom.

Second, in order to understand the broader impact of digital communication technologies on police/media/public relations, I draw on the work of Burt (1992, 2002) on 'structural holes' and 'bridge decay' to conceptualise the changes in this relationship. Burt's work draws on the fields of sociology, economics and computer science; the idea of the 'structural hole' was originally introduced in an attempt to explain the origin of differences in social capital. Burt's theory suggests that individuals hold certain positional advantages/disadvantages from how they are embedded in neighbourhoods or other social structures. A structural hole is understood as a gap between two worlds that are structurally unconnected. An individual who acts as a mediator between two or more groups of people is known as the 'tertius' – the third who bridges the structural hole between the two parties.

From a network analytic perspective point of view, crime journalists traditionally occupied a bridging position between two worlds that are unconnected – the police and the public. I draw on structural hole theory to understand the advantages accruing to crime journalists in the 1980s and 1990s as the main 'bridge' between police and public. However, since the 1990s, technology has given a wider number of citizens the ability to speak directly to the public. Whereas the 'notion of direct police–public communications [was] once something that only occurred in personalised contexts such as "on the beat"' (Lee and McGovern, 2014, p 114) the police are now able to communicate directly with the public through social media platforms. At the same time, the role of the journalist as 'bridge' between police and public has been weakened – and in later chapters, I draw on 'bridge decay' theory to understand how a number of factors, including the advent of digital communication technologies, undermined the traditional position of the press as 'tertius' between news sources – in this case, the MPS – and the public.

Third, I argue that the advent of digital technologies has been a contributory factor in the emergence of non-profit news organisations; and I suggest that this has led to a new and more complex network of 'bridges' forming between the new journalism start-ups, news sources, legacy media organisations and the public over the last decade. In order to conceptualise this, I use communication infrastructure theory (CIT), a theory developed to understand the role communication plays in building and maintaining community cohesion. I draw on this theory to explore how, in the community-centred reporting of the non-profits, the journalist is only one actor in a larger network of bridges where other actors, such as local citizens and community groups, all have agency in creating, in this case, crime and investigative news. I argue that this form of working can be conceptualised as 'a storytelling island' and explore how this new method of creating investigative journalism – reporting with communities rather than about them, particularly on *The Bristol Cable* and the *Bureau Local* in the United Kingdom – has contributed directly to the reimagining of crime news and to the reduction of representational harm to marginalised and stigmatised communities in their work.

Methods

Research for this study was carried out in three stages over a period of eight years from 2012 to 2020 though, as I shall explain, this was more through happenstance than by conscious design on my part. The first phase of my research began in July 2012 and ended in October 2013 and was intended to be a small-scale study on the effect of recommendations made by the Filkin (2012) and Leveson (2012a, 2012b) Reports on police and media relations. During this first phase of my research, I carried out observation of working practices on four national newspapers: *The Guardian*, *The Observer*, *The Times* and *The Telegraph*. Other national newspapers were also approached, but without success.

I sat in on daily story meetings, where the editors would pitch stories brought in by reporters for the following day's edition, and also on the smaller, more informal meetings led by crime editors or home affairs editors, depending on the newspaper I was working with. I also carried out semi-structured interviews with many of the staff at each organisation. A number of the crime correspondents I spoke to offered to introduce me to other journalists and to their own police contacts. Interviews with these contacts then led to personnel working in the Press Bureau at Scotland Yard. In all, interviews were carried out with 23 crime correspondents, working on national newspapers, of whom 22 were male and one was female. Five interviews were carried out with current and former senior employees of the Scotland Yard Press Bureau, all of whom were male. Seven interviews were carried out with senior Metropolitan Police officers from specialist squads, whose work brought them into contact on a daily basis with press officers and heads of communication. All of these respondents were male. The experience of journalists interviewed for this study ranged from eight years to more than 30 years; similarly, press officers and senior officers interviewed for the study had from ten years to more than 30 years' experience. It follows, then, that the older participants in this research would have been at the early stages of their careers at the time of the early studies of crime news reporting (Chibnall, 1977; Hall et al, 1978), allowing me to re-evaluate some of the findings in those studies.

I carried out a second stage of follow-up interviews with two journalists and two press officers from Scotland Yard in 2014, to reflect any further changes in the police/news media relationship since 2012, including the impact of digital communication technologies on that relationship. When I carried out my initial research, the use of social media by both the MPS and the journalists I interviewed was still a comparatively recent phenomenon and, while younger journalists and press officers were enthusiastic about its use in their work, older journalists and retired press officers expressed a more cautious view.

My third phase of research started in October 2018 and continued on and off until August 2020. The aim of this phase was to understand the impact of the new non-profits on the field of crime and investigative journalism; whether or not these organisations' news processes were similar to those of traditional commercial journalism; and, at a time when it seemed legacy media crime journalists were less able to fulfil their Fourth Estate role, whether the new non-profits could fill that gap. During this period, I carried out interviews with two freelance journalists and ten journalists, managing editors and community organisers from non-profits, focusing particularly on *The Bristol Cable*, *The Bureau for Investigative Journalism* and the *Bureau Local* (a project of *The Bureau for Investigative Journalism*) as the case studies for this book. My initial aim was to find out how their news processes might differ from those of traditional media. This led me to realise that the non-profits were making two significant contributions to the field of crime and investigative journalism: first, by researching and reporting stories in innovative ways; and second, by expanding the remit of traditional crime news.

The findings from this study come from a 'grounded theory' (Strauss and Corbin, 1998) approach. Grounded theory is a research method concerned with the generation of theory which is 'grounded' in data that has been systematically collected and analysed. It is used to uncover such things as social relationships and behaviours of groups, known as social processes. There are three main stages in the process of analysis. The first stage involves finding concepts or categories in the data. The second involves finding relationships between these categories. The third stage is to conceptualise those relationships at a higher level of abstraction (Punch, 1998).

What all this means, in practical terms, is that the theoretical insights described throughout the book – the 'strategies' used by the police to control the flow of information; the 'tactics' used by the media to resist that control;

the role of the journalist as 'bridge' between the police and public; and the subsequent decay of that role over the last ten years, to be replaced by a myriad of new bridges between old and new media and the public – were all gleaned through this process. I have also attempted to provide details of my fieldwork throughout the book in each chapter to make clear how this 'sense-making' (Konieczna, 2018, p 27) happened.

Outline of the book

In Chapter 2, I revisit the classic texts of the 1970s and 1980s on police and media relations and suggest that, even in a pre-internet age, the police/news media relationship was even more complex and contingent than these texts suggest. Although, from the 1970s onwards, police press officers started to take a more open stance with the media, inviting journalists on occasion to cover sensitive investigations to limit harmful or inaccurate reporting, access to the media was never guaranteed. As a result, many key investigations were not covered as they were not deemed newsworthy. Senior police officers from this period also suggested that they often felt vulnerable in their dealings with the press. The press had the power to quote officers out of context, to make or break reputations and the power of the last word. As a result, and in contrast to the classic criminological texts from this time, police respondents believed the press in this period were extremely powerful and frequently had the upper hand.

In Chapter 3 I explore, from the perspective of journalists, the complex and contingent web of relations – both official and unofficial – that existed between the Metropolitan Police and national crime journalists from the 1980s to the early 2000s. I suggest that there were two cultures of journalists: the inner circle, who usually worked for popular news outlets and who often established close friendships with police officers; and outer circle journalists, who mainly worked for broadsheets or were freelance and were more critical of the police in their work. I suggest that, while inner circle journalists depended on the police for routine stories, this was not the case for outer circle journalists, who drew on a much wider circle of contacts, including members of the public, victims, witnesses, relatives of people in prison, solicitors and barristers. For both cultures, having informal contacts within the force was crucial but for inner circle journalists, this sometimes came at a price – having to turn a blind eye to police malpractice. Although outer circle journalists stressed their detachment from the police, I explore how, on occasion, officers would use them to leak stories about police corruption or abuses of power – stories that would otherwise go unreported.

Chapter 4 explores the impact of the recommendations of the Filkin and Leveson Reports (2012) on relations between the Metropolitan Police and the national news media. The main recommendation of both Reports was the recording of all contact between the press and the police. However, almost immediately, both inner and outer circle journalists reported a clampdown on all contact with the Metropolitan Police Service, both official and unofficial. Inner circle journalists suggested that they were no longer being given even routine stories, while outer circle journalists suggested that their ability to carry out their Fourth Estate role had been compromised. Whereas, in the past, the majority of stories about police malpractice or corruption had come from within the organisation, they believed that this channel was now firmly closed and that control over the flow of information to the public and to the press was very much in police hands. However, I suggest that police respondents contested this view, arguing that journalists would find alternative sources only too willing to co-operate, and expressed concern that restrictions on contact would lead to inaccurate or speculative reporting.

In Chapter 5, I argue that, at a time of already beleaguered relations between the Metropolitan Police Service and the national news media, following the recommendations of the Filkin and Leveson Reports (2012), the advent of new digital technologies further damaged relations between the police and the news media. Through the use of social media platforms, the MPS have been able to communicate more directly with the public than ever before but also to exert even more control over the flow of policing information to the press and to the public. Of course, it is also true that new digital technologies have allowed both the public and the press more sophisticated ways in which to monitor the police and publicly disseminate and circulate images and narratives of police brutality in real time on YouTube and Facebook — a recent example being the murder of George Floyd in Minneapolis in May 2020, which triggered worldwide demonstrations and protests. Nevertheless, the police still have considerable control in these situations — bystander video footage of police brutality can be dismissed as a partial representation of events, while new technologies such as body worn cameras afford the police greater powers of surveillance.

In Chapter 6, I explore the impact on the field of crime and investigative journalism of three new investigative journalism start-ups and projects in the United Kingdom: *The Bristol Cable*, the *Bureau Local* and *The Bureau for Investigative Journalism*. I focus on how they are challenging journalistic norms through very different working practices, and how this is leading, in turn, to an expansion of the remit of stories. I suggest that all three are doing this through the practice of engaged journalism. On *The Bristol Cable*, this takes the form of working with communities and co-creating stories. I argue that this enables journalists to give voice to under-represented communities. *The Bureau for Investigative Journalism* challenge journalistic norms through collaborations and the use of big data in their work, enabling them to report crimes often under-investigated by mainstream media such as corporate crime and crimes of corruption. The *Bureau Local* combine both these methods — the use of big data and collaborations with citizens — to produce 'transformational' journalism, working with citizens to bring what they term the societal or systemic harms they are reporting upon to wider societal attention, with the aim of sparking societal change and amelioration of these harms.

In Chapter 7, I explore how, as a consequence of their working practices, the non-profits are changing crime reporting. I focus on three aspects of crime and investigative reporting that have received particular attention over the years in qualitative criminological research: the 'othering' of marginalised or stigmatised communities; the under-reporting of certain crimes, particularly crimes of social harm; and the concentration on crime as a discrete event, without discussion of causes or effects. I suggest that the very different working practices on the non-profits have sought to address these problems – that by not needing to meet the demands of a daily publishing cycle, non-profit journalists are able to spend time forging meaningful relationships with marginalised and hard-to-reach communities and ensure a greater range of perspectives are included in their reporting, thus giving a voice to communities that are often negatively portrayed in the media. I also explore how the non-profits are broadening the content of crime news in two respects: by focusing on crime as systemic harm rather than crime as discrete event; and by exploring the causes and effects of these social harms, through the emphasis on evidence and data shared as part of their reports on their websites.

In Chapter 8, I explore how the Fourth Estate now works in terms of crime reporting. The last ten years have seen what Beckett (2018) calls a paradox of power for journalism. As argued throughout this book, the traditional crime journalists' ability to fulfil their Fourth Estate role has been greatly diminished – by technological changes, the global crisis in the news industry and by the impact of the Leveson and Filkin Reports (2012) on police/news media relations. At the same time, as Beckett (2018) also suggests, individual journalists or acts of journalism have had more impact than ever before. Outlets such as the *Bureau Local*, *The Bureau for Investigative Journalism* and others are radically changing journalistic norms and changing the nature of crime news. Nevertheless, although the start-ups may be transforming crime news, one key source – the police – increasingly controls the flow of policing news to the press and the public. If knowledge is power, the question of who controls the production and distribution of information is more important than ever in an era of fake news and disinformation. The Fourth Estate may have transformed radically over the last ten years, allowing millions of new entrances to public life to open, but in the case of the police in the United Kingdom, the Fourth Estate has never been so hamstrung in its ability to speak truth to power. This chapter argues that the only way forward is a re-establishment of relations based on trust and reciprocity between the MPS and new and old media – but that such a renewed relationship may take some years to achieve.

Conclusion

In this opening chapter, I have set out my reasons for wanting to write this book and why I hope it is both timely and important. Following the murder of George Floyd in Minneapolis in 2020, the content of crime news has come under intense scrutiny, with journalists themselves calling for change in newsrooms. But in order to understand why, as Callison and Young (2020) put it, journalism 'legitimizes, amplifies, and reinforces some experts, views, and perceptions of events and problems in the world – and their potential range of solutions – over *other* experts, views and perceptions' (Callison and Young, 2020, p 11), I argue that it is necessary to understand how production processes, working practices (particularly those between sources and journalists) and the ideological values of those involved in the news-making process all shape the content of crime news – whose stories are told and whose stories never make the cut.

Although I suggest that many of the problems now dogging mainstream crime journalism, and crime journalists' relationships with the police in the United Kingdom, have their roots in the 1970s and the 1980s, I also suggest that there may be some cause for optimism for critics of the content of crime news: that the new start-ups, particularly those featured in this book, *The Bureau for Investigative Journalism*, the *Bureau Local* and *The Bristol Cable*, may be succeeding in gradually 'repairing' (Konieczna, 2018) and, in particular, reducing representational harms by widening the media frame in their reporting of vulnerable communities.

2

The Metropolitan Police

Introduction

I started my research on this book in October 2011. It was both a good and bad time to be starting such a project – good in that police/news media relations were front page news daily, but bad in that I initially found it – and understandably so – very difficult to interview journalists. No one would answer my emails. In the end, I resorted to desperate measures, and gatecrashed a private book launch, at which I managed to speak to a prominent journalist. He very kindly agreed not only to grant me an interview, but also to introduce me to some of his colleagues, many of whom, like him, had retired or were on the brink of retirement.

At first, I wasn't sure how useful this might be, as my initial plan had been to interview journalists and press officers who were currently in post. After the first interview, I realised that it was absolutely vital for a study of this kind to be able to set the current crisis in context. The more interviews I conducted, the more I realised that the complexities of the current police/ media/public relations had their roots in the 1980s and 1990s. In this chapter and in Chapter 3, I draw on interviews with former senior police officers, former MPS press officers and journalists whose careers spanned the 1980s to the present day.

A considerable body of literature explores the relationship between the police and the news media in the last quarter of the 20th century (Chibnall, 1977, 1979; Hall et al, 1978; Ericson et al, 1989, 1991; Ericson, 1995; Innes, 1999; Mawby, 1999). A key recurring theme is the issue of power in the relationship between the police and the media. In *Law-and-Order News*, Chibnall (1977) suggested that, while the police perspective might be challenged on occasion, the relationship between the police and the press is always asymmetrical – 'the reporter who cannot get information is out of a job, whereas the policeman who retains it is not' (Chibnall, 1977, p 155). Similarly, Hall et al (1978) argued that time pressures, and the need for media statements wherever possible to be grounded in 'objective' and 'authoritative' statements from 'accredited sources', lead to a 'systematically structured over-accessing to the media of those in powerful and privileged institutional positions' (Hall et al, 1978, p 58) or, as they termed them, 'primary definers' (Hall et al, 1978, p 59) such as the police. Subsequent studies in Canada in the late 1980s (Ericson et al, 1987, 1989, 1991) and in the United Kingdom in the 1990s (Schlesinger and Tumber, 1994; Mawby,

1999) took a more nuanced view, stressing the importance of economic factors as well as working relationships between sources and reporters in shaping the news. Ericson et al (1989) argued that from the perspective of the police, the media were in possession of key resources that 'frequently give them the upper hand' and that 'sources who realize they can only respond within an established news frame or … who are limited to a twelve-second clip, feel that it is they who function as … secondary definers for the news media' (Ericson et al, 1989, p 378). Schlesinger and Tumber (1994) suggested that access was not always automatic, even for 'primary definers' such as the police, while Mawby (1999) questioned the extent to which the police were actually able to set the news agenda, using a series of case studies from 1998, 'a kind of *annus horribilis* for the British police image' (Leishman and Mason, 2003, p 43).

However, all studies were united in suggesting that, in certain key respects, the police held power. In their interactions with journalists, the police were controllers of 'the primary definitions of the subject of address (crime, criminality and its control by police)' (Ericson et al, 1989, p 124); and in attending to 'the definition of social problems', the news media routinely draw on 'the preferred solutions of accredited bodies' (Ericson et al, 1987, p 35). As Ericson et al (1987) explain, '[w]hen there is a problem – ranging from urban riots in Britain … to violence against women in Toronto … politicians [and] police … offer a cause of the troubles' (Ericson et al, 1987, p 35). In the context of the news media, the police define what is seen to be a crime or criminal behaviour and the correct response to the event.

This chapter revisits these classic texts and argues that, even in a pre-internet and pre-smartphone era, the police–media relationship was possibly never 'the easily manageable process it might once have seemed' (Mawby, 1999, p 279) and was always complex and contingent. It starts with a brief history of the Press Bureau and how it operated in the 1970s through to the turn of the century, before moving on to an exploration of the relations – both official and unofficial – of press officers and operational officers with the national news media. The discussion in this chapter focuses on these relations from the perspective of the MPS; Chapter 3 considers that same relationship from the perspective of journalists.

The history of the Press Bureau

Policing – and by extension police legitimacy – has 'always been a matter of symbolism as much as substance' (Reiner, 2003, p 259). From the formation of the Metropolitan Police in the 19th century to the present day, the police have been heavily involved in 'image work', defined by Mawby as 'all the activities in which police forces engage and which construct and project images and meanings of policing' (Mawby, 2002a, p 5).

Although before the First World War there were no crime correspondents as we would understand the term today (Chibnall, 1977), there was nevertheless a huge appetite for crime news on the part of the British public. As popular journalism expanded in the 1910s and competition for a 'scoop' between papers increased, 'information about the earlier stages of the criminal justice process took on a greater importance' (Chibnall, 1977, p 49). The police exercised 'virtually monopolistic control over such information and were by no means predisposed to release it' (Chibnall, 1977, p 49). As a result, informal arrangements sprang up between police and press, with officers selling information over a drink to reporters (Chibnall, 1977; Rock, 2014). When concerns over these arrangements reached the level of parliamentary complaints, the then Commissioner, Sir Nevil Macready, formalised police/press relations by establishing the Scotland Yard Press Bureau in 1919.

Apart from its intent to dissipate the culture of bribery in the MPS, Macready also suggested that one of the main functions of the new Press Bureau would be to increase transparency between the police and the public (Rock, 2014). However, Rock argues that while '[p]ublicly, the Commissioner and the Home Office were open about these two purposes upon which the Press Bureau was founded ... private internal correspondence indicates that the Bureau aspired to manage public perceptions of the police' (Rock, 2014, p 27).

Initially, the Bureau consisted of one civil servant, who collected information from Scotland Yard's departments and issued two press releases a day (Mawby, 2002a, p 12). This arrangement persisted through the 1920s until the mid-1940s (Mawby, 2002a) and the appointment of Sir Harold Scott in 1945 as Metropolitan Police Commissioner. Scott increased the functions of the Press Bureau, appointed a Public Relations Officer, who had been a former employee of the BBC and War Office, arguing that 'the appointee to the new post must know Fleet Street well if satisfactory relations were to be built with the press' (Mawby, 2002a, p 14).

The next big development in the running of the Press Bureau came in the mid-1960s. While the period that followed Scott's appointment, from 1945 to the end of the 1950s, has been described by some scholars as 'the "Golden Age" of public confidence in the police' (Reiner, 2000, p 144), Mawby suggests that 'by the turn of the 1960s cracks in the image were appearing' (Mawby, 2002a, p 16). The decline of the police image occurred towards the end of the 1950s (Emsley, 1996; Reiner, 2000) as crime rates increased and the police became more distant from the community as they moved from foot patrol to car patrol. There were increasing confrontations with a largely middle-class section of the public at demonstrations, which Mawby describes as 'taking place in a society which was becoming more questioning of policing and more generally of the powers of the state and its institutions' (Mawby, 2002a, p 18). At the same time, there had been only limited developments in police image work since Scott's time and 'rudimentary channels of communication with the media … were no longer appropriate' (Mawby, 2002a, p 19).

As a result, a new head of public relations, G.D. Gregory, was appointed, 'brought in from industry after putting the "Schhh" in Schweppes' (Mawby, 2002a, p 20). He promptly set about 'a task of image-reconstruction' (Chibnall, 1977, p 72), appointing a number of 'men with newspaper experience into his staff and making sure that the Public Relations Department was never considered a quiet field into which ineffectual policemen could be put out to graze' (Chibnall, 1977, p 72). He also sponsored a freelance journalist, Peter Laurie, to spend time at the MPS to research a book, including a spell of observation in the Press Bureau. But, as Mawby (2002a) notes, when Laurie's book, *Scotland Yard: A Personal Inquiry*, came out in 1970, the Press Bureau was described as having 'a low position in the hierarchy and was not geared to positive explanation of the police problems and activities' (Laurie, 1970, p 21).

The appointment of Sir Robert Mark as Commissioner of the MPS in 1972 led to significant changes in police/press relations. In 1969, *The Times* had published a story on police corruption in the MPS and demanded an inquiry. When the case came to trial, '*The Times* happily reported the praise of its journalists voiced by Lord Justice Edmund-Davies, that "it was, it would appear, mainly their intrepidity and skill which laid bare a hideous cancer which, if unchecked, could have done even greater and incalculable damage to law enforcement"' (quoted in Rowbotham et al, 2013, p 186).

At the time of becoming Commissioner, Mark described the relationship between the press and the MPS as one of 'mutual distrust and dislike' (Mark, 1978, p 123). At the same time, he also believed that 'acceptability of the police in a free society depended, amongst other factors, on our willingness to be an accountable and open administration. A free and open relationship with the Press was, in my view, the best way to demonstrate this' (Mark, 1978, p 135). He embarked upon a new press policy, significant on two counts. First, officers were encouraged to speak to the press, including officers of lower rank than inspector, providing they had been given authorisation by a superior officer. This was a challenging move for a police force 'whose officers were traditionally suspicious of liaising with the media' (Mawby, 2002a, p 22). However, Mark himself had a somewhat ambivalent attitude towards the press, once describing the relationship between the MPS and the media as 'an enduring, if not ecstatically happy, marriage' (Reiner, 2003, p 259); he tempered this apparent 'transparency and accountability' with 'the strict control of "Press Identification Cards"' (Mawby, 2002a, p 22). Information from the Press Bureau was given only to card holders, and cards were issued to the press at the discretion of the MPS, 'ensuring that they controlled the flow of information' (Mawby, 2002a, p 22).

Mark's media policy saw greater co-operation and less hostility in police/news media relations during his time as Commissioner, and his thinking was endorsed by successive Commissioners. Although police/news media relations deteriorated somewhat under Mark's immediate successors, Sir Robert McNee and Sir Kenneth Newman, both Reiner (2000) and Schlesinger and Tumber (1994) suggest that this was 'not so much a consequence of personalities'; rather, it was 'a symptom of the politicized state of policing' (Reiner, 2000, p 145). Both Newman's and McNee's periods of office coincided with the years of the Thatcher government and periods of social and industrial unrest, including nationwide riots in 1981, the 1984–5 Miners' Strike and clashes with striking print workers at the News International plant at Wapping in 1986–7. The police were deployed to act with force in these disputes, 'raising fears of police alignment with the Thatcher government' (Mawby, 2002a, p 23).

In the late 1980s, there was another 'discernible shift in police image work' (Mawby, 2002a, p 28) with the appointment of Peter Imbert as Commissioner. Imbert came to the MPS with a reputation for supporting openness with the media and, as Chief Constable of Thames Valley Police, had allowed film-maker Roger Graef to produce a 'fly-on-the-wall' documentary simply called *Police*. One of the episodes depicted bullying of a rape victim by police officers, which was instrumental in leading to changes in procedures for rape complaints.

Addressing the 1989 International Police Exhibition and Conference, Imbert argued that '[o]penness must be central to the policing of a democratic and pluralist society' (Imbert quoted in Schlesinger and Tumber, 1994, p 113). At the same time, Imbert was aware that continuing adverse media comment was 'causing frustration, low morale, and a lack of confidence in management' (Schlesinger and Tumber, 1994, p 108). As a result, he decided to take 'image work into a new phase' (Mawby, 2002a, p 43), by commissioning the corporate identity consultants Wolff Olins to undertake an audit of internal and external attitudes to the MPS. One of the key findings was that the MPS needed to improve its internal and external communications. A larger infrastructure was developed to support its media and public relations policies. By 1997, the Directorate of Public Affairs and Communications (the DPA) had a staff of nearly 100 and a £9 million budget.

The Directorate of Public Affairs and Communication

In their book, *Policing and Media*, Lee and McGovern (2014) draw on the work of De Certeau (1984) to analyse the complex and contingent relationships between the police and the media. De Certeau's most influential work is *The Practice of Everyday Life* (1984), in which he explores power relations between producers and users of social representations and how people reappropriate rituals, laws and representations imposed upon them by organisations or institutions. He argues that these power relations can be conceptualised in terms of 'strategies' of power or 'tactics' of resistance. Strategies can be used by those within organisational power structures, whether large or small, such as the state, a corporation or a proprietor, and are deployed against an external entity, such as adversaries, competitors or clients, to institute a set of relations for proper or official ends. In order to pursue 'strategies' of power, De Certeau argues that any institution or business first needs a 'place that can be delimited as its own' and can 'serve as the base from which relations with an exteriority composed of targets or threats ... can be managed' (De Certeau, 1984, p 36). In the case of the MPS, the physical base was the DPA (later known as the Directorate of Media and Communication).

During the 1980s and 1990s, there were four branches of the Directorate: News; Publicity and Advertising; the Secretariat; and the Briefing and Planning Department. In 1986, the Directorate spent just over £2 million; by 1992, its operational budget had risen to £12.5 million (Schlesinger and Tumber, 1994, p 117), reflecting the increasing importance of public relations to the organisation and to successive Commissioners. Of those four branches, the News Branch was the main point of contact for the media, including specialist crime journalists.

The News Branch was, in turn, divided into three further sections – the News Group, the Press Bureau and the Area Liaison Unit. The News Group was set up primarily to monitor radio and television programmes for news items relating to the MPS, while the Press Bureau and the Area Liaison Unit were press officers for the force on a national and local level respectively.

There was an overall head of the Directorate whose duty it was to act as press secretary to the Commissioner. Daily briefings would be held each day between the Commissioner and the head of the Directorate to discuss news coverage involving the MPS, future news initiatives and the preparation of the annual Commissioner's Report. Below the head of the Directorate was the head of the News Branch, who managed a team of approximately 40 press officers in the Press Bureau and the Area Liaison Unit, as well as a smaller team manning the News Group. Below the head of the News Branch was a Chief Press Officer, who was responsible for the day-to-day running of the Press Bureau and the Area Liaison Unit.

The Press Bureau employed approximately 20 staff to man the office on a 24-hour basis. Each day, a tape-recorded log of main news stories would be made available to the press. Journalists were also able to phone at any time to talk to a press officer. Within the Press Bureau, there were also designated 'press desks' for each of the specialist squads, such as the Flying Squad[1] and Counter Terrorism.[2] An additional 20 press officers were employed within the Area Liaison Unit. At that time, the MPS was divided into four main areas – north, east, west and south London – and there would be a designated officer dealing with each area and serving as a point of contact for local journalists within those specific areas.

Relations between the Press Bureau and the press

Ericson et al (1989) argue that the two main aims of any news source are to achieve positive publicity while protecting the organisation against unwelcome intrusion. However, the press officers who had worked in the Press Bureau in the 1970s noted that they had an additional task in implementing Sir Robert Mark's new policy of openness – to convince senior officers, long suspicious of the media, to co-operate with them in giving them information for the press.

Despite his objective to make his force more accessible to journalists, 'Mark was far from dewy-eyed about the police's relationships with the media' (Schlesinger and Tumber, 1994, p 111). In 1974, he told the London Press Club that the police were without doubt 'the most abused, the most unfairly criticised and the most silent minority in this country' (cited in Reiner, 2010, p 183). Mark clearly understood 'that without public confidence in their ability to deal with crime, or in their professionalism and integrity, the [police would] not receive public co-operation' (Schlesinger and Tumber, 1994, p 113); nevertheless, Schlesinger and Tumber noted that there had been, in recent years, 'a feeling within the police that the public and the media have overlooked the good work that they do' (Schlesinger and Tumber, 1994, p 113). As a result, there was a wariness of the media at all levels within the force – a wariness that extended to the new civilian press officers appointed under Mark.

As one former press officer explained:

'When we joined, corruption was endemic. And a lot of that corruption was to do with journalists, the brown envelopes thing, taking cash for information. So I think certain officers, those who were involved in the whole brown envelope thing, didn't want to get involved with us, because we'd been brought in to put an end to those cosy relationships. And those that weren't involved had been brought up not to trust the media, and they saw us as an extension of the media and therefore not to be trusted. So yeah, those early days were tricky … as my boss told me when I joined, he used to go up to CID and before he'd even opened his mouth, they'd be straight in, "And you can fuck right off for a start".'

There were a number of other objections to the appointment of an all-civilian press office. Even as late as the 1990s, many forces still had public relations departments run by serving officers, or a combination of civilian and police staff manning the department. One initial worry about appointing an all-civilian press team was that a journalist coming into the police as a press officer might 'over-identify' with the police, while 'a police officer, rotated every two or three years, was not at risk in this kind of way' (Schlesinger and Tumber, 1994, p 132). Another objection to civilian press officers seemed to be a fear that they would lack 'the authority to demand the release of information' (Chibnall, 1977, p 147). However, despite this initial hostility on the part of some officers towards Press Bureau staff, respondents suggested that this was a temporary state of affairs and that, over time, senior police officers in particular came to rely upon the judgement of Press Bureau officers in both handling the press and protecting the public image of the MPS.

De Certeau (1984) argues that by establishing a base – in this case, the DPA – organisations are able to achieve the following key objectives: 'to capitalize acquired advantages, to prepare future expansions, and thus to give oneself a certain independence with respect to the variability of circumstances' (De Certeau, 1984, p 36). First, the Bureau benefited considerably from the 'acquired advantages' of civilian staff. As a former press officer explained:

'We were essentially negotiators. Mediators even. As a press officer, I was no good to the media unless I had a foot in the police camp. I was no good to the police unless I had a foot in the media camp.'

When asked why he thought the Press Bureau came to be more valued by operational officers, he suggested that it was this factor – that press officers were intermediaries between operational officers and the press. He argued that press officers had a unique understanding of the police's needs to balance openness with privacy and protection of sensitive information in dealing with the press, while at the same time understanding that, for most journalists, the most interesting stories are often in the 'back regions' (Goffman, 1959) or private spaces of an organisation, where 'decisions are taken but which are open only to the purview of those who are officially authorized to be there' (Ericson et al, 1989, p 9).

He gave an example of this, describing his organisation of a press conference after the shooting of an MPS officer:

'So the Borough Commander called me and said, "I want you to look after X [the officer's widow] and to tell me what I should be doing to protect her as well". So I arranged for X to meet the media in what I would call a controlled way. I invited them all in to speak to X, to stop them hanging round the house and trying to take pictures of the kids. So I said, "Here's a picture of the four kids. One person will ask questions and that's it." We arranged for a lady crime reporter to sit at the front and ask questions very gently and I stood at the back to make sure it went to plan. Now I have never seen anyone who doesn't cry when the press asked them questions about their loved ones. But the Borough Commander said, "You've got to stop this, we can't have X crying". But I said, "No, I can't do that, this is all just part of her answering honestly how she feels". And then the next day, the lady crime reporter wrote the most amazing article about X, and people sent in about three hundred thousand pounds for X and her family and set them up for life. And I think that was one of the turning points for us as press officers, that the top brass could see we could harness the press.'

A more proactive approach to dealing with the press

Another advantage for institutions of power in establishing a base, according to De Certeau, is being able to plan 'future expansions' (De Certeau, 1984, p 36). As Ericson et al comment, '[a]ll organizations control knowledge of their activity in order to sustain the view publicly that they are operating with procedural regularity, and are therefore accountable' (Ericson et al, 1989, p 92). As respondents in this study noted, before the arrival of civilian staff, the Press Bureau had been traditionally reactive in its approach to news communication, 'either defending their actions when questioned, or simply enclosing on knowledge' (Ericson et al, 1989, p 92). One of the key changes in the Press Bureau introduced by the new civilian staff in the 1970s was a more proactive approach in preparing media strategies for future serious emergencies. As a former press officer explained:

'So we had an operation called Atlantic Blue. This was preparing us for a serious event like 9/11 to be run in a bubble at Hendon where we would have police officers and press officers reacting to and dealing with a real emergency event. We needed to plan how we would react, what information we would give out and when and to whom. And we would do this as if in real time, with press conferences, and with information coming in all the time, casualty figures, multiple bombs going off. So that was one of the first times where we realised we could not just react but had to be prepared.'

Another key change was a more proactive approach generally in disclosing knowledge to the press. As one former head of news explained, part of the change in strategy was realising the ramifications of too rigid enclosure of 'back region' (Goffman, 1959) knowledge in relation to the press and to the public. He gave an example of this:

'A child was assaulted in a South London park. The police had a very detailed description and decided to stake out the park but not tell the media. But somehow an editor of a local paper on that patch found out, rang me and asked why the media hadn't been informed. So I said I'd find out and ask the officer concerned and the officer said they hadn't given details as they believed they were going to catch him. So the editor wrote a piece in his paper and said, "Okay, your job is to catch him, my job is to inform the public of danger. So can you guarantee right now, that man is going to be caught without striking again?" So that made me think very hard about what we should be doing as press officers. So every case from that point on, where an officer wasn't going to give information – barring exceptional circumstances – I would ask officers, "Is that in the public's interest to withhold that information? Because if not, you will have to justify that secrecy in a court of law".'

A third advantage of establishing 'a place appropriated as one's own' is the ability for an organisation to achieve 'a certain independence with respect to the variability of circumstances' (De Certeau, 1984, p 36). Ericson et al argue that one key way in which the police promote a positive image is through 'publicity about their law-enforcement crackdowns on the presumption it will have a general deterrent effect and, not incidentally, affect the supportive sentiments of citizens' (Ericson et al, 1989, p 150). At the same time, Ericson et al argue that all news sources 'must appreciate the bad-news emphasis in the media' and that by participating 'in the public conversation ... [a source] must come to terms with the fact that the news formula for translating the local knowledge of her organizational activities into the common sense is to focus on procedural propriety in her organization' (Ericson et al, 1989, pp 378–9). But while both Ericson et al (1989) and Chibnall (1977) argue that the overriding aim of the police in dealing with the media was to 'ensure that the general tenor of journalists' accounts remains "helpful" to the overall goals of the control agency' (Chibnall, 1977, p 178), press officers from this period discussed how they pursued what might appear to be a counterintuitive policy in order to promote the organisation's transparency and accountability by releasing 'bad news' stories pre-emptively to the media. An example of this was given by a former press officer:

'I learnt the value of this from one Commissioner after the shooting of Cherry Groce.[3] We put out an apology on the Saturday morning, and in *The Guardian* on Monday, there was an editorial, "Fresh winds blowing in Scotland Yard, for the first time they've apologised about something they've done wrong".'

In their study of relations between the police and the media in a Canadian context in the 1980s, Ericson et al noted that, by a policy of greater openness with the press, organisations 'can close off incursions that make the organization more vulnerable and its environment more equivocal' (Ericson et al, 1989, p 93). Similarly, the same press officer observed:

> 'If you leave a vacuum for the press, particularly when there's been an institutional cock-up, that's a vacuum waiting to be filled by bullshit.'

Trying to reduce organisational 'leaks'

One final 'strategy' of power available to organisations, according to De Certeau, is 'a mastery of places through sight' or a 'panoptic practice', which De Certeau suggests as 'proceeding from a place whence the eye can transform foreign forces into objects that can be observed and measured, and thus control and "include" them within its scope of vision' (De Certeau, 1984, p 36).

Ericson et al noted, in their Canadian study, the 'limited nature of journalists' methodology' (Ericson et al, 1989, p 126) in regard to the police. They suggested that the journalists they interviewed were rarely allowed direct observation; and when they did 'ask to do something other than to conduct an interview, to attend a news conference, or to scrutinize a news release, they were usually refused' (Ericson et al, 1989, p 127). However, Chibnall's (1977) study of relations between the police and the media in the 1970s took a slightly different stance. He suggested that, on very rare occasions, journalists were subjected to a technique he terms 'buttering-up' or being afforded privileged or particularly hospitable treatment in order to develop 'affective bonds between the reporter and individual members of the control agency' (Chibnall, 1977, p 181) and, hence, ensure favourable coverage.

Those senior press officers that I interviewed who had worked at the Press Bureau in the 1970s and 1980s spoke of giving journalists access to sensitive operations – partly as a way of preventing dangerous 'leaks', or information not already processed through official channels, which might endanger the lives of those involved and jeopardise the investigation, but also as a way of preventing inaccurate reporting:

> 'We had planned a raid on a big estate in North London. And the CPS had made it very clear that to catch the people who were operating there, they would need to have been caught in the act. The strategy I had already evolved with the Deputy Assistant Commissioner was that we would take TV people along with us. They could see whatever they wanted, report what they want and that way no one could say the

infamous "we have been told that". We wanted to avoid inaccurate reports of police brutality, basically.

But in the run up to it, when things were still very, very quiet, two daily newspapers, one daily newspaper, one Sunday newspaper, approached us and said they'd heard about the raid and wanted to be there. That operation was extremely sensitive as our guys were still in the OPs [observation points] and would have been at risk of their lives, if they'd been discovered. So I said, "Okay, I know you won't tell me but who told you?" And they said, "We're not going to tell you". So I said, "Okay, you'd better confirm to me that you've told no one else or this operation is off." And they said they hadn't. So we built them into the arrangement.'

Chibnall argues that a key strategy open to press and operational officers in the 1970s was 'freezing-out' (Chibnall, 1977, p 178) reporters who had either published stories critical of the police or potentially jeopardised investigations. However, this press officer argued that this was a technique he had never used and nor had his colleagues. In this case, rather than 'freezing-out' these reporters, he instead decided to do what he termed "placing the moral monkey on their shoulder". As he explained:

'If they decided to leak anything they shouldn't have, they would have been potentially responsible for officers losing their lives. Now these crime reporters were well known to us, they were as trustworthy as anyone could be in that respect. And this was a measured decision on our part. They could come in, they could report what they liked but they would have to take the consequences if, through their actions, someone was killed. And that was our technique on a number of operations. Pass the moral monkey to sit on the journalist's shoulder.'

The power of the press from police perspectives

Certainly press officers had a number of 'strategies' of power (De Certeau, 1984) at their disposal in terms of dealing with the press. But while the dominant view in early studies of police/news media relations was that the police/news media relationship was asymmetrical in favour of the police (Chibnall, 1977, 1979; Hall et al, 1978), Chibnall's (1977) study was mainly grounded in the perspectives of journalists, with only one interview with a Scotland Yard press officer, while Hall et al's (1978) study was not based on empirical research at all. Although press officers agreed that they 'controlled the primary definitions of the subject of address (crime, criminality and its control by police)' (Ericson et al, 1989, p 124), they also suggested that, from their perspective, the media were actually 'very powerful, in possession

Figure 2.1: Crime reporter as *'tertius gaudens'*

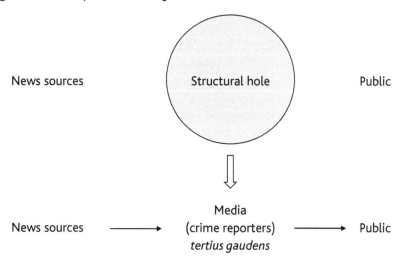

of key resources that frequently give them the upper hand' (Ericson et al, 1989, p 378).

Before the advent of the internet, journalists were extremely powerful in that they occupied 'a bridging position between two worlds that are structurally unconnected: the sources of news and the members of the audience' (Boczkowski and Mitchelstein, 2017, p 22). By forming a 'bridge' between the police and the public, journalists in the 1980s and 1990s could also be said to be bridging a 'structural hole' (Burt, 1992), as illustrated in Figure 2.1.

Burt introduced this concept in an attempt to explain the origin of differences in social capital. His theory argues that individuals hold certain positional advantages/disadvantages from how they are embedded in neighbourhoods or other social structures. A structural hole refers to an 'empty space' between contacts in a person's network and, according to Burt, '[t]hese holes in social structure – or more simply, structural holes – create a competitive advantage for an individual whose relationships span the holes' (Burt, 2002, p 337). He explains that the hole between these two groups does not mean that 'people in the groups are unaware of one another. It only means that the people are focused on their own activities such that they do not attend to the activities of people in the other group' (Burt, 2002, p 337). Accordingly, structural holes are 'an opportunity to broker the flow of *information* between people, and *control* the projects that bring together people from opposite sides of the hole' (Burt, 2002, p 337, emphasis in original). The person who brings these two worlds together is known as the *'tertius gaudens'* or the one who benefits, by controlling a flow of 'accurate, ambiguous or distorted information' (Burt, 2002, p 338) between these two worlds.

Until the early 1990s and the advent of the internet, 'making appeals directly to citizens while bypassing intermediaries' such as the news media was 'a relatively rare strategy available only to important figures such as the president of a country' (Boczkowski and Mitchelstein, 2017, p 23). This meant that, for the greater part of the 20th century and until the early 2000s, the main way in which the police could communicate with the general public – to ask for help with investigations, to appeal for witnesses or to promote police successes – was through the media and, in the case of this study, through crime reporters. In the context of crime news, the police might be the 'primary definers' (Hall et al, 1978, p 59) of information relating to crime or policing; yet journalists were arguably in an equally, if not more, powerful position in being able to control 'the information flow between newsmakers and their audiences' (Boczkowski and Mitchelstein, 2017, p 22).

Although early studies of police/news media relations (Chibnall, 1977; Hall et al, 1978) argued 'that the prevailing tendency of the media is towards the reproduction ... of the definitions of the powerful' (Hall et al, 1978, pp 65–6), these were not based on empirical research. Schlesinger and Tumber's (1994) study was, and they argued that, even among the privileged, primary definers' access to the media was not guaranteed. Similarly, respondents in this study described how stories had to be shaped to meet normative news values and appeal to the particular demographic in order to be released, with the result that many investigations were simply not covered by the media. As a former press officer explained:

'There's a borough called Southwark and in the Met it's called M district. And that became M for murder. And we had a Greek priest murdered in his church. And then you get a little old lady who just happened to be mugged in Brixton. And fallen, broke her arm and then died of pneumonia. That's a murder inquiry. But that was impossible to generate interest. Stories about little old ladies aren't seen as sexy or interesting. Whereas there was a case of a girl who was an ex-Playboy model who was found murdered in the East End. So that had all the right ingredients. Beautiful young girl, element of sleaze, found murdered. So that story ran and ran.'

Chibnall (1977) identifies a number of core news values or imperatives, which act as an implicit guide to the construction of news stories, including dramatisation, personalisation and immediacy. Jewkes (2004) updates this list, suggesting that a number of other news values also now determine an editor's perception of whether a story will appeal to his or her outlet's audience. These include stories that feature children as victims or offenders, stories with a celebrity angle, stories featuring crimes of a particularly violent or sexual nature, and stories featuring crimes with a strong element of spectacle, such as arson, rioting or police clashes with citizens. She also identifies proximity, both spatial and cultural, as an additional news value. Spatial proximity relates to the geographical nearness of an event while cultural proximity relates to the 'relevance' of an event or crime to an audience or readership. For example, Jewkes suggests that the likelihood of the national news media lending its weight to a campaign to find a missing person is far higher if that missing person is a child or a young woman who is White, middle-class and of British descent. By contrast, if a missing person or victim of a crime is older, of African, Caribbean or Asian descent, is working-class or has had previous convictions, 'reporters perceive that their audience is less likely to relate to, or empathize with, the victim, and the case gets commensurately lower publicity' (Jewkes, 2011, p 57). Thus, when wishing to access media assistance with certain investigations, press officers knew in advance that not all cases would fit the press's definition of newsworthiness (Fenton, 2009) or events that have met a 'certain level of perceived importance or drama' (Jewkes, 2011, p 45).

Another problem for the press office was when individual police officers used the news media to fight internal policy or conduct personality battles through the press:

> 'One of the hardest things for us was where police officers would go public to air their grievances. You'd often find in those situations that the officers had lodged Employment Tribunals [ET] against the organisation. So we were completely restricted about what we could and couldn't say because obviously we didn't want to prejudice the ET, for a start. But in those situations, our hands were tied, they knew it and that's why they did it.'

As Silverman comments, in this respect 'the corporate factionalism of the Met was not so very different from that of other large organizations' (Silverman, 2012, p 123). But as Ericson et al argue, 'because they are in the media spotlight constantly, the police are especially vulnerable to having their procedural strays focused upon' (Ericson et al, 1989, p 97) and any story where the Met had failed significantly would be 'seized on by print and broadcast journalists' (Silverman, 2012, p 124). In these circumstances, while disclosure might have allowed them to portray the organisation in a better light, press officers were 'organizationally constrained to stay mum' (Ericson et al, 1989, p 132).

Nevertheless, despite Chibnall's suggestion that the Press Bureau was 'jokingly referred to as the *Sup*press Bureau and its mobile representatives – Divisional Liaison Officers – [were] sometimes known as the Don't Let Ons'

(Chibnall, 1977, p 148, emphasis in original), press officers at the Bureau during this period seemed to have relationships with the press that were largely based on respect and reciprocity.

Senior police officers' relations with the media

Strategies to 'control' media relations

Although later studies of police/news media relations were grounded both in police press officers and journalists' perspectives (Ericson et al, 1987, 1989, 1991; Schlesinger and Tumber, 1994; Ericson, 1995; Innes, 1999; Mawby, 1999, 2002a), only Schlesinger and Tumber's (1994) study additionally draws on interviews with senior police officers whose work brought them into close contact with the press. For this study, I also interviewed senior police officers, including heads of specialist squads whose careers spanned this period.

Although senior officers admitted that, during their training at Hendon, they had been warned "never to speak to the Press and certainly never, ever trust a journalist", they also acknowledged that valuable early lessons they had learned while rising through the ranks were not only to cultivate good relations with the press but also to actively understand how the media functioned. As one officer explained:

> 'Something that wasn't taught then, but something you had to work out for yourself early on, was how to phrase things as an SIO [Senior Investigating Officer] when you release things to the media. You need to think what it is you want the media to hear, in terms of public relations and the public's understanding of what this crime is, and why the public need not bolt all their doors and lock up everything they possess tonight, because actually this is not a random attack. And I think once you learned that, you were less likely to be burned by the media.'

Many officers spoke of how their first contact with the press had been early on in their career, often as a sergeant:

> 'At certain times of the week, local papers would come in and you would go through the occurrence book, the accident book with them, and if you thought it suitable, you would give them background on incidents and then they would decide whether or not it was suitable.'

Respondents suggested that they often retained contacts in the press from those early days and kept in touch as both officer and journalist climbed up the career ladder. This partially echoes Chibnall's findings where he argues that through these informal or 'unofficial' contacts, '[r]eporters and policemen often develop an intimate knowledge of each other's family life' and that '[t]he pursuit of information provides a growth of friendship which is reinforced by a reciprocation of help and co-operation' (Chibnall, 1977, p 150). Certainly, some of the police respondents in this study noted, as did Chibnall's (1977) respondents, occasions on which crime reporters had been able to supply them with valuable information relating to an ongoing investigation:

> 'So for example, during my term in [X], the local newspaper decided it would run a campaign of its own to match a police operation called Operation Eagle, which was partly about education and partly about enforcement about drugs. And the paper brought in stacks of information – so much we didn't have time to look properly through it – but it was "go down to Granny so and so, she may seem as clean as a whistle but there's half a ton of gear in the bedroom". And the thing was, no one would want to seem a grass or a snout to the police, but they would talk to someone impartial in order to get this scourge out of their community.'

Another former senior police officer described how a colleague's relations were so good with one particular editor that they were able to suggest a steer as to how events might be reported in a particularly sensitive case:

> 'It was a difficult case about a Sikh man who had allegedly committed suicide in custody after beating up the woman he was living with. There were so many elements that were difficult, particularly as he'd taken his turban off and put it down the toilet and this was all utterly unacceptable to the family. They could not believe any of it – that he had beaten up a White woman, that he was drunk – and my colleague had to find ways of reporting the case which would not cause stress and grief. So he talked to the Home Affairs Correspondent and they put together an understanding of how they would report these cases.'

A final 'unofficial' way in which police officers used the press when trying to crack a case was what they termed a 'trigger event' (Chibnall, 1977; Campbell, 2016). According to Chibnall, this involved 'utilizing news as a medium of private communication with either the conscious or unconscious help of journalists' (Chibnall, 1977, p 192). However, police respondents in this study were adamant these ploys were only used with the express consent of the press outlets involved. One respondent described how a 'trigger event' worked:

> 'We would be interested for the purposes of an investigation how particular suspects would react to a story in the public domain. So we

would engineer a particular story in the media, or particular details in the hope that our suspects would say, "Blimey, what's all that about" while we would have ways of being able to listen into that conversation. Journalists were taken into confidence, written into the disclosure process. So we were actually involving them in a fairly complicated covert police operation.'

Similarly, Chibnall describes how, in the kidnapping of Muriel McKay,[4] the police planted information in the press to 'convey an exaggerated impression of Mrs McKay's urgent need for special drugs in the hope that her captors would panic and attempt to buy the drugs from chemists' (Chibnall, 1977, p 193).

Chibnall argues that, in the 1970s, the Press Bureau had 'a reputation for censorship' (Chibnall, 1977, p 148); however, senior police officers from this era described how, on the contrary, Press Bureau staff were often the first to put reporters phoning in for information in touch with senior investigating officers. As one former head of a specialist squad commented:

'I think it was very valuable for both sides. They would be able to get help and guidance from us and, in turn, we would be able to make sure that whatever went out was accurate and not the press taking a punt.'

Police respondents in Chibnall's study described requests from the Press Bureau staff for information as 'an annoying complication to their investigations' with one police officer commenting that he often had to 'fight the Bureau to prevent them getting stuff I knew but didn't want to get out' (Chibnall, 1977, p 146). However, those senior officers that I interviewed described how they frequently worked out media strategies with the Press Bureau:

'The Press Office were our bridge into the media. So when we went official for any reason at all, either we were approached or I was approached to talk to a journalist about something, I always made a point of doing it through the Press Office because I thought that was the best way to make sure that everybody was onside.'

At the same time, officers also spoke of how they used the Press Bureau as 'a safety net' – particularly on occasions when they did not want to disclose information to the press – and, in those circumstances, referred reporters back to the official channels (Ericson et al, 1989).

Police work is characterised by secrecy (Punch, 1983, 1985; Reiner, 2010). As Sir Robert Mark suggested, police officers have 'an almost unconscious but natural bent towards reticence and secrecy' (quoted in Chibnall, 1979, p 135). Police officers are also secretive in relation to each other (Ericson et al, 1989; Reiner, 2010). As Ericson et al comment, '[t]his secrecy is sometimes related to the desire to gain personal or subunit credit for work and/or the need to appear credible and "cover ass" with superiors' (Ericson et al, 1989, p 126). But this secrecy also comes into play '[i]n relation to the court system, [where] there is a need to control accounts of cases to achieve outcomes the police deem both just and justifiable' (Ericson et al, 1989, p 126). Disclosing information too soon to the press might jeopardise the integrity of an operation, might have a detrimental effect on citizens involved in a case or on victims' families, or give 'the "criminal element" information that would be to their benefit' (Ericson et al, 1989, p 128).

A former head of a specialist squad echoed Ericson et al's (1989) findings by explaining key reasons for withholding certain information from the press:

'Obviously, power over the release of information rests with the police and there's a good reason for us to keep a lot of that back from the press. So for example, when we're in an interview situation, and the suspect says, for example, that the victim was strangled, and we know that's never been released anywhere, we can get right in and say, "Oh, how do you know that then, as it's never been in the press". So it's a tactical device.'

Thus, a valuable 'strategy' of power (De Certeau, 1984), open to operational officers not wanting to disclose certain information to the press, was to refer journalists to the Press Bureau or 'the base from which relations with an exteriority composed of targets or threats ... can be managed' (De Certeau, 1984, p 36).

Another 'strategy' of power (De Certeau, 1984) used by operational officers to manage the press, was to employ a 'panoptic practice' (De Certeau, 1984, p 36), keeping possible competitors or attackers under close surveillance. While press officers employed this tactic by taking the press on police raids to ensure accurate reporting, police officers used the Press Bureau and its staff to hold 'controlled' press conferences, where the media would be given confidential information in the express knowledge that, if they printed it, they would be jeopardising critical MPS operations. A former head of a specialist squad gave an example:

'The accusation at the time was that we were exaggerating the terrorist threat, in order to support British foreign policy in Iraq. We had a lot of terrorist cases in the pipeline, where the evidence would eventually come out, but it was taking two or three years and we couldn't tell the public what we'd found. So there was a clear public interest in informing editors, we've found plans for dirty bombs, so that they didn't then rush off writing things which were wrong ... which would undermine our ability to mount effective investigations.'

This example signifies a constant dilemma for senior police officers in their dealings with the national media. If they remained secretive about sensitive operations, they ran the risk that reporters might seek out alternative sources over whom they would have very limited control, including accounts from citizens or even other police officers leaking the information from within the organisation. A paramount consideration for all officers leading sensitive cases was that if they did not talk to the press, the press could and would often "go away and dig things up by themselves", as one respondent claimed. As Ericson et al note, the source 'must consider the value of the story to the reporter and predict what length he will go to if denied access' (Ericson et al, 1989, p 132).

The problem of 'leaks' for operational officers

Ericson et al argue in their study of crime news reporting that 'control of knowledge is always partial' in any large organisation, and that 'police effort to control knowledge is a perpetual struggle' (Ericson et al, 1989, p 129). While 'unofficial' contacts with the press were often of benefit to operational officers, leaks – or 'knowledge that has not been screened or processed through official channels prior to release to reporters' (Ericson et al, 1989, p 135) – were highly problematic. When asked whether leaks were more of a problem with senior or junior staff, respondents suggested that they occurred at all levels:

> 'The worst case was one particular Assistant Commissioner who showed off. And, you know, he's then giving away other people's information. And these people sometimes forgot. They thought they were talking to journalists and being listened to as experts or even just fellow human beings. They're not. They're being listened to as senior police officers. Everything they say has that baggage.'

One police respondent described how he had endeavoured to keep secret the impending arrests of the four men involved in the attempted London bombing on 21 July 2005, to the extent that he had not even given the operational details to the Directorate of Media and Communication, "simply because you put anyone who has that information in an awkward position if there is a problem". However, as he recounted, the information was leaked to a television reporter:

> 'who was standing outside Parliament the day the arrests were made. Could have been the Met. Could have even have been inside Number Ten. Could have been both. But what I do know is the organisation is a sieve.'

Police respondents also noted that some reporters had access to systematic sources of police information (Ericson et al, 1989). As one respondent recalled:

'When I was at the Yard, it was known that one of the Murdoch[5] papers had on its books an ex-Detective Sergeant who was clearly able to screw information out of the system for them.'

When asked why they thought colleagues would leak information to the press, respondents suggested that it was for a variety of reasons and would vary according to the rank of the officer and the nature of the interaction he or she would have with the press (Ericson et al, 1989; Silverman, 2012). Some suggested that, at street level, officers might leak information to the press "for a sense of importance, getting one over on their colleagues, a bit of self-aggrandisement". Others suggested that ambition was a motivating factor at street level and above. As one police officer observed:

'You're a young ambitious cop, you want people to notice you so you need cuttings. And to get cuttings you need a tame reporter to highlight what you're doing.'

Feeling vulnerable in dealings with the press

In his study of police/news media relations, Mawby describes how he and a colleague interviewed two detectives from the Fred West[6] investigation team. He discusses the 'media pressures that the investigation had encountered' (Mawby, 1999, p 277), including detectives being followed into local pubs and eavesdropped upon by journalists, as well as journalists accessing key witnesses and paying for their stories, concluding that control over the media was problematic even in pre-internet days. While Chibnall asserted that 'in the final analysis the relationships are asymmetrical because the journalist is always in an inferior negotiating position' (Chibnall, 1977, p 155), senior police officers in this study believed themselves to be quite dependent on journalists in the process of co-operation with them. Senior officers argued that journalists could take snippets from interviews to give a context completely the opposite to that intended by the officer. Others talked about being interviewed by the media and being put in a compromising position by journalists:

'It was during the Southall riots in the 1980s. I had spent a lot of time working with the community leaders and what was very clear was that the riots in Southall were not riots against the police, they were rebelling against the restrictions of their families, seeing the freedoms Western friends had and wanting those freedoms too.

And when I spoke to the leaders, we made it very clear that we would be there as back-up but we would prefer if they were able to defuse the situation. In the middle of this I was asked if I would do a television interview.

An officer from the Press Bureau was there and we said that we would not be interviewed alongside any community leaders from the Asian community, it had to be a separate interview. We did not want it to be in any way that this was a clash between Asian youths and us. When I sat down in front of the camera, there was an Asian man there and again I said I wanted to be interviewed separately. The interviewer said it would be fine and he would deal with us in turn. Then the interview started and it was clear the interviewer wanted to set up a fight between the two of us, the Asian guy and me, which was the last thing I wanted as there was no conflict between me and the Asian community.'

The officer then explained how, in this instance, he had nevertheless managed to have 'the ultimate power, the last word' (Ericson et al, 1989, p 380):

'So when I thought the interview was coming to an end, I asked the Asian gentleman where he lived. He said he was from the East End of London and I said our community is Southall and he said, "Well, I know a lot of people there, who work there" and I asked, "Have you ever lived there?" and he said "No" and I asked, "What do you know about the community, about this incident?" and bang, it virtually ended there, and I felt I'd won the day.'

Officers also talked about how they felt personally under attack in the press in times of crisis, as the "public face of the force". One officer talked at length about a particularly confrontational press conference he had experienced:

'The case involved an individual who had a very on-off relationship with his wife and he decided to take a gun to the party that his wife and her mother and sister were having. He shot all three of them and two of them dead, and one of them died before we could get the ambulance there because basically my firearms officers thought they were dealing with another Hungerford. So the issue was all about how fast we got there and about one person dying in the process who probably would have died anyway, but the inquest found that that was a bit of a fine line. I did a big press conference, the day after, and I must have had over a hundred different press outlets, which is a lot by any stretch, most of whom were baying and the first question was, "Are you going to resign?" which is not a great start. So yes, you do feel vulnerable.'

In her update of Chibnall's (1977) news values, Jewkes (2004) adds a new category, 'simplification' (Jewkes, 2011, p 47). She argues that the media 'engage in a process of personalization in order to simplify stories and give them a "human interest" appeal, which results in events being viewed as the actions and reactions of people' (Jewkes, 2011, p 49), as in the case of this senior officer. Unlike a press officer who would almost certainly be at a press conference and help to shape the public account of events, the officer leading the conference is the one in the public eye, and the one facing condemnation by the press.

In contrast to press officers from this period, who suggested that they largely had a symbiotic relationship with the press, senior officers in this study suggested that, from their perspective, the media often held a lot of power (Ericson et al, 1989) – the power to edit, to deny access, to leak sensitive information into the public domain. As one former head of a specialist squad noted:

> 'Anyone who thinks they can manipulate the British media is mad. You can try and inform them, you can try and make sure that what they say is based on accurate information but the idea that you can manipulate or control the media is mad. The media will write what they want and are fearsomely independent.'

Conclusion

In this chapter, I have explored relations between the MPS – both press officers and operational officers – and national crime reporters from the 1970s to the millennium. In revisiting the body of literature on police/news media relations from the 1970s through to the late 1990s (Chibnall, 1977; Hall et al, 1978; Ericson et al, 1987, 1989, 1991; Schlesinger and Tumber, 1994; Mawby, 1999), I suggest that these relationships were even more complex and contingent than these earlier studies suggest. Drawing on De Certeau's (1984) work on strategies of surveillance and control, I explore the 'strategies' of power (De Certeau, 1984, p xix) used by MPS officers in their dealings with the national press.

From the 1970s, I suggest that press officers adopted a proactive stance in their dealings with the media, in contrast with their predecessors who tended to take a more reactive stance. One 'strategy' of power was to be more proactive in preparing how to deal with the media in the case of future serious emergencies. Another strategy was to release bad news pre-emptively to the press with the aim of limiting harmful and inaccurate reporting; while a third strategy was to give journalists access to sensitive operations as a way of preventing dangerous 'leaks', or information not already processed through official channels, which might endanger the lives of those involved and jeopardise the investigation. However, despite these strategies, press officers also noted that access to the media was never guaranteed (Schlesinger and Tumber, 1994) and that stories had to be shaped to meet normative news values and appeal to the particular demographic in order to be released, with the result that many investigations were simply not covered by the media. In the case of missing persons, in particular, appeals for help by the police were often not covered by the press.

I also interviewed senior police officers and heads of specialist squads whose work regularly brought them into contact with the press and whose careers spanned the early 1980s to the early 2000s. Although many officers interviewed for this study recalled that, as part of their training, they were warned not to trust the press, all of them spoke of the importance for them personally and operationally of getting the press onside as they progressed through the ranks. Respondents talked of how crime correspondents often had more 'underworld' contacts and were able on occasion to help officers 'crack' cases through their contacts. However, one problem noted by all senior officers interviewed for this study was that of 'leaks', which they suggested happened at all levels and for a variety of reasons, including self-aggrandisement, ambition or a desire to wound colleagues. Others commented that, at times, they believed themselves to be personally attacked and beleaguered by the press, when investigations did not turn out as planned, or evidence of police malpractice or abuses of power were revealed. In contrast to the press officers interviewed for this study, these senior officers suggested that, from their perspective, the press in this period were extremely powerful and frequently had the upper hand.

3

Police 'control' and the UK national press

Introduction

One of the earliest crime reporters in the United Kingdom was Charles Dickens, who started his career as a court reporter at the age of 17 in 1829 – the same year in which the Metropolitan Police was set up by Sir Robert Peel. As noted by Duncan Campbell, the veteran crime reporter and writer, Dickens was both fascinated by and friendly with the new police force, 'notably detectives, with whose arrival in British fiction he is often credited' (Campbell, 2016, p 25). Dickens was, according to Campbell, 'expansive in his admiration of the police, who responded by allowing him unprecedented access', including 'travelling into criminal redoubts and spending a night at Bow Street police station' (Campbell, 2016, p 25). Campbell comments that the newly formed Metropolitan Police force must also have realised that allowing writers and journalists access would have considerable benefits for them; as 'allowing someone to see how they work often leads to sympathy and understanding' and might encourage those observers to 'side with the people who are looking after them and ... be tempted to ignore their flaws' (Campbell, 2016, p 26).

Greer and McLaughlin (2011b) argue that a key component of past research on news media and police relationships is Becker's (1967) concept of the 'hierarchy of credibility', a model proposing that, in any society, it is taken for granted that governing elites have the power to 'define the way things really are' (Becker, 1967, p 241). Chibnall argued that the journalist was always in an inferior negotiating position, and suggested that, because of that dependence on the police, reporters were 'obliged to make [their] stories acceptable to [their] personal contacts' (Chibnall, 1977, p 155). Although this model influenced early studies of crime reporting in the 1970s (Hall et al, 1978), subsequent studies in Canada in the late 1980s (Ericson et al, 1987, 1989) and in the United Kingdom in the 1990s (Schlesinger and Tumber, 1994) stressed the importance of economic factors and organisational behaviour as well as working relationships between sources and reporters in shaping the news, and suggested that '[p]owerful sources still have to pursue goal-oriented action to achieve access, even though their recognition as "legitimate authorities" is already usually inscribed in the rules of the game' (Schlesinger and Tumber, 1994, p 26).

This chapter explores, from the perspective of journalists, the complex and contingent web of relations – both official and unofficial – that existed between the Metropolitan Police and national crime journalists from the 1980s to the early 2000s. It examines the ways in which journalists attempted to circumvent 'the often limiting structured access they have to information and the content of the information being released to them' (Lee and McGovern, 2014, p 191) and also explores the under-researched 'tactics' of resistance (De Certeau, 1984) used by Metropolitan Police Officers to fight internal policy or personality battles using the media (Silverman, 2012). It argues that, during this pre-social media era, from a network analytic perspective, journalists occupied a 'bridging position between two worlds that are structurally unconnected: the sources of news and the members of the audience' (Boczkowski and Mitchelstein, 2017, p 22). Far from being in an inferior negotiating position with the police during this era (Chibnall, 1977), it suggests that crime reporters derived considerable power as the '*tertius gaudens*' (Simmel, 1950; Obstfeld, 2005) or the third party who benefits from brokering information and access between other players.

The end of the 'golden age' of crime reporting

In his study of crime reporting, Duncan Campbell describes how, in the 1950s and 1960s, some crime reporters were 'better known than the villains and detectives whose activities they covered' (Campbell, 2016, p 91) and how the world of what he terms 'the Sultans of the Newsroom' (Campbell, 2016, p 91) was one of 'booze and tobacco and camaraderie and cheerfully creative expenses' (Campbell, 2016, p 98). He describes how 'many of the Sultans had individual detectives with whom they were particularly close'; in particular, how *The Telegraph*'s crime correspondent, Tom Sandrock, who died in 2004, was on very friendly terms with a Detective Superintendent in the Flying Squad, who would reportedly 'brief his officers in a corner of the St Stephen's dive bar, off Whitehall, and would then tell Sandrock which stories he could print' (Campbell, 2016, p 102). Relations between this particular officer and Sandrock were so close that, according to his obituary in *The Telegraph*, if Sandrock was drinking with detectives when a tip-off came in, he would sometimes be asked to act as a driver to take them to the scene of the crime.

During the 1960s, reporters even had their own press room – and bar – at Scotland Yard. As one reporter said:

'When I first started, you could just walk into Scotland Yard, press the buzzer on the ground floor, give your name, and then you'd go up to the press room. There was an old armchair in there, and you'd usually see some old crime reporter slumped in that, waiting for someone else to come along. And there were little old fashioned booths where you could file a story. And you'd say, "Do you want to go for a drink?" And then we might see a Press Officer or we'd ring them and they would come for a drink as well.'

The same reporter went on to recount how he was actively encouraged by his editor on a national daily to stop working from his employer's newsroom and instead set himself up more or less permanently in the police newsroom:

'I remember one of my first weeks on the paper, I was in the office, on my own in the little reporters' pen. And the News Editor came over and said "Is everything alright? You're not ill, are you?" And I said "No". So he said, "Well fucking hell, what are you doing here? Get out, man and get down to the Yard".'

As Reiner notes, the mid-1960s were 'glowing ones for press treatment of the police' (Reiner, 2010, p 183) perhaps in part due to the seemingly close relations between the MPS and certain sections of the British press. Chapter 2 described the modernisation of the Press Bureau, but the 1960s were also a period of profound reorganisation for the police as an institution, centring on the new Unit Beat system of patrol. Under this new system, 'area constables would have the function of preserving close relations with the local communities, the [new] panda cars would provide a faster emergency service, the collator would analyse information provided by the patrol officers for use in detecting offences, and all police officers would gain enhanced status and job interest' (Reiner, 2010, p 79). Although, as Reiner notes, there was in practice a shortage of manpower to implement this properly, these changes were singled out by the press 'as a modernizing breakthrough', and the MPS's 'gang-busting successes' (Reiner, 2010, p 183) against the notorious gangs of the 1960s – the Krays and the Richardsons – were also celebrated.

But this police–press accord was seriously threatened by the series of scandals uncovered by the press from the late 1960s onwards. In 1969, *The Times* revealed evidence of widespread corruption within the MPS and this was followed by two further major corruption scandals relating to the MPS, one involving the Drug Squad, the other involving the Obscene Publications Squad. Both revealed systematic malpractice and led to the imprisonment of several senior detectives.

Although Chibnall's (1977) study of Fleet Street reporters suggested that a majority saw it as their responsibility to present the police in a favourable light, Reiner (2010) suggested that, from the 1980s onwards, the picture changed considerably. While specialist crime reporters 'used to be found only on tabloid newspapers' and 'tended to see themselves as extensions of the working team of detectives whose crime-busting exploits they glamorized and celebrated' (Reiner, 2010, p 181), in the 1980s, broadsheet newspapers as well as the BBC and ITV started to employ specialist crime correspondents, although often under labels such as 'home affairs' or 'legal correspondents' rather than specifically crime (Schlesinger and Tumber, 1994). According to Schlesinger and Tumber, this was in part due to a change in 'public discourse about crime' shifting 'from predominantly offering descriptions of crimes ... to a wider one that now include[d] police accountability and government policy on law and order' (Schlesinger and Tumber, 1994, p 147) – particularly on the broadsheets competing for upmarket audiences 'that included solicitors, barristers, and others working in the legal profession' (Schlesinger and Tumber, 1994, p 148).

Although many of the correspondents on tabloid newspapers traditionally 'established close affinities with police officers' (Ericson et al, 1989, p 104), relations between the police and correspondents on the broadsheet newspapers – and freelancers working for them – were less harmonious. Chibnall notes that '[h]arassment [was] a feature of police dealings with members of the fringe or radical press, but similar allegations are also occasionally made by journalists working for "respectable" Fleet Street papers' (Chibnall, 1977, p 183); reporters working for *The Guardian* 'rarely forged close ties with police contacts' and 'felt that their paper was unpopular with the police who ... regarded it as a little too libertarian' (Chibnall, 1977, p 183). Chibnall also notes that, although the exposé of corruption in the MPS by *The Times* in 1969 was carried out by a special team of reporters working independently of the paper's regular crime reporters, 'the repercussions of the story were wide-ranging', with one reporter from *The Times* suggesting that police contacts were 'not as available as before' (Chibnall, 1977, p 163).

General coverage of police matters from the 1980s onwards became increasingly critical. Reiner argues that news footage of the miners' strike[1] in the mid-1980s revealed apparent police abuses; and while coverage of the 1990 anti-poll tax demonstration[2] in Trafalgar Square 'initially portrayed the police favourably', it was subsequently subject to 'media analyses probing allegations of mishandling and malpractice' (Reiner, 2010, p 185). The media were also 'prominent in the process by which the major *causes célèbres* of police abuses leading to miscarriages of justice have been revealed, notably the Guildford Four, the Birmingham Six, and the Tottenham Three.[3] In each case individual investigative journalists ... were pivotal factors in discrediting the police evidence' (Reiner, 2010, p 185).

Nevertheless, Reiner argues that, in the 1990s and early 2000s, the overall presentation of the police in the media remained 'highly-favourable' but 'volatile and ... constantly liable to be sabotaged by scandals or spectacular failures' (Reiner, 2010, p 183). An example was the murder of Stephen Lawrence, a Black British teenager who was murdered in a racially motivated attack while waiting for a bus in Eltham in 1993. After the initial inquest, five suspects were arrested but not charged. The Lawrence family subsequently launched a private prosecution, which collapsed, but there was a second inquest in February 1997. Following the five suspects' refusal to answer any questions, the *Daily Mail*, a paper 'known for its traditionally reactionary stance on race issues' (Greer, 2010a, p 264), printed a front page headline accusing the suspects of Lawrence's murder and giving the names and photographs of the suspects. It was a newspaper event that epitomised the 'brittle character of the representation and public standing of the police in the 1990s' (Reiner, 2010, p 185).

The police as official source for journalists

The last chapter described how, according to De Certeau, the first key strategy of power for any organisation is to establish a 'base from which relations with an exteriority composed of targets or threats (customers or competitors, enemies [...]) can be managed' (De Certeau, 1984, p 36). In the case of the Metropolitan Police and its relations with the national press, this base was the DPA, and within that base, the Press Bureau was the official point of contact for crime reporters.

Respondents in this study said that they routinely listened to the Press Bureau's audiotape of breaking stories, which ran continuously through the day and was updated every hour. The other back-up used by crime correspondents was the Press Association, which also reported on crime news at regular intervals (Schlesinger and Tumber, 1994).

The other 'official' channel for crime reporters to make contact, particularly with senior officers, was the Crime Reporters' Association (CRA). This was formed in 1945 with the 'dual function of pressure group for better facilities for gathering information, and business-like organization whose members the police could distinguish from less responsible practitioners of Fleet Street journalism' (Chibnall, 1977, p 50). In January every year, the CRA would hold a reception to which they would invite the Home Secretary, senior Metropolitan Police officers as well as chief constables. According to Schlesinger and Tumber (1994), this was an informal occasion, where reporters could get to know senior police officers better and exchange ideas. There was also a special membership tie embossed with a crossed quill pen and handcuffs (Campbell, 2016). In London, CRA members also belonged to a 'lobby' organised by the Metropolitan Police – an initiative started by Sir Robert Mark, then Commissioner, in the 1970s – and this took the form of a monthly briefing by the Commissioner.

Journalists interviewed for this study suggested that openness or otherwise of relations between the MPS and crime journalists varied according to successive Commissioners' policies on official and unofficial contact with the press, to individual press officers' attitudes to their role, and to relationships of trust between those officers and individual reporters. One journalist gave an example of this:

'For years, I'd had this vision of the Met as this impenetrable fortress. But when Imbert took over, he wanted genuinely to know what was wrong. And during his time, I wrote a long piece about racial violence and was taken out in Southall by the Chief Superintendent, openly saying, "I don't know how to talk to these people and I know that's a problem for our force".'

But he also suggested that access could be stopped or restricted at any time, due to a change in Commissioner or a change in Press Bureau personnel:

'There was a new head of the Press Bureau and I needed access to some officers for a story and I called her up and she said, "What's in it for us?" And I realised in that second that the world had changed yet again and the easy flow of information I'd had was about to be stopped.'

However, for most journalists, the real stories are to be found in the back regions of an organisation, areas not usually open to them or other members of the public. One way in which journalists try to circumvent the official control of information is to establish their own inside contacts and sources. In De Certeau's work, the concept of 'tactics' of resistance is used to explore how people use mass culture, altering objects, representations or rituals imposed upon them by 'producers' to make them their own – or as De Certeau puts it, 'poaching … on the property of others' (De Certeau, 1984, p xii). In terms of the police/news media relationships, journalists also resist 'strategies' of power by 'poaching' and operating within 'enemy territory' (De Certeau, 1984, p 37) through the establishment of unofficial contacts within the police organisation (Chibnall, 1977; Ericson et al, 1989; Schlesinger and Tumber, 1994; Mawby, 2010, 2012; Lee and McGovern, 2014; Colbran, 2017). These contacts are able to provide journalists with 'information beyond the official information release' and are 'not just one-off instances of information exchange in reaction to particular events or stories' but 'operate as structured allegiances that can be seen as competing and/or operating in tandem with official channels of information' (Lee and McGovern, 2014, p 195). This was suggested by a number of reporters who participated in this study. One stated:

'So for example, I might have heard a story on the tape and if I know the police officer concerned, I can ring him up and say, "is this right or who else do I need to talk to about this" and it's going to be much faster than if I ask the press office to set me up. So I wouldn't knock the press office entirely. They do try to be helpful but they don't have detailed knowledge.'

While many studies of police/news media relations suggest that the police were the primary source of stories for crime journalists, on both official and unofficial levels (Ericson et al, 1989; Schlesinger and Tumber, 1994; Lee and McGovern, 2014), a significant number of journalists in this study, particularly those working for the broadsheets or as freelance reporters, stated that the police were not, in fact, a primary source of stories and that their main contacts were drawn from a wider field, including barristers, solicitors, victims and offenders. But for all respondents, 'the use of contacts [was] practically essential to being able to carry out their investigative roles impartially' (Lee and McGovern, 2014, p 195).

The two cultures of journalism

In their study of police/news media relations in Toronto, Ericson et al (1989) identified two distinct cultures of crime journalists, each with their own approach to news management. The first culture consisted of what they described as the 'inner circle', who generally but not always worked for popular news outlets, with a focus on reporting crime incidents, and who often established close affinities with police officers. 'Outer circle' journalists, on the other hand, often either worked for 'quality' outlets or were freelance and were professionally more detached from the police, with 'the important mission of policing the police rather than only policing with them' (Ericson et al, 1989, p 110). Similarly in this study, respondents in the United Kingdom appeared to fall into these two cultures – inner circle or crime correspondents, working on the day-to-day reporting of crime incidents, and thus dependent on police sources for information, and who generally worked for tabloids; and an outer circle or group of investigative journalists, either working freelance and contributing to the radical or fringe press, or writing for quality broadsheets, whose stories tended to focus much more on police impropriety or inefficiency, and who were consequently not as dependent on police sources for their stories.

Making contacts

Inner circle journalists

There seemed to be two main paths into crime reporting for both inner and outer circle journalists. The first path, which was principally – but not exclusively – taken by inner circle journalists, was to complete an approved training course in journalism and then secure a job on a local paper. Many inner circle journalists described how they made their first informal police contacts while working for local papers, and maintained those relationships as they – and their police contacts – rose through the ranks. One inner circle journalist described how he made his first police contacts in the 1960s, by visiting his local police station every week to go through the station 'crime book' with the sergeant in charge of collating it:

'And I had to go to these police stations, twice a week, and go through all these hard copy, leather bound crime books – major crime book, minor crime book, motor vehicle crime book. So you'd be told something like "There was a Post Office robbery, two men came in, armed with a knife and stole two and hundred and fifty pounds". So then I'd ask "Who's the officer dealing with it", and sometimes that officer would be helpful, sometimes they would be downright rude, but quite often you'd strike up a bit of a rapport, especially with the younger Detective Constables, as we'd be interested in the same sort of thing – football, fishing, chasing women.'

Campbell (2016) notes that many crime reporters on local papers often shared 'the same class background' as the officers they were working with – usually a working-class background, leaving school at 16, either to become a police cadet or to train as a reporter at a local college of further education – and that this aided a working and indeed natural affinity between them (Chibnall, 1977; Mawby, 2010).

Outer circle journalists

By contrast, outer circle journalists or investigative reporters were usually university-educated, did not complete a formal journalism training course, and often started their careers working as a freelance for radical or alternative publications with a definite anti-authority and anti-police stance:

'I started through local radio, then *Time Out* magazine, erm, which used to have a big news section in the 1970s. Then *City Limits* and then a London evening paper and then *The Guardian*. These were all publications that would be seen as more critical of the police, so inevitably we wouldn't be given stories some of the tabloids might get, as they would be seen as more sympathetic to the police point of view.'

But not all outer circle journalists started their careers with a conscious anti-police bias. Sometimes they started working for underground presses or alternative outlets because it was often easier to find lower-paid and freelance work on these titles, without prior experience on local papers or formal journalistic training (Campbell, 2016). One outer circle journalist explained that his attitudes towards the police had changed radically as a result of the investigations he was asked to carry out by the editor of an outlet known for its radical stance on the police and on the criminal justice system:

> 'I was covering a case about a young Black woman who was charged with various offences and it was clear that the police were giving very questionable evidence against her. And I got talking to her defence lawyer, who was an Asian barrister, who later became a QC and became a close friend. And a lot of them were very angry about these issues. And that, in turn, very much influenced me in my attitudes towards the police at that time. And I began to see the police, as the lawyers did, as an institution that was repressive and evil and badly in need of radical reform.'

Most outer circle journalists suggested that the police were rarely a primary source of stories for them. One respondent said that his relations with the MPS were so bad that "If I ring the Met, I hear them making noises at the sound of my name at the other end of the phone". As Ericson et al note, 'the police reporter in the quality news outlets had a very different work experience than his counterpart in the inner circle', and there was often 'a "running battle" between outer-circle reporters and the police' (Ericson et al, 1989, p 112). In the case of this respondent, this was in part due to the reputation his particular news organisation had gained over the years, for breaking several major stories of police corruption and malpractice, and also due to the anti-police stance in his reporting. However, other outer circle journalists acknowledged that they did occasionally use unofficial police contacts, but that they needed to be careful not to make these contacts public or they would alienate their other sources, who were, as one outer circle journalist described, "members of the public, victims, witnesses, relatives of people in prison, solicitors and barristers".

In the same vein, when asked about sources other than the police, inner circle journalists acknowledged that they would like to have a wider circle of contacts than they did, but were fearful of alienating the main source of what they termed "bread and butter work" from the police. As one inner circle journalist explained:

> 'So if you're at the Old Bailey on a regular basis, you probably would come into contact with barristers, in particular, or defence lawyers who would specialise in defending, say, armed robbers. But then if you got too close to them, that would in turn poison your relationship with detectives.'

For many of the older outer circle journalists, the criminal underworld was a particularly rich seam of contacts and source of story material. One veteran outer circle journalist explained how he came to make so many contacts within this world:

'I was working on *Time Out* and someone told me to cover this case – it was a murder, very gruesome murder, a torso was found in the Thames. So I went along to the Old Bailey, the trial went on for seven months, and I got to meet people on the periphery, people who were involved in this world. And then one person introduces you to another. And because I already had a reputation for covering miscarriages of justice, people started coming to me with other cases they thought I should know about.'

Establishing trust with contacts

Chibnall (1977) also notes how a system of sponsorship often existed on local newspapers, whereby seasoned and senior crime reporters would introduce new recruits to their contacts. As one inner circle journalist explained:

'When I started on a local paper there was a tradition. So I replaced a long established crime reporter, and he left me a list of contacts, so I could follow in his footsteps and introduce myself as his successor.'

But as the same reporter explained, 'that just got my foot in the door'; trust had to be established over a period of time. Chibnall describes how, in order to be accepted by police contacts, the crime reporter was often subjected to 'a lengthy period of probation' (Chibnall, 1977, p 151). As one reporter told me:

'They wanna get to know you, they want to know, can we trust this bloke? You know, if we tell him a few things about a villain, then let's see what he does with it, does he go to some dodgy solicitor or something. So that's your test and if you pass, then they gradually give you a bit more.'

Just as inner circle journalists had to go through a period of 'initiation' with their police contacts (Chibnall, 1977), outer circle journalists also had to prove that they were trustworthy to the criminal fraternity:

'I had one story where somebody claimed that they were not guilty of a murder, a mass murder in fact. Escaped from prison, went on the run ... contact was made with us and we agreed to do an interview on the basis that we wouldn't turn him in and so on and that he would give himself up as soon as he had got enough publicity for his story. Obviously, the police saw it and wanted to know who'd set up the interview and we just said no comment. So they threatened that they would take it to the DPP [Director of Public Prosecutions] for obstruction and perverting the course of justice. But he gave himself up three weeks later, and then he was found innocent, a few years after that. But once you get a reputation that you can be trusted, people will come forward.'

Although inner circle journalists were adamant that they had never paid for information from their police contacts, beyond paying for the odd meal or drink, outer circle journalists acknowledged that the situation was somewhat different with contacts in the underworld. As one freelance respondent explained:

'Criminals don't go to the press to further their career. Generally, it's because they've been fitted up. But the other reason is that, especially if they're in prison, selling their stories to the press can be a nice little earner.'

As another outer circle journalist suggested, the relationship between the press and the criminal underworld was not without its benefits for reporters. Having connections in the criminal fraternity meant that reporting on issues such as drugs or organised crime would be based on informed insider information:

'I think that's why we see such naive reporting at times by the mainstream lot, because they don't have any knowledge of that world. So police or Customs might tell them that they'd got a haul with a street value of three million, but if you knew anything at all about that world, you'd know the street value would be more like half a million. But obviously no one's going to phone up on behalf of the Federation of Drug Traffickers and say actually the value was much less than they were claiming.'

Unsurprisingly, many outer circle journalists interviewed for this study were critical of inner circle journalists, expressing 'their distance from the values and practices of the inner circle' (Ericson et al, 1989, p 110). One outer circle journalist commented that:

'They are very reluctant to write stories that might piss off the police, and I think you can point to a whole host of corruption cases or serious wrong-doing and misconduct that have been under-reported by them.'

Outer circle journalists also argued that what they were doing was of greater 'value both professionally and for society' (Ericson et al, 1989, p 110) than the work of inner circle journalists, described by one outer circle journalist as "cheerleaders for the Met". Conversely, some inner circle journalists expressed their distance from outer circle journalists, expressing some derision and disbelief that outer circle journalists "did not want to sully their hands by getting too close to the police".

Tactics of resistance: inner circle journalists' relations with the police

Self-censorship

As described earlier in this chapter, 'tactics' of resistance (De Certeau, 1984) operate in the 'space of the other', and are manoeuvres 'within enemy territory' (De Certeau, 1984, p 37) – in this case, crime journalists utilising informal contacts within the police organisation. However, as a number of inner circle journalists explained, there was a distinct culture of openness with the Press Bureau for much of the 1980s and 1990s, with the Press Bureau often actively encouraging journalists to talk to investigating officers so that they could report more accurately on a case and avoid printing any sensitive material that might jeopardise a case. But as Ericson et al also note, the 'perfection of knowledge-control is to have reporters censoring themselves, routinely enclosing knowledge that is not helpful to the police and disclosing knowledge that is helpful' (Ericson et al, 1989, p 152).

Chibnall comments that, having made contacts within the police organisation, the inner circle journalist also needs 'to invest effort in cultivating suitable sources' with reporters, suggesting that the development of friendships with detectives involves 'hard work and hard drinking' (Chibnall, 1977, p 150). Similarly, respondents in this study talked about the need to "keep contacts sweet" and ringing them regularly "even if you hadn't had a story from them for a year or two". Often, as inner circle journalists suggested, over time these informal drinks or meals out would develop into friendship, with reporters and police officers developing intimate knowledge of each other's lives – and carrying on those friendships as they both rose up the ladder in their respective fields (Schlesinger and Tumber, 1994). But as the veteran journalist, Roy Greenslade, noted in Duncan Campbell's (2016) study of crime reporting in the United Kingdom:

[Y]ou were locked into a culture where your job was to turn over villains not the police. The idea that the police were any more corrupt than the occasional cuff over the ear did not form part of the culture. You depended so much on them. Your stories were on the effects of crime and the only way you got them was by being friendly with the police. (Greenslade, quoted in Campbell, 2016, p 144)

In the same vein, another inner circle respondent explained that the price of staying on the good side of police contacts was often to turn a blind eye to police misdemeanours and, in the case described in the following quote, protecting police informants:

'I can remember having conversations with detectives and saying "Yeah, this bloke whose been stabbed, you know, last night at the Wanstead flats? Is there any chance I could get a word with him?" And, you know, I've actually had officers say "Er, listen, erm, listen now, er, no I don't think so, I don't think he'd wanna talk to you." And you had these awakening moments, if you see what I mean, and I'd say, you know, "Sorry, why not?" And they'd say, "He wasn't where he was supposed to be, right. But he's a nice bloke, you know, he's not a villain, he's been stabbed, so we've told his wife he got stabbed somewhere else doing something".'

As Ericson et al note, the 'cultural spirit' of inner circle journalists 'was with the police, matching where they spent their time and who they most often related to socially' (Ericson et al, 1989, p 108). Relations with police sources were based primarily on friendship, but that meant that '[w]hen the values of journalism collided with the values of police culture, the police culture usually prevailed' (Ericson et al, 1989, p 108). At the same time, winning the trust of police sources 'provided many gains for these reporters' (Ericson et al, 1989, p 108). As the inner circle respondent quoted previously also explained:

'I know there were a lot of journalists who would have said to me about that story about the stabbing, that they would have written it. But I knew how the police work and I played the long game and it worked for me. I never ever went up to those sources and said, "You owe me a favour". But every now and again, I'd be contacted, someone would say, "Do you remember me, I was a detective at [X] and I'm somewhere else now but you did me a really big favour all those years ago. So if you pop in to see me, I think I've got something big for you".'

Losing police trust and the consequences

According to De Certeau, the art of the tactic is 'an art of the weak' (De Certeau, 1984, p 37) and what a tactic 'wins it cannot keep' but 'must accept the chance offerings of the moment, and seize on the wing the possibilities that offer themselves at any given moment' (De Certeau, 1984, p 37). Inner circle journalists might have access, both official and unofficial, to officers at all levels, but that access would come at a price and could be withdrawn at any moment. As Campbell argues, 'if the police thought that a reporter was aiming to expose or denigrate their colleagues, cooperation would swiftly end and the tip-offs and inside information, on which crime reporters relied, would soon cease' (Campbell, 2016, p 145). A journalist gave an example of this:

'The then Commissioner wanted to give me an interview about miscarriages of justice just before the Birmingham Six were released, and he was saying he was quite sure the conviction was going to be quashed. Which was very controversial. So it came out in *The Observer*, and he hit the roof. I was phoned up by the Press Bureau and they were furious saying I'd let them down. And I said, "He's not actually disputing he said these things, so what are you on about?" But clearly they or this person in particular expected reporters, specialist crime reporters, to be up the Met's arse. And very quickly after that, I realised I was blacklisted.'

As Ericson et al (1989) also argue, there is 'considerable variation in who controls the process, depending on the context, the type of sources involved, the type of news organizations involved, and what is at issue' (Ericson et al, 1989, p 378). While the majority of inner circle journalists were cognisant of the need to keep police sources onside, this did not mean that the power in those relationships to control news accounts was always in the hands of police sources.

In Chapter 2, I suggested that one way of theorising the complexity of the ebb and flow of these relationships was through Burt's (1992, 2002) theory of structural holes. I argued that, before the advent of the internet, crime journalists occupied a privileged position as the bridge or '*tertius gaudens*' (Simmel, 1950) between the two unconnected worlds of news sources such as the police and the general public. By controlling the flow of information to the public, crime journalists in the 1980s and 1990s possessed 'fundamental assets that put them in a powerful position' (Ericson et al, 1989, p 378) from a police perspective. Not only were the media the main facilitator of 'the police-public relationship through the reporting of police activities to the community' (Lee and McGovern, 2014, p 114) but they also possessed 'the power to deny a source any access; the power to sustain coverage that contextualizes the source negatively' and 'the power of the last word' (Ericson et al, 1989, p 378). But both inner and outer circle journalists had another key asset for individual police officers. As the bridge or '*tertius gaudens*', they had the power to make or break police reputations (Silverman, 2012).

Tactics of resistance by the police

Using the press to make or break colleagues' reputations

As Lee and McGovern argue, journalists 'are not the only ones in these relationships who actively resist attempts to govern their activities'. They suggest that '[t]he police themselves can also resist the efforts of police hierarchies and/or governments to closely manage and monitor their role in communications with the media and the public' (Lee and McGovern, 2014, p 199). Silverman (2012) suggests that one key element missing from past studies of police/news media relationships is the use made of the press by individual officers to further their own personal agendas. In his study, he quotes Richard Offer, the then head of the press office at the Police Complaints Authority, on these 'tactics' of resistance by police officers:

> The thing I noticed about the Met was that every single person who had a grievance went rushing off to the media – and each section fought its case through the press. I was always teasing John Steele [the *Daily Telegraph* crime correspondent] that he was the official spokesman for the firearms unit because they trusted him and he picked up a lot of stories from the unit. Similarly, whenever a squad was threatened with cuts or disbandment, the story would appear in the *Evening Standard*. (Offer, quoted in Silverman, 2012, p 123)

According to Silverman (2012), this was a problem that particularly affected the MPS and that was not seen in other forces – mainly because of the large number of senior officers in the MPS, all with their own personal political agenda and the desire to move up the career ladder. As a result, he suggests that one tactic of resistance used by senior police officers to ensure promotion was to use the press to discredit their rivals.

A respondent interviewed for this study gave an example of this. He was given in confidence a story about a senior police officer's sexual indiscretion by one of the officer's colleagues. However, as the journalist explained, the motive for divulging this secret was not merely to discredit a colleague but to bring about, by using the leverage of adverse publicity in the press, the officer in question's resignation. As the respondent explained:

> 'I thought long and hard, was this in the public interest? So I was taking soundings from other senior police officers who were independent, who didn't have an axe to grind against that man. And I came to the conclusion that it had to be. He was a senior officer who came within a whisker of losing his job over a high profile murder case. Who had exercised poor judgement. And had gone on holiday in the first 24 hours of a major investigation, two missing girls, it had tragedy written

all over that case in the first 24 hours. If he'd had a clean slate, so to speak, beforehand ... then I might, I might not have done it.'

As Burt (1992) comments, the structural hole argument is one 'of negotiated instead of absolute control' (Burt, 1992, p 7) and the process of negotiation by the *tertius* with one party seeking to communicate with another through the *tertius* is 'about initiating and sculpting the deal' (Burt, 1992, p 6). This example shows very clearly that type of 'negotiated control' in the interaction between some police officers and some inner circle journalists. But it could also be seen as an example of what Bizzi (2013) calls the 'dark side of structural holes' (Bizzi, 2013, p 1555). While Burt's (1992) study concentrates mainly on the benefits to the *tertius* in bridging unconnected ties in the workplace, both Bizzi (2013) and, in an earlier study, Obstfeld (2005) argue that structural hole theory can also be seen as being 'built on the idea of adversarial relationships, on manipulating others for one's own personal benefit, and on playing people off against one another' (Bizzi, 2013, p 1555) – in this case, a game played by both police and press. Finally, this example also demonstrates the complexity and contingency of those relationships. While stories criticising the police as an organisation might pose problems for inner circle journalists seeking to maintain good relationships with both official and unofficial contacts within the MPS, it could be argued that criticism of individual officers might cause embarrassment to the MPS but would not attract the same opprobrium – not least because such offending could be explained away by what Reiner terms 'a "one bad apple" framework' (Reiner, 2010, p 181), or as an isolated procedural stray. In this framework, stories of police malpractice could be seen as an unfortunate one-off incident, 'implying that the discovery and punishment of the rare evil individual was proof that the police institution remained wonderful' (Reiner, 2010, p 181).

Using the press to break stories about police corruption

Although many outer circle journalists emphasised their detachment from the police, a number of this group also acknowledged that there were times when unofficial police sources would bypass the official MPS channels of communication and approach them with information about police corruption and malpractice.

Many studies have stressed the codes of behaviour that enjoin officers to back each other up in the face of external investigations (Stoddard, 1968; Westley, 1970; Punch, 1985; Kleinig, 1996; Newburn, 1999; Loftus, 2009). The crime correspondent Sandra Laville, echoing these findings, commented in an article in *The Guardian*: 'Within the Met, *The Guardian* knows of at least two cases where whistleblowers have been bullied, isolated and investigated for spurious disciplinary offences which have never been proven, after making complaints to superior officers about bad practice, including racism and sexual assault' (Laville, 2012a). For that reason, as one interviewee explained, rather than making complaints through official channels, whistleblowers in the police organisation have preferred to make contact anonymously with journalists not perceived to be part of the inner circle. One such case concerned information about alleged corruption and brutality against suspects in the Enfield Crime Squad, given by an unofficial source to the press and cited by Sandra Laville in her witness statement to the Leveson Inquiry (Laville, 2012b). Another case where details were leaked anonymously to the press, though in this case concerning an incompetent investigation on the part of the MPS and not police corruption, was the case of Kirk Reid.

> Reid – a serial rapist and sexual abuser was finally brought to justice after years of incompetence and failings by the Met police. ... His case was taking place very shortly after that of another serial rapist – John Worboys – whom the Met had also failed to apprehend for years because they did not believe the string of young women who claimed he had raped them.
>
> Despite the experience of the Worboys case, the Met did not through official channels make journalists – and therefore more importantly the public – aware of the case of Reid. It was through informal contacts with a police officer that I found out about the case. (Laville, 2012b, p 19)

As Reiner (2010) notes, one of the big changes in crime reporting in the 1990s was the virtual disappearance of court reporters. Reiner argues that this was in part due to the 'increasing news emphasis on celebrities, to a point where even the sensational murder story is squeezed out' but also due 'to the more commercial orientation of the multimedia conglomerates that own an increasing number of news outlets, which has restricted editorial budgets severely' (Reiner, 2010, p 181). As a result, many major cases, some of them involving police abuse and malpractice, fail to attract any attention. In an article for *The Guardian* in 1999, the crime reporter, Nick Davies, described how he had been in Nottingham covering an unrelated incident and, by chance, decided to follow up a story reported in the *Nottingham Evening Post*:

> [T]his case – which involved Scotland Yard breaking just about every rule in the book in their handling of a Jamaican Yardie informer – had been running for months without a single word of national coverage. Nothing. It had crept into the local press. And that was all. *The Guardian*'s involvement, and the subsequent national attention, was sheer fluke. (Davies, 1999)

Thus, in many cases, tip-offs from anonymous police officers, using 'tactics' of resistance (De Certeau, 1984) to make contact with outer circle journalists and to bypass official channels of communication, were invaluable in allowing the press to bring cases of police malpractice to light that would otherwise have gone unreported, due to the disappearance of court reporters.

Tactics of resistance: outer circle journalists' power in negotiating with the police

In structural hole theory, the successful *tertius* is one whose network is not necessarily large but one which connects them to a number of nonredundant contacts, or contacts who are likely to have different forms of information to trade with the *tertius*. As Burt (1992) explains, 'contacts who, regardless of their relationship with one another, link the player to the same third parties, have the same sources of information and so provide redundant benefit to the player' (Burt, 1992, p 47). Structural holes can be seen 'as the gaps between nonredundant contacts' and a network 'rich in nonredundant contacts is rich in structural holes' (Burt, 1992, p 47). According to Burt (1992), a *tertius* whose network is full of structural holes, meaning that the *tertius* is able to obtain information that does not overlap from a variety of sources, also has an advantage in negotiating their relationships.

Outer circle journalists had more diverse contacts than inner circle contacts. Although the *tertius gaudens* acts as a bridge connecting two disconnected worlds, or two disconnected clusters of contacts, Burt (1992) notes that this does not preclude information flowing back to those contacts. In the case of outer circle journalists, with a wide circle of contacts including underworld contacts, they were often able to provide favoured unofficial police sources with valuable information or tip-offs. As such, contacts were often 'more likely to give information to a journalist than to a policeman' (Chibnall, 1977, p 154). One crime reporter gave an example of this:

'There was a case of a wealthy woman who went missing, she was apparently a millionairess, lived in Marylebone, worked in Libya. Or so we thought. Then I spoke to the detective leading the case and he was adamant she was comfortable, but not a millionairess, she had maybe four hundred grand in the bank and a flat but wasn't in that league. Then I spoke to the family and they didn't seem to know anything about what she'd been doing in Libya or anything she'd been up to. And everything you heard slightly chipped away at the crime story about this wealthy oil executive going missing. And then I got a tip off from someone that actually she was an escort and she was on this escort website and he'd used her. So I rang my detective and said I'd had a tip off and then an hour later, he said he'd phoned the family and had a chat and that they were now going down this line of enquiry, she was an escort who'd been working in Libya.'

Burt (1992) argues that there needs to be a relationship of trust and equality between the *tertius* and their contacts. As he explains: 'If a contact feels that he is somehow better than you … your investment in the relationship will be taken as proper obeisance to a superior' (Burt, 1992, p 15). In the case of the inner circle journalist, although relationships with police sources were characterised by friendship, trust and mutual reciprocity, such co-operation could be, and was, withdrawn if the reporter was deemed to have written something that was not acceptable to that source or to the MPS as an organisation. The inner circle journalists therefore had a vested interest in keeping their sources onside.

But as Burt also argues '[p]layers with relationships free of structural holes at their own end and rich in structural holes at the other end are structurally autonomous' (Burt, 1992, p 49). This was only partly the case for inner circle journalists. Although, as we have seen, they had a certain degree of power in their relationships with the police, both on an official and unofficial level, as the main 'bridge' between the police and the public, they were nevertheless dependent on those sources, particularly for information on breaking stories or 'scoops' that would give them a competitive edge over their news rivals. They therefore had networks that were not free of structural holes at their end. As a result, their contacts always had 'the option of replacing [them] with one of [their] colleagues who provide[d] the same network benefits that [they did]' (Burt, 1992, p 44).

Outer circle journalists did not have that dependence on police sources for their day-to-day reporting, and therefore had networks that were free of structural holes at their end. These were the 'players best positioned for the information and control benefits that a network can provide' (Burt, 1992, p 49). In particular, '[w]here there is any uncertainty about whose preferences should dominate a relationship, there is an opportunity for the tertius to broker the negotiation for control by playing demands against one another' (Burt, 1992, p 33). An outer circle journalist gave a good example of this *tertius gaudens* strategy:

'I had a story that this detective did not want me to run. So in exchange for me not running it, he basically grassed up someone else's operation. It was about smuggling handguns into the UK. And he gave the exact number and I said, "Do you know any more than that" and he said no. So I started thinking who do I know does firearms and started ringing all of them. Tried the Met, the Association of Chief Police Officers [ACPO], then I rang someone I'd known for years in Merseyside who specialises in guns and gangs and I could tell by the minute's silence, that I was on the right track. So she said she'd have to get back to me and I thought, okay, here we go. And when she came back, she offered me a deal basically, that they would give me a full briefing on the operation but you'll have to sit on it because someone's been nicked already and we're about to nick some people here in two months' time.'

To sum up, while both inner and outer circle journalists were in a powerful position as the bridge or *tertius* between the police and the press, it could be argued that the negotiating power of inner circle journalists was weaker than that of their outer circle counterparts, because they were more dependent on police sources for their day-to-day crime reporting. In contrast, outer circle journalists had far more power in negotiating with the police because of their lack of dependence and their 'mission of policing the police rather than only policing with them' (Ericson et al, 1989, p 110).

Conclusion

In this chapter I explore, from the perspective of national crime journalists, the complex and contingent web of relations – both official and unofficial – that existed between them and the Metropolitan Police from the 1980s to the early 2000s; and the 'tactics' of resistance (De Certeau, 1984, p xix) used to circumvent 'the often limiting structured access they have to information and the content of the information being released to them' (Lee and McGovern, 2014, p 191).

In their Canadian study, Ericson et al (1989) identified two distinct cultures of journalists: the 'inner circle' and the 'outer circle'. Similarly, in this study, respondents in the United Kingdom appeared to fall into these two cultures. Although most of the early British studies of police/news media relations (Chibnall, 1977; Hall et al, 1978; Schlesinger and Tumber, 1994; Mawby, 1999, 2002a) suggested that the police were the primary source of stories for the press, I argue that, while this was the case for inner circle journalists, outer circle journalists rarely depended on the police for stories; instead, they drew on a much wider circle of contacts, including members of the public, victims, witnesses, relatives of people in prison, solicitors and barristers.

Lee and McGovern (2014) argue that having 'informal links to the police is paramount in the search for a news scoop or an update on a breaking story, and most certainly for information about police corruption' (Lee and McGovern, 2014, p 191). I argue that, for inner circle journalists, gaining informal access to the police and 'exclusives' sometimes came at a price – either turning a blind eye to police malpractice or taking the risk of being denied future access. However, I also argue that power between the police and the media ebbed and flowed and that, as police respondents in the previous chapter argued, both inner and outer circle journalists were in possession of several key resources – particularly, the power to make or break police reputations. Although outer circle journalists interviewed for this study emphasised their detachment from police sources, those who did have 'unofficial' contacts within the MPS explained how they were often used by those contacts to 'leak' stories of police corruption or abuses of power – stories that might otherwise go unreported. I also suggest that, in some respects, outer circle journalists had more power in their relations with the MPS – official and unofficial – than did their inner circle counterparts, who were by and large more dependent on police favour for a steady flow of crime news. Overall, I conclude that the balance of power in police/news media relations often tipped in favour of crime journalists.

4

The phone-hacking scandal

Introduction

On 4 July 2011, it was reported by *The Guardian* that journalists working for the *News of the World* had hired private investigators to hack into missing schoolgirl Milly Dowler's voicemail inbox shortly after her disappearance in March 2002. It was alleged that they had deleted some messages, giving false hope to police and to Dowler's family, who thought that she might have deleted the messages and therefore might still be alive, and also potentially destroying valuable evidence both about her abduction and against a potential abductor and murderer. Two days later, the *Daily Telegraph* reported that the voicemail accounts of some relatives of British soldiers killed in action in Iraq since 2003 and Afghanistan since 2001 had been listened to by employees of the *News of the World*.

On 8 July, Rupert Murdoch took the decision to close down the *News of the World*, sacking over 200 employees. However, over the coming days, senior MPS officers also came under scrutiny, with allegations in the press of inappropriate relations between the MPS and members of News International and suggestions that these senior MPS officers had known about the practice of phone hacking for some time but had failed to act on warnings of media misconduct. In the coming weeks and months, over 250 journalists were arrested and/or interviewed under caution. Forty-five journalists and public servants were charged and convicted, including Andy Coulson, the former *News of the World* editor and the media advisor to the then British Prime Minister, David Cameron. The Commissioner of the MPS, Sir Paul Stephenson, and his Deputy Commissioner, John Yates, also resigned as a result of the scandal. There were estimated to be over 5,000 victims of the phone-hacking scandal.

In Chapter 2, I described how the start of my research coincided with these events and how I found it extremely difficult initially to make contact with journalists or MPS press officers. Through speaking to a number of former national crime journalists and former MPS officers, however, I was able to gain introductions to journalists and press officers who were currently in post – and in the case of two journalists, to whom I am extremely grateful, introductions to their 'unofficial' police contacts within the MPS. Over the next 18 months, I spoke to many people – national crime journalists and senior police officers. I talked to people in their homes, at Scotland Yard, at their offices and in a couple of cases out of town in tucked-away dark pubs or coffee shops, far from where my interviewees could be spotted.

During this period, three separate inquiries were being undertaken: the first headed by Her Majesty's Inspectorate of Constabulary (HMIC, 2011); the second by Dame Elizabeth Filkin (Filkin, 2012); and the last to report by Lord Leveson (Leveson, 2012a, 2012b). All three inquiries had the aim of formalising the terms of police/news media contact. However, as I was to find out in the course of my research, even before all three inquiries had reported, the MPS had seriously restricted formal contact with the press and, in effect, suppressed all informal contact. Most of my interviewees – both police and press – agreed that there had been some improprieties in police/news media relations; but, with the exception of one or two police interviewees, all respondents believed this clampdown on contact would have a deleterious effect on future relations – and, from the perspective of the press, severely restrict their ability to carry out their Fourth Estate role.

I start this chapter by exploring the events leading up to the phone-hacking scandal of July 2011, drawing on interviews with press officers, senior MPS officers and journalists. I then discuss the impact of the recommendations made by the three inquiries (HMIC, 2011; Filkin, 2012; Leveson, 2012a, 2012b) on police/news media relations. Drawing on Burt's (1992, 2002) work as before, I argue that, as a result of the restriction on police/news media contact imposed by the MPS, the 'bridge' between the MPS and the press effectively 'decayed' (Burt, 2002) almost overnight.

The background to the phone-hacking scandal

Although the phone-hacking scandal became a news story of international importance in July 2011, the origins of the scandal go back to 2005, when Buckingham Palace staff reported to the Royalty Protection Department of the MPS that the voicemail messages of Prince William's and Prince Harry's personal secretaries had been intercepted and details of these messages had been appearing in the column of Clive Goodman, the Royal editor at the *News of the World*. Peter Clarke, the head of the anti-terrorism branch of the MPS (known as SO13) was asked to lead the investigation, known as Operation Caryatid. The investigation confirmed that Clive Goodman had been involved in phone hacking. It also confirmed that another private investigator, Glenn Mulcaire, was involved and that the phone hacking was not limited to the Royal Family. However, the decision was made to close Operation Caryatid, as Clarke believed that the priority of SO13 needed to be focused on counter-terrorism, particularly in the wake of terrorist attacks in London in July 2005. Although, at the time, the *News of the World* passed off Goodman's activities as 'those of one rogue reporter' (Mawby, 2016, p 491), work by the investigative journalist Nick Davies, writing for *The*

Guardian, made it very clear that the matter was far from being resolved. Davies also claimed that Andy Coulson, the former editor of the *News of the World* who had subsequently become the communications advisor to the then Prime Minister, David Cameron, knew that journalists on his paper were carrying out these practices.

The then MPS Commissioner, Sir Paul Stephenson, asked the Assistant Commissioner, John Yates, to investigate *The Guardian*'s claims and to see whether the case should be reopened. After spending eight hours considering the case (Davies, 2014; Mawby, 2016), Yates made a statement to the press, in response to Davies's articles, and commented that 'in the vast majority of cases there was insufficient evidence to show that tapping had actually been achieved' (Leveson, 2012a, p 362).

On 15 December 2010, *The Guardian* reported that some of the documents seized from Glenn Mulcaire in 2006 by the MPS implied that *News of the World* editor, Ian Edmondson, specifically instructed Mulcaire to hack voice messages of the actors Sienna Miller and Jude Law, and several others. The documents also implied that Mulcaire was engaged by *News of the World* chief reporter Neville Thurlbeck and assistant editor Greg Miskiw, who had then worked directly for editor Andy Coulson. It was apparent that Yates's decision not to pursue investigations further into the cache of these documents belonging to Glenn Mulcaire in July 2009 had been seriously flawed (Mawby, 2016).

On 26 January 2011, the Metropolitan Police announced that it would begin a new investigation into phone hacking known as Operation Weeting, following the receipt of new information regarding the conduct of *News of the World* employees. In June 2011, the issue of computer hacking was addressed with the launch of Operation Tuleta. News International attempted to forestall investigation by hiring former Director of Public Prosecutions Ken Macdonald to review the emails that News International executives had used as the basis of their claim that the only *News of the World* journalist to engage in phone hacking was Clive Goodman. However, Macdonald suggested that irrespective of whether other journalists had been involved in phone hacking, there was clear evidence of criminal activity, including payments to serving police officers. Macdonald turned this evidence over to the MPS, which led to Operation Elveden, an investigation into bribery and corruption within the MPS.

On 4 July 2011, *The Guardian* reported that the *News of the World* had hacked murdered schoolgirl Milly Dowler's mobile and gained illicit access to her phone messages. A week later, the *News of the World* was closed down and the House of Commons Home Affairs Committee (HAC) took evidence on phone hacking from, and criticised, senior MPS officers.

Three major enquiries into the ethics of the relationship between the police and the media were subsequently commissioned. On 13 July 2011, the Prime Minister, David Cameron, announced that a public inquiry would be chaired by Lord Justice Leveson, to examine the culture, practices and ethics of the British press following the News International phone-hacking scandal. On 20 July 2011, HMIC, a body set up for the purpose of inspecting the efficiency and effectiveness of individual police forces, was formally commissioned by the then Home Secretary, Theresa May, to consider instances of undue influence and inappropriate contractual arrangements and other abuses of power in police relationships with the media and other parties. At the same time, the then Commissioner of the MPS, Sir Paul Stephenson, appointed Elizabeth Filkin, a senior civil servant, to conduct a review into the relationships specifically between the MPS and the media.

The findings of the three reports

The HMIC Report

The first of the three reports to be published was the HMIC Report (2011), entitled 'Without fear or favour'. The review set out to explore what controls were in place to prevent relationships that might create a conflict of interest for police officers, including systems to proactively seek out wrongdoing and corruption, the work of governing bodies, corporate governance and oversight, training, intelligence and enforcement. The Report found that, while there was no evidence of endemic corruption within the media, the current guidance on police dealings with the media were of 'variable quality and currency' and that only three forces provided 'clarity around managing and maintaining relationships between staff and the media, and even they do not seek to define the boundaries of appropriate relationships' (HMIC, 2011, p 30). The Report made the recommendation that 'forces and authorities should record all interactions between police employees and media representatives' and that the 'time and date of the meeting, brief details of purpose, content and persons involved should be recorded' (HMIC, 2011, p 31).

The Filkin Report

The second report to be published was the Filkin Report (2012). The aim of the review was to explore ethical issues arising from the relationship between police and the media and to recommend steps that 'should, or might, be taken to improve public confidence in police/media relations' and 'to improve transparency of police/press relationships' (Filkin, 2012, p 5). The Filkin Report (2012) was more critical of police and media relationships than the HMIC Report (2011). The report suggested 'that there is contact – which is neither recorded nor permitted – between the media and police officers and staff, at all levels' and that this had, on occasion, resulted in 'improper disclosure of information which is damaging to the public, the MPS and to the policing of London' (Filkin, 2012, p 13). This included the leaking of information for 'vanity, "buzz", flirtation, a sense of power and control and professional advantage during employment within the MPS or to gain future employment elsewhere' (Filkin, 2012, p 14). Filkin also noted the practice of 'trading' within the MPS – providing 'inappropriate information … to the media, to dilute or prevent the publication of other information which could be damaging to the MPS or senior individuals within it' (Filkin, 2012, p 15).

In order to combat leaks and other improper practices, Filkin recommended that contact with the media should be 'permissible but not unconditional' (Filkin, 2012, p 45), that officers should be required to make a record of all contacts with the press and that these records should be randomly and regularly audited by senior officers. Although the HMIC Report (2011) had made a similar recommendation, the Filkin Report was more trenchant in its suggestions and included an appendix listing tactics used by some in the media to cajole information from police officers. These tactics included the plying of officers with alcohol, flirting and the offer of money. Filkin also suggested that police officers should assume that all conversations they had with reporters were likely to be recorded.

The Leveson Report

The third report to be published was the Leveson Report (2012a). There were four modules in the final report. Hearings for the first module took place from November 2011 to February 2012, and considered the relationship between the press and the public. The second module (February and March 2012) examined the relationship between the press and police.

In his opening statement to Module Two on 27 February 2013, the lead counsel for the Inquiry, Robert Jay QC, summed up the key issue of concern – that 'the relationship between the police and the media, and News International in particular, was, at best, inappropriately close and if not actually corrupt, very close to it' (Jay quoted in Leveson, 2012a, p 741). Central to this module was to determine whether or not Peter Clarke's decision to close Operation Caryatid in 2006 and John Yates's decision in 2009 not to reopen the investigations had 'been made on an objective basis or had been influenced by particular relationships that existed between senior MPS officers and employees of [News International]' (Mawby, 2016, p 492).

Although the Report did not find evidence of corruption, Leveson was nevertheless critical of the judgement, attitudes and actions of some senior officers (Mawby, 2016). On the subject of Operation Caryatid, he suggested that there had been a series of poor decisions but made clear that there was no doubt that the decision made 'by Peter Clarke not to expand the investigation was wholly justified given the threat from terrorism and the enormous counter terrorism operations then in play' (Leveson, 2012a, p 415). However, the Inquiry also heard evidence that, while the majority of relationships between the MPS and the press included 'close working relationships that had developed over years and facilitated information exchange and understanding', other relationships had 'crossed over into suspected preferential treatment of an inner circle of reporters and, more seriously, the provision of personal benefits unrelated to the working relationship' (Mawby, 2016, p 494). The Inquiry heard how a close personal friendship existed between John Yates, the former Assistant Commissioner, and Neil Wallis, a former deputy editor of *The Sun* and executive editor of the *News of the World*, and how Yates also socialised regularly with Lucy Panton, crime correspondent on the *News of the World*. Yates was openly criticised by Leveson in the Inquiry, who noted that 'the general thrust of the article in *The Guardian* in July 2009 was to the effect that phone hacking involved a conspiracy which embraced others at the *News of the World* and one which possibly went quite high up in that organisation'; and that, given that 'at the time of events, his friend Neil Wallis was the deputy editor of the paper and at the time of the article, he was the executive editor ... it was inadvisable for Mr Yates to have been involved in any way in any exercise of review, reconsideration or reflection upon Operation Caryatid' (Leveson, 2012a, p 917).

The Inquiry also suggested that access to the DPA was provided unequally, and that this perception of inequality appeared to have grown 'as a result of a particular style of leadership within the DPA' (Leveson, 2012a, p 853). A number of crime journalists who had given testimony to the Inquiry suggested that the then Director of Public Affairs, Dick Fedorcio, had a 'favoured grouping or "inner circle" of journalists' (Leveson, 2012a, p 857) and that, on one occasion, Fedorcio allowed one of the 'inner circle', Lucy Panton, to file an article on his computer in his office. It was also revealed that Fedorcio had a close friendship with Neil Wallis. After his resignation from the *News of the World* in 2009, Wallis was hired by Fedorcio 'to provide strategic communication advice and support to the MPS' (Leveson, 2012a, p 885). However, once appointed, 'there was some question as to the transparency and internal visibility of Mr. Wallis's role within the DPA', to the extent that 'Sara Cheesley, the senior information officer on the specialist operations press desk in the DPA ... only [became] aware of the existence of Mr Wallis' contract with the MPS in July 2011' (Leveson, 2012a, p 884).

Aside from the evidence of phone and computer hacking and payment to public officials by the press, details also emerged of the numerous ways in which News International had attempted to pervert the course of justice or to intimidate those seeking to expose the corporation's corrupt practices. The

Inquiry heard how the *News of the World* stalked and harassed an MPS officer, Dave Cook, and his wife, Jacqui Hames, another officer and a presenter on *Crimewatch*. Cook had reopened an investigation into the death of Daniel Morgan, a private investigator. Morgan's partner in the agency, Jonathan Rees, worked on various assignments for the *News of the World* and it had been suggested that Morgan had been killed as he was about to reveal the corrupt practices in the agency (Campbell, 2016).

However, as Mawby noted, when the Leveson Inquiry published its four-volume report in November 2012, 'overall the police escaped unscathed' (Mawby, 2016, p 496). Mawby suggests that this was due to a number of 'impression management techniques' on the part of the police witnesses at the Leveson Inquiry, deploying 'a repertoire of tactics ... which distanced current MPS leadership and practices from those in place during the phone-hacking crisis' (Mawby, 2016, p 497).

Although the police emerged from the scandal largely unscathed, the same could not be said for journalists. According to an article published in *The Guardian* in December 2015, Operation Weeting, the investigation into phone hacking, had led to 41 arrests and nine convictions. Under Operation Elveden, the investigation of payments by the press to police officers and other officials, there had been 90 arrests and 34 convictions. Under Operation Tuleta, the investigation into computer hacking, there had been 23 arrests and two convictions (*The Guardian*, 2015). Andy Coulson, former editor of the *News of the World*, was convicted of conspiring to intercept voicemails and was jailed for 18 months. Rebekah Brooks, the other former editor of the *News of the World* who was charged with the same offences, was found not guilty. The *News of the World*'s former chief reporter, Neville Thurlbeck, and two former news editors, Greg Miskiw and Ian Edmondson, were all jailed, for six months, six months and eight months respectively.

Despite these findings, all three reports highlighted the importance of the media's public function and warned against a disproportionate response to their findings. In his Report, Leveson (2012b) made it clear that in his view, journalists and the police have important roles to play in a liberal democracy:

> In our mature democracy, policing must be with the consent of the public not least because it has to involve the public in the reporting and detection of crime. The public must be kept aware of policing concerns and must engage in the debate. Therefore the press also has a vital role: it must encourage the public to engage in the criminal justice system by coming forward with evidence; it must facilitate that assistance and it must applaud when criminals are brought to justice as a result. The press must also hold the police to account, acting as the eyes and ears of the public. (Leveson, 2012b, p 20)

However, as the crime correspondent Duncan Campbell suggested, 'the big chill on relations between police and journalists had already started some months before the Leveson Report was completed' (Campbell, 2013, p 197), with official and unofficial contact between the press and the police being severely restricted, and officers being threatened with disciplinary proceedings in the event of any unauthorised disclosures being made to the press.

The pre-Leveson relationship between the police and press

The expansion of police corporate communications

Writing in the early 2000s, Leishman and Mason suggested that the relationship between the police and the media in the United Kingdom was in the main symbiotic (Leishman and Mason, 2003). However, in the late 2000s – and immediately prior to the phone-hacking scandal – two studies by Cooke and Sturges (2009) and Mawby (2010) suggested that the asymmetric police–media relationship identified by Chibnall (1977) and Hall et al (1978) not only endured but had 'ha[d] become more pronounced in terms of police dominance of the relationship' (Mawby, 2010, p 1073). Both studies suggested that this was due to two factors: a national expansion of police corporate communications throughout the 1990s and 2000s; and organisational changes in the news industry at the same time, including severe staff cuts.

In the MPS, this change started in the late 1980s, when the then Police Commissioner, Peter Imbert, hired the corporate identity consultant Wolff Olins to 'undertake an audit of internal and external attitudes towards the Met' (Mawby, 2002a, p 43). The government, led by Margaret Thatcher, was concerned that 'additional resourcing of the police had failed to control crime and that the service was not providing value for money' (Mawby, 2002a, p 32). The Wolff Olins report suggested that the MPS needed to 'improve its communication techniques both internally and to the world outside' (Wolff Olins, 1988, p 15); and by 1997, the DPA employed a staff of nearly 100 and had a budget of nine million pounds. Nationally, from the late 1990s, communication departments increasingly undertook a wide range of activities, 'including internal communications, delivering media training and facilitating police officers' direct communication activities, formulating media strategies for major cases and incidents, and the proactive marketing of campaigns' (Mawby, 2010, pp 1065–6).

The crisis in the news industry

Concurrently, there had been significant changes in the news industry, which Mawby argued had weakened the ability of crime reporters 'to act as the prime conduit of policing news and to hold the police to account' (Mawby, 2010, p 1066). Two of the biggest changes were the introduction of 24-hour rolling news and the advent of the internet (Davies, 2008). In 1994, the *Daily Telegraph* launched its first online national news operation, followed three years later by the BBC's news website. By the end of the 2000s, online websites were viewed as essential for all newspapers, major broadcasters and news agencies.

At the same time, a cut in advertising revenue forced newspapers to cut back on staff. Pressure in newsrooms to produce more articles in less time led to fewer journalists gathering stories outside the office and, in its place, the rise of 'churnalism' (Davies, 2008) – journalism based on the reuse of material obtained from sources such as press releases or syndicated news reports, rather than original research. The financial crisis of 2007–9, the worst economic crisis to date since the Great Depression (Reuters, 2009), led to further decline in advertising revenue, even more cutbacks and 'foreboding about the future of journalism and democracy' (Birnbauer, 2019, p 5). Mawby's (2010) study echoed those fears, arguing that as a result of these changes, 'PR, primary definers and corporate control remain the dominant forces in media narratives of crime' and that, as a result, 'crime reporters find it increasingly difficult to make their independent, sometimes dissenting, voices heard' (Mawby, 2010, p 1073). However, Mawby's (2010) study concentrated mainly on the relationships between crime reporters on regional newspapers and heads of communication from forces outside the London area; and the crisis in the newspaper industry hit provincial papers hardest (Davies, 2008; Dean, 2012). Although, throughout the 2000s, staff cuts also hit national broadcast and print journalism – the Trinity Mirror group made 1,700 workers redundant in 2009, while *The Guardian* and *The Times* lost 200-plus workers between 2008 and 2010 – the picture was nevertheless less bleak for crime reporters on national outlets. Serious broadsheets such as *The Times*, *The Guardian* and the *Daily Telegraph*, and the tabloids including the *Mail*, the *Mirror* and, up to its demise, the *News of the World*, protected their investigative units from devastation (Rowbotham et al, 2013).

The rise of News International

But throughout the 1990s and 2000s, another factor also complicated the relationship between the MPS and some sections of the national press – the continuing rise of the Murdoch-owned newspaper industry, including such titles as *The Times*, *The Sun* and the *News of the World* (Rowbotham et al, 2013; Davies, 2014).

At the end of the 1960s, newspapers 'came steadily under the stewardship of commercially minded media conglomerates headed by figures like Rupert

Murdoch' (Rowbotham et al, 2013, p 174). According to Rowbotham et al, under Murdoch's stewardship there was a 'shift towards a greater minimalism in terms of the complexity of newsprint offerings' and a move 'away from factual, if summary, headlines towards impact-driven headlines' (Rowbotham et al, 2013, p 174). As Rowbotham et al note, the influence of proprietors on newspaper content has always been significant, but a new development occurred under the Murdoch stewardship – 'political attitudes taken by titles in reflection of the parties they supported began to shape their commentary on law-and-order (and so crime) issues' (Rowbotham et al, 2013, pp 175–6).

As Greer and McLaughlin comment, the tabloidisation of the UK press introduced by the Murdoch corporation had 'fundamentally transformed newspapers' sense of their power' (Greer and McLaughlin, 2017, p 266). Central to this, and of particular salience to the police and to MPS senior officers, was the emergence of what Greer and McLaughlin term 'trial by media', which they describe as 'a dynamic, impact-driven, news media-led process by which individuals – who may or may not be publicly known – are tried and sentenced in the "court of public opinion"' (Greer and McLaughlin, 2011b, p 138). These practices are not limited to the Murdoch-owned media. The targets and processes of 'trial by media' are diverse and 'may range from pre-judging the outcome of formal criminal proceedings against "unknowns" to the relentless pursuit of high-profile celebrity personalities and public figures deemed to have offended in some way against an assumed common morality' (Greer and McLaughlin, 2011b, p 138).

The targets also included senior MPS police officers. Silverman (2012) details how former Commissioner, Sir Ian Blair, came under attack from the press. In February 2005, Blair lost an employment tribunal case brought by three MPS officers, who had claimed racial discrimination after being disciplined for making racist remarks on a MPS training day. The *Daily Mail* ran a 'headline on the case "The police chief who hung his officers out to dry" (*Daily Mail*, 28 June 2005)' (Silverman, 2012, p 125). A few weeks later, Blair came under further attack, following the killing of Jean Charles de Menezes, who was shot dead by firearms officers as part of the investigation into the 7/7 terrorist attacks on London. At a hastily arranged press conference, Blair stated that the shooting was 'directly linked to the ongoing and expanding anti-terrorist operation' (IPCC, 2007, p 6). As Silverman notes, at this point 'a number of his senior colleagues were already aware that an innocent man had been killed but ... Blair, himself, was in ignorance until the following morning' (Silverman, 2012, p 125).

As Greer and McLaughlin (2011b) suggest, Sir Ian Blair's 'trial by media' was important for two reasons. First, it demonstrated 'what type of Commissioner and policing philosophy' was acceptable to certain sections of the press and, at a time when conservative and tabloid commentators were calling for a tougher law-and-order response to crime, Blair was seen as a soft option, the representative of a 'brand of "politically correct" (New Labour) policing' (Greer and McLaughlin, 2011b, p 140). Second, and even more crucially for police/news media relationships at this time, Blair's treatment at the hands of the press marked a further shift in power between the police, particularly the MPS, and the national press, particularly the tabloid and conservative news outlets. While relationships between the police and the media had always been complex and contingent, the media and particularly the Murdoch-owned titles had now become a significant stakeholder in deciding who was suitable to steer the MPS and on what terms.

Favouritism by the Press Bureau towards journalists working for News International

In interviews with crime reporters active during the 2000s, one of the key changes many of them saw in their relationship with the Press Bureau was overt favouritism towards certain journalists and news organisations. As one respondent commented:

> 'From the Met's point of view, as has become clear, *The Sun* and the *News of the World*, *The Times* to a lesser extent, were seen as places where they would, and the *Mail*, were seen as places where the police would be treated favourably and therefore they would reward the paper concerned or the journalist concerned with exclusives. Papers like *The Guardian* and *The Independent* and *The Observer*, that might be more critical of the police, inevitably would be given less stuff.'

One of the tactics open to players negotiating with a problematic *tertius*, as we saw in Chapter 3, was simply to withdraw from the relationship or cluster of relationships to focus resources on other channels. Another tactic open to a player or an organisation dealing with a problematic *tertius* is to expand 'the boundary of the network to include a new contact to compete with the offending constraint' (Burt, 1992, p 232). As Burt notes, this is potentially a risky strategy – the old and new contacts might become 'too aware of one another' and getting together 'they could find reason to cooperate in forcing [the other player] to meet their mutually agreed-upon demands' (Burt, 1992, p 232). In the case of crime reporters during the 2000s, all the players were certainly aware of each other, but those reporters working for News International had an added advantage in the relationship – the power of the Murdoch empire to cause reputational damage and more both to the MPS as an organisation and to individual officers. Whereas in the past, inner circle journalists working for tabloid papers with a pro-police stance were rewarded by 'scoops' or 'exclusive information', these were increasingly only given to reporters working for Murdoch news outlets, according to a number of respondents, echoing findings of the Leveson and Filkin Reports (2012).

Chapter 3 discussed the 'dark side of structural holes' (Bizzi, 2013, p 1555). Bizzi argues that structural hole theory can also be seen as being 'built on the idea of adversarial relationships, on manipulating others for one's own personal benefit, and on playing people off against one another' (Bizzi, 2013, p 1555). He suggests that *tertii* or brokers who take this approach to their relationships with 'alters' – two worlds that are structurally unconnected – 'have more opportunity to engage in unethical behavior, which generates negative emotional responses from proximal individuals' (Bizzi, 2013, p 1561). He also suggests that '[e]motional tensions among brokers in the same environment' – in this case, other journalists – 'could rise because brokers may decrease each other's opportunities through simultaneous brokerage behaviors' (Bizzi, 2013, p 1561).

Inner circle journalists not working for News International commented that, as a result of this favouritism, their work had become harder. Staff cuts meant that their jobs were more office-based than before, making it difficult for them to make new contacts within the police, and the same cutbacks had also led to fewer resources being available to them to pursue long investigative stories. They also discussed how, in the past, they had been given privileged treatment by the Press Bureau and allowed to accompany the police on raids, but this practice had stopped:

'I remember going on raids and just storming in behind the police, into people's houses and sitting around in someone's living room and the suspect might say "Who's this bloke here? With the camera" and the cops would just say, "Don't worry about him, he's one of us". Nowadays you have to sit outside the house, you're not allowed in anymore and that's if you're really lucky to get that far.'

The same respondent also noted that:

'There's a lot of pressure certainly on me to fill the paper with stories and the thing is, I'm not getting them, the exclusives or the titbits of information that I used to get in the past. So you have to give your editor what you have which is often just a press release from the Bureau or something like that. I try to give it a bit of context or to try and put the other side of the story if I can, but yes, there are fewer investigations and we are just dependent on what the police give us which is not that much any more.'

In addition to favouritism being shown to certain inner circle journalists and news organisations by the Press Bureau in the 2000s, respondents also alleged that money often changed hands between journalists and some MPS officers, despite the fact that the Filkin and Leveson Reports (2012) found no evidence of widespread corruption within the MPS. All respondents were keen, however, to distance themselves from any suggestion that they had taken part in these illegal transactions. Two inner circle respondents who had not worked for Murdoch-owned newspapers both described how, at the start of their careers, their editors had made it clear that money was available to them, should they want or need to pay public officials, including the police, for confidential information; and both made it clear that they had not availed themselves of this. But although respondents denied ever paying officials for information, many commented that on occasion they could see it "might be necessary, as the police is such a secretive organisation and sometimes it's the only way to get stories about abuse or malpractice out there". However, respondents reserved particular censure for employees at News International, whom they suggested had paid for stories but, in their eyes, had "paid for rubbish ... not in the public interest ... gossip about celebrities".

Reluctance of left-wing press to run stories on police corruption or abuses of power

While outer circle journalists were less affected by the apparent favouritism shown by the Press Bureau to certain reporters, as they were not dependent solely on police sources for news stories, a number of them explained how editors on national newspapers were becoming more risk-averse, particularly when it came to running stories on police corruption or malpractice. The crime reporter Duncan Campbell suggests that a key factor in this was the readiness of the Police Federation, created in 1919 to support rank and file officers up to the rank of chief inspector, to bring cases against the press on behalf of members who believed they had been libelled. As Campbell (2016) notes, newspapers frequently settled out of court; once a case went to court, the cost escalated dramatically and most newspapers avoided that risk even if they had a reasonable case. Campbell (2016) recounts how he and *The Guardian* successfully fought a libel case brought by certain police officers, after *The Guardian* broke a story about cases of corruption in eight different MPS stations. Despite the judge showing partiality to the police officers who appeared in court, telling the jury they could award up to £125,000 per person in damages, the jury returned a judgement in *The Guardian's* favour. Further actions by the Police Federation against the press dwindled in number after this case (Campbell, 2016).

The *Reynolds* v *Times Newspapers* case in 1999 further complicated the picture, particularly for outer circle journalists. This was a House of Lords case in English defamation law concerning qualified privilege for publication of defamatory statements in the public interest. *The Times* had published an article to the effect that Albert Reynolds, the then Taoiseach or Prime Minister of Ireland, had misled the Irish Parliament. The article was published first in Ireland, then in the United Kingdom – where the version omitted the explanation for the events given by Reynolds – and he brought an action for defamation. A number of outer circle journalists suggested that, as a result, editors were increasingly wary of running investigative stories, particularly against the rich or powerful, for fear of expensive court cases. As one outer circle journalist described:

> 'I've done stories that we've paid out that we should have fought and won and we've settled them because the lawyers have basically said to me "it's too expensive to fight". A few years ago, I had researched a story about … a warehouse from which charity operations were being collected but that money collected in that charity was funding Al-Qaeda. Anyway, I put one man right at the centre of it, that he owned the warehouse but we ended up having to pay out quite a substantial sum of money because we had not written that this guy had resigned as director of the charity. But even though he'd resigned, he still owned the warehouse. He was still collecting donations to go to Al-Qaeda. Once upon a time we would have fought that but he had a top defence so we paid out of court. But what it means is that you censor yourself.'

In their study of Canadian newsrooms in the 1980s, Ericson et al make the point that '[t]he law was highly salient' in the newsrooms they observed, and that '[m]ost salient were the laws of defamation, libel, and contempt of court, which restrict what can be published or broadcast' (Ericson et al, 1987, p 318). Increasingly, for outer circle investigative journalists working in the United Kingdom in the late 1990s and early 2000s, one of the key considerations in deciding whether or not to pursue a story was whether it might involve the newspaper they worked for in possibly ruinously expensive court cases.

It could be concluded then that relationships between the police and the press in this period were even more tangled and contingent than they had been in previous decades. Some inner circle journalists, particularly those working for Murdoch-owned titles, appeared to enjoy a favoured relationship with some press officers, not least because of the immense power the organisation had in shaping public and political opinion. Other inner circle journalists reported increasing dependence on police press releases for stories, echoing Mawby's (2010) findings; while outer circle journalists reported a greater caution on the part of their editors in running investigative crime stories or stories involving the police, for fear of litigation.

The process of bridge decay between the police and the press

According to Burt (1992), in addition to withdrawal and expansion, two further tactics available to players caught in a 'constraint-generating network' (Burt, 1992, p 233) are 'embedding it in a second relationship over which you have more control' (Burt, 1992, p 233) or seeking an 'arbitrator to whom you and your contact turn to settle disputes' (Burt, 1992, p 234). Burt describes this as the 'governance mechanism invoked to legitimate "fair" behaviour in the relationship' (Burt, 1992, p 234). He gives an example of this in describing how, in Evans–Pritchard's (1940) work on Nuer tribesmen, the 'leopardskin chief' mediated troubled relations between the tribesmen, acting as a second and higher level *tertius*. The second level *tertius* had, according to Burt (1992), the power to 'define what the other ... players may, must, can and cannot do in the final negotiated relationship' (Burt, 1992, p 235). This negotiation is 'subject to the further constraints of social structures in which negotiated relations are embedded' (Burt, 1992, p 234).

In the case of the relationship between the police and the press, and more specifically the MPS and national crime reporters, this was turned over to independent arbitrators – HMIC (HMIC, 2011), Dame Filkin (Filkin, 2012) and Lord Justice Leveson (Leveson, 2012a, 2012b) – to renegotiate the terms of that relationship. The links between the MPS and certain journalists working for the Murdoch press could not have been renegotiated in any other way, as any attempts at exclusion – replacing these journalists by other more favoured contacts or withdrawing from those contacts altogether – were not an option, given the power of these titles in shaping public opinion for or against either individual police chiefs or the organisation. However, the suggestions made by the Filkin and Leveson Reports (2012) to formalise the terms of that relationship by requiring police officers to record all details of meetings with the press had an inadvertently deleterious impact on that relationship. It also heralded the first stage in 'bridge decay' between the MPS and the national press.

The effect of the Leveson and Filkin Reports on police/news media relations

Journalists' perspectives

Following the recommendations of these reports, the clampdown on the flow of communication between the police and the news media had most adversely affected the traditional crime reporter or inner circle journalist. Despite being more sympathetic to the police in their coverage of news stories (Chibnall, 1977; Hall et al, 1978; Ericson et al, 1987, 1989, 1991; Schlesinger and Tumber, 1994; Mawby, 2010), a number of inner circle journalists suggested that they were no longer being given even routine stories. As one inner circle journalist commented:

'One of the worst examples of how bad it's got recently was the attempted murder of the Russian banker, German Gorbuntsov.[1] We didn't know about it until it was published in a newspaper in Moscow. We knew there had been a shooting because they'd put out the day afterwards saying a man was shot and that Operation Trident Officers are investigating. That's mainly gangs, Black on Black crime and so of course we thought that's not news, two Black gangsters having a shoot-out in Wapping and one of them dying is not news. And in fact it wasn't a shoot-out and it was a hit organised by someone in Moscow.'

Both inner and outer circle journalists reported that they had received calls from Scotland Yard but did not wish to elaborate on the identity of the person making the calls. They said that they had been asked to supply a list of their official and unofficial contacts at the Yard. All journalists I interviewed said that they had refused to comply, as they saw this as a betrayal of sources. Many journalists were also angry at the guidance given by Dame Elizabeth Filkin (2012) to police officers in their dealings with the press. As one reporter commented:

'The thing that really got up our noses was the bit about assuming all conversations are being taped. Firstly it's not true and secondly it's going to put off all the officers just coming through now ever talking to the press about anything.'

The same respondent also noted how any meetings between officers and journalists were now under intense scrutiny by the Yard:

'So for example, a colleague of mine was tipped off that Reg Traviss, the former boyfriend of Amy Winehouse, had been arrested for rape. So she rang the Press Bureau and the answer comes back, "We can confirm that a 27 year old man has been arrested in connection with a rape". So that's your confirmation that the name is correct. But apparently the colleague had had a coffee two weeks before with a Press Officer, he's now under investigation and accused of leaking the information to her while she gets an email from the Director of Professional Standards asking her if she met so and so on such a date and if they discussed this particular arrest. I think that's really sinister and goes against freedom of speech, the lot in this country, if the police can now check up on who journalists are talking to.'

Inner circle journalists also pointed out that, even if they were given 'exclusive' information by one of their police contacts, by publishing that information they would be automatically putting their contacts at risk of arrest and possibly losing their careers:

'The way things are, if you put anything out that someone had given you, people at Operation Elveden will jump all over it and say that's completely unauthorised because we never put that in an email from the Press Office and they will then try and found out where we'd got that information from. Quite frankly, I don't know how we're going to be able to carry on doing our jobs at this rate.'

But while inner circle journalists worried that they would no longer receive 'exclusives' from their contacts in the current climate, outer circle or investigative journalists also worried that their ability to hold the police to account, through the unofficial information they receive from police sources, would also be severely curtailed. In her witness statement to the Leveson Inquiry, the British crime reporter Sandra Laville gave her reasons for seeking to circumvent 'official' channels of information:

Journalism, as is widely accepted, has a legitimate role in a democratic society to interrogate, challenge and question in the public interest, to be the peoples' eyes and ears. My job is therefore to make sure I can get information from the Met from a variety of sources, both official and unofficial, both on and off the record, to ensure that I can hold the police to account, question their version of events – for example during the recent riots – and make sure that the police – an enormously powerful organ of the state who have had a history of secrecy – are not abusing their powers. (Laville, 2012b, p 3)

As she went on to explain:

The Met officially is very bad at answering questions when things have gone wrong, or at giving out information on incompetent investigations that effect the public, or have put the public at risk. They are also bad at promoting the good work of some of their rank and file officers. The official channels – the press bureau – are too slow to respond to requests on many occasions. For example during the August riots I was researching a piece on what the police had been through night after night, any violence they suffered, the length of shifts they were having to work etc.

The official media channels of the Met police did not seem able to provide me access to officers, they were slow to react and therefore quite useless to me – who was writing to a deadline and needed to access the voices of ordinary officers working on the frontline. (Laville, 2012b, p 3)

But under the new regime, she explained that her Fourth Estate role had been severely compromised and that the police now had more control over the flow of information to the press and to the public than ever before – a development which she argued did not sit well with democratic practices in the United Kingdom:

> If information is restricted to formal briefings in which the flow of information is tightly controlled, it is very difficult for a journalist to interrogate the truth. What is vital and goes to the heart of a journalist's role in a democracy is for me to have this ongoing and informal dialogue with police officers with whom I have built a relationship of trust, to help me do my job as the eyes and ears of the wider public and hold the police to account. (Laville, 2012b, p 4)

While the majority of outer circle journalists interviewed for this study suggested that restrictions on police contact with the press were yet another step in what one respondent termed 'the process of giving power back to the powerful', there were a few dissenting views, though these were very much in the minority. One outer circle respondent welcomed the sea-change in police and media relations, arguing that the new restrictions would lead to healthier and more ethical interactions between the two:

> 'I think there's a parallel here with the world of politics because 20 years ago Westminster operated in a very similar way but there was a backlash against it, where a few journalists just totally rejected the lobby system and said no, we just don't agree with it. And what I think they wanted was to swap this hierarchical access for greater transparency, and that's what I hope we will see coming out of Leveson.'

To sum up, the majority of inner and outer circle journalists suggested that their ability to carry out their work had been severely impaired by the recommendations made by both the Leveson and Filkin Reports (2012). While inner circle journalists were hardest hit by these restrictions and suggested that they were no longer being given even routine crime stories, outer circle journalists believed that their ability to carry out their Fourth Estate role had been severely compromised. Whereas in the past, the majority of stories about police malpractice or corruption had come from within the organisation, they believed that this channel was now firmly closed to them and that control over the flow of information to the public and to the press was very much in police hands.

MPS operational and press officers' perspectives

The Filkin Report received a warm welcome from the then newly appointed MPS Commissioner, Sir Bernard Hogan-Howe. Speaking at the launch of the Report, Hogan-Howe commented: 'There should be no more secret conversations. There should be no more improper contact and by that what I mean is between the police and the media – that which is of a selfish, rather than a public interest' (Hogan Howe quoted in BBC, 2012). However, the MPS operational and press officers interviewed for this study did not entirely share his view of the situation. Just as journalists had been asked to give details of their contacts to Scotland Yard, press officers had also been asked to give details of their media contacts:

> 'So they have a database at Scotland Yard where if you have friends or family who are criminals, they keep that data. Which is fair enough. But I stood my ground on this and said, if I give you the names of friends who are also journalists, does that mean they are kept on that same database? And I refused to give them that information.'

One former press officer suggested that part of the problem was that staff from the Press Bureau had not been consulted during the Filkin and Leveson Inquiries as to how they thought the police/news media relationship should be regulated. His observation was that the reviews in both cases had been carried out by operational staff who had no "understanding of the complexities of the police/media relationship and the benefits to both parties". While he was adamant that the review had been carried out "without malice" and that "given two Commissioners have had to resign, something had to change", he nevertheless believed that the recommendations could only do serious harm to the police/news media relationship:

> 'I think people believed that these recommendations were coming from the Commissioner. It's not the Commissioner. The problem is the way the Met is structured, it's very much a silo mentality and that's no criticism of my colleagues because that works when you're dealing with investigations and other operations. But I think what went wrong here was first of all, the decisions were not made by senior staff and secondly instead of trying to understand how the relationship worked with the press and how it had always worked, instead I think they thought, "Okay. What sort of structure do we have in place already that we can bring to bear on this situation". So for example, the decision about recording all contacts with the press, that was made by a Detective Sergeant, and I found out only by accident. And if it hadn't come onto my desk, then a system would have been implemented and

then we'd be getting a whole load of bad news stories with the press saying, "The Met has now decided all journalists have to be put on a criminal database" and then we'd be there firefighting the damage.'

Another problem of the Reports for operational and press officers was the clampdown on unofficial contact with the media. As described in Chapter 2, these off-the-record meetings were of particular importance to officers working on sensitive operations where disclosure of information about an operation at too early a stage might jeopardise that investigation by 'affecting the production and later value of evidence' (Ericson et al, 1989, p 127). Other reasons for off-the-record briefing were to prevent unnecessary distress to victims and their families and to avoid 'giving the "criminal element" information that would be to their benefit' (Ericson et al, 1989, p 128). As one police respondent commented:

'I always found with reporters if you could tell them why you weren't going to give that information, they might not like it, but they would understand. And before Leveson, pre-Filkin, the personal relationship I had with some of the reporters was really good. I mean, there was one who'd ring up and ask questions and then when you wouldn't answer, he'd just do a long pause and I'd say, "Listen mate, I'm not going to tell you for these reasons but I can give you some guidance, some background but it'll be really unhelpful to us and to a lot of people if you use that right now". And they'd honour that. But I think those days have gone. If we don't respond, they're going to turn to less reliable sources or just make guesses at what they don't know.'

Both operational and press officers expressed concern that, as a result of these restrictions, more and more inaccurate reporting would find its way into the press. A police respondent described how, following the death of Gareth Williams, an employee of Government Communications Headquarters (GCHQ),[2] whose naked body was found in a padlocked holdall in his home in August 2010, the press made wild conjectures about his lifestyle. One paper had suggested police had found links to the fetish club Torture Garden, while another paper claimed that the victim liked to be trapped in confined spaces. The police respondent noted that the only information released to the press at this point had been that toxicology reports revealed that no toxic substances had been found in the victim's body.

Press officers also believed that the new restrictions had made their job harder. One press officer explained that, in a climate in which colleagues had been investigated for having a coffee with a press contact, using discretion to decide what could or could not be given as background to a journalist was a luxury they could no longer afford:

'Leveson has made our job harder too. Whereas in the past, if someone was writing a story, we'd say, "Okay, we'll give x a call and get back to you". But now you don't know if that's counted as off the record. So we play safe. And we don't give out any information until we're sure of it.'

Finally, police respondents expressed concern that this breakdown in communication would seriously damage police and media relations in the long term:

'I appreciate there was a need to actually reset the boundaries between the police and the press because it was quite clear that the Met had got too close with certain national newspapers and I'm the first one to put my hand up to that and say that was pretty obvious and we should have not been put in that position. Instead of saying we have a problem, and trying out various things, various stages of implementation, of controlling the leaks, we've gone to the extreme. Now every interaction has to be recorded. And instead of acting like a grown up organisation, allowing our employees to interact with the media and trust them to use discretion, integrity, we've taken away that trust. And I think we are storing up problems for the future.'

Ericson et al argued that the 'silent source loses any control over accounts of the matter at issue' (Ericson et al, 1989, p 381). They also suggested that '[a] source organization that is expected to engage the public conversation but fails to do so sews the seeds of long-term hostile relations with journalists, and sometimes with members of other source organizations' (Ericson et al, 1989, p 381). Similarly, police respondents believed that, by restricting contact with the media, more rather than fewer stories criticising the police would find their way into the press. They also expressed concern that while, in the past, they were generally able to depend on journalists to have 'the good sense, and common sense, not to publicize something at a time when it might affect the organization negatively' (Ericson et al, 1989, p 381), that trust had, in their eyes, been eroded by the recommendations of the Leveson and Filkin Reports.

Conclusion

This chapter has explored how the recommendations of the Filkin and Leveson Reports led to the first stage of 'bridge decay' (Burt, 2002) between the MPS and the national press. Inner circle journalists appeared to be hit hardest by the restrictions on official and unofficial contact with the MPS. Even though they were traditionally pro-police in their reporting, many reported that they were no longer being given even routine crime stories. Outer circle journalists, who were not as dependent on the police for news sources, were not so affected, but reported a greater caution on the part of their editors in running investigative crime stories, or stories involving the police, for fear of litigation.

However, the recommendations of the Filkin and Leveson Reports (2012) had a transformative effect on both inner and outer circle journalists' relationships with the MPS. The main recommendation of both Reports was the recording of all contact between the press and the police. However, almost immediately, both inner and outer circle journalists reported a clampdown on all contact with the MPS, both official and unofficial. Inner circle journalists suggested that they were no longer being given even routine stories, while outer circle journalists suggested that their ability to carry out their Fourth Estate role had been compromised. Whereas in the past, the majority of stories about police malpractice or corruption had come from within the organisation, they believed that this channel was now firmly closed and that control over the flow of information to the public and to the press was very much in police hands. However, police respondents contested this view, arguing that journalists would 'find alternative sources only too willing to co-operate, and that co-operation [might] include visualizing impropriety on the part of the source who remains silent' (Ericson et al, 1989, p 381).

While the restrictions on contact between the press and the police undoubtedly put a strain on that relationship, the relationship at that stage still remained intact, if somewhat damaged. But, as described in the next chapter, the advent of the internet and the widespread adoption of social media by the police meant that 'traditional media and professional journalists [were] no longer the only news brokers' (Boczkowski and Mitchelstein, 2017, p 23). For the first time, police organisations could communicate directly with citizens 'through modes previously unimaginable ... bypass[ing] the traditional media altogether' (Lee and McGovern, 2014, p 114). As a result, crime journalists in the United Kingdom saw their hitherto privileged and powerful position as *tertius gaudens* between the police and public severely eroded. The process of 'bridge decay' (Burt, 2002) was accelerating.

The effect of digital platforms on the police and the media

Introduction

During 2013 and 2014, a period of severe ill-health interrupted my research. When I was well enough to go back into the field, I decided to touch base with a couple of contacts to review my initial research findings and to see if the impasse between the police and the national news media was still in place or if relations had thawed since I carried out my first interviews. To my surprise, however, my contacts sounded even more bleak than they had previously about police and media relations and about their ability to carry out their Fourth Estate role. They suggested that part of this was due to the continuing restrictions on both official and unofficial press contact, but they also identified another factor contributing to the breakdown in police/news media relations – the police's newfound interest in and use of social media.

In 2011 and 2012, when I carried out my initial interviews with press and senior police officers and with national crime journalists, the use of social media and new digital technologies was still in its infancy. The older journalists I spoke to initially were dismissive and suggested that social media could never be a replacement for making face-to-face contacts, while the younger journalists were enthusiastic about the potential of social media for researching and crowdsourcing stories. The police press officers I interviewed also had mixed responses; while some saw social media as a way of communicating more directly with the public than ever before, particularly communities who might not read mainstream news, others suggested pitfalls in terms of spreading disinformation to the public.

However, three years on from these interviews, my reporter contacts had a more cynical view of the police's interest in social media, arguing that it allowed the police to control the flow of information more tightly than ever before. They told me that, although crime incidents were being reported daily on the Metropolitan Police's Twitter feed and news website, when they rang the Press Bureau for background information or to speak to investigating officers, they were invariably fobbed off. One reporter commented succinctly:

'The less information we get, the less bad news we can print. Forget about Fourth Estate roles. Most of us can't even carry out our day-to-day jobs.'

This chapter explores how, at a time of already beleaguered relations between the MPS and the national press, the advent of social media enabled the police to bypass or 'withdraw' (Burt, 1992) from the legacy media even further. It suggests that police uptake of social media was initially slow in the UK, with the riots of August 2011 – one month after the phone-hacking scandal – being a decisive turning point, as the MPS used social media not only to reassure the public but also to call for witnesses and information about the rioting.

I follow Lee and McGovern (2014) by arguing that, over the last 15 years, three key objectives have informed the MPS's official relationship with the press: promoting the public image; management of risk; and increasing trust in the organisation. I argue, as do they, that the use of social media has enabled the police to pursue all these aims more effectively than ever before and, as a result, increase their control over the flow of information to the public. Although these technologies have also provided the public with new ways to monitor the police (Lee and McGovern, 2014), the chapter argues that, with a few highly publicised exceptions (most notably in recent times the murder of George Floyd in Minneapolis in 2020), the power of the press and of the public to hold the police to account through these new technologies is limited.

In order to analyse my findings, I draw on Burt's (2002) work on bridge decay, to explore how, at a time of already straitened relations between the MPS and national crime reporters, technological and organisational transformation further weakened the position of journalists and legacy news organisations as bridge between sources and the public. I also follow Lee and McGovern (2014) in using De Certeau's (1984) work to explore in more detail how new technologies allowed the MPS to use different 'strategies' of power in their relations with the press and the public; and to understand how much resistance or 'anti-discipline' (De Certeau, 1984) is possible on the part of the press – and the public – in this new media landscape, and with what consequences for police accountability and transparency.

Police use of social media

In the UK, police forces began experimenting with the use of social media in 2008, initially on the basis of initiatives by individual officers and with 'varying degrees of official support' (Crump, 2011, p 1). However, according to Crump (2011), two events in 2010 and 2011 changed police perceptions of the importance of social media for policing on a symbolic and operational level.

The first event occurred on 14–15 October 2010, when the Greater Manchester Police (GMP) published a short message about every incident notified to their control room over a 24-hour period, using the social networking site Twitter. The aim of the exercise, according to Peter Fahy, then Chief Constable of the GMP, was to 'raise awareness of the diverse and complex role of policing, explaining how much time officers spend with non-crime matters' (Fahy cited in Crump, 2011, p 1).

The second event that proved to be a turning point for police interest in the use of social media (Procter et al, 2013) was the shooting of a young man, Mark Duggan, by police in Tottenham, North London in August 2011, which was followed by rioting across the United Kingdom. During the riots, a number of politicians, including David Cameron, called for social media such as Facebook and Twitter to be closed down temporarily to stop information about looting and unfounded rumours spreading. Subsequent research (Lewis et al, 2011) indicated that most of those involved in the rioting were actually using the free messaging service available on BlackBerry phones – known as 'BBM' – to communicate and plan in advance of riots. By contrast, the police were overwhelmingly in favour of keeping the networks open. In an interview with *The Guardian*, Kevin Hoy, then web manager at GMP, said that Twitter allowed the police 'to give "direct reassurance" and "dispel rumours … in a way that we could never have achieved previously"' (Halliday, 2011).

Following the riots, a number of studies emerged exploring the police's use of social media during the crisis. Procter et al suggested that the police were not 'making effective use of social media services such as Twitter' (Procter et al, 2013, p 433), though they also stressed that 'police resources were very stretched, both in communication centres and in local police teams' (Procter et al, 2013, p 434). However, another study of police use of Twitter by Denef et al (2013) noted marked differences in use of Twitter by the GMP and the MPS. The study suggested that the MPS took what they termed an 'instrumental' or more formal approach to their communication, using Twitter largely to inform the public about their performance and citing numbers of arrests. By contrast, the GMP took a more personal or 'expressive' approach, the most frequent type of tweets being messages of reassurance, with information gathering and dissemination being a secondary consideration.

A number of other studies internationally have explored how the police have used social media to interact with the public. Early studies (Brainard and McNutt, 2010; Crump, 2011; Liebermann et al, 2013) suggested that the police in a number of jurisdictions mainly used social media to send out information to the public, without any attempts at engagement with them.

Conversely, later studies (Meijer and Thaens, 2013; Lee and McGovern, 2014; Schneider, 2016; O'Connor, 2017) have identified police use of Twitter and other social media to engage the public, promote the police image and to work on 'community-building' (O'Connor, 2017). However, in a study of five British constabularies, Bullock suggested that police use of social media still failed to elicit interaction with the public, suggesting that this was largely due to the 'scepticism and risk aversion of some leaders and the apathetic response from some officers' (Bullock, 2018, p 255) towards the use of social media in their work.

A number of studies in Canada, the United States, the United Kingdom, New Zealand and Australia have also explored the use by police departments of humour on social media (Schneider, 2016; Raymond, 2018; Hu and Lovrich, 2019; Kalish, 2019; Wood, 2019; Zhou, 2019; Wood and McGovern, 2020) to increase audience engagement with content and enhance the public image of the police. However, Wood and McGovern argue that these humorous posts have another function. At a time when 'certain forms of police misconduct have never been so visible' (Wood and McGovern, 2020, p 306), they suggest that these posts may 'serve as a tool of distraction ... presenting a "sanitised" version of police work that is at odds with the reality of policing' (Wood and McGovern, 2020, p 314).

The effect of social media and digital platforms on police interaction with the press remains comparatively under-researched at this time, albeit with a number of notable exceptions. In a study of relations between regional and national crime reporters and eight regional police forces, including heads of communications within those forces, Mawby (2010) argued that an expansion in police corporate communications had coincided with a worldwide crisis in the news media. He commented that the asymmetric police/news media relationship identified by Chibnall (1977) and Hall et al (1978) endured, and that the advent of new technologies and social media would only strengthen that asymmetry, arguing 'that the strategic choices of forces are likely to be in the direction of direct communication that bypasses the traditional media' (Mawby, 2010, p 1073).

While Mawby's (2010) focus was mainly on police/news media relations, in a case study focusing on coverage of the 2009 G20 Summit Protests in London, Greer and McLaughlin (2010) explored the news-making process from another angle, arguing that new technologies could, on occasion, enable members of the public to produce information challenging the 'official' version of events. They discuss how mobile phone footage produced by a bystander showed that the death of a newspaper vendor, Ian Tomlinson, was due to police brutality rather than natural causes – the version of events given to the press by the MPS – and how, as a result, the 'news media focus at G20' changed 'from "protestor violence" to "police violence"' (Greer and McLaughlin, 2010, p 1041).

In a 2014 study, Lee and McGovern examine how the New South Wales (NSW) Police Force are increasingly utilising social media and other forms of new communication technologies to interact with the public in innovative ways. They argue that the use of social media enables the police to communicate more directly with the public than ever before but also has opened up 'a range of possibilities for both image work and operational policing' (Lee and McGovern, 2014, p 60). Press officers are no longer just engaged in 'information dissemination, they are actively working with operational police to identify and apprehend offenders, to deliver public safety messages and to receive intelligence through their "networks"' (Lee and McGovern, 2014, p 72). While, in the past, police organisations would have achieved many of these objectives through the media, Lee and McGovern argue that these new technologies are increasingly enabling the police to 'bypass the traditional media altogether' (Lee and McGovern, 2014, p 114). Ellis and McGovern (2016) also explore the impact of social media on the police's relationship with the media and the public. They comment that, while the advent of digital platforms has resulted in 'a greater volume of, and easier access to, police-generated operational information ... the police maintain the premium on that information and control it more tightly than ever' (Ellis and McGovern, 2016, pp 956–7). They argue that, consequently, the police are less open than before to 'critical scrutiny ... by journalists' and that the public are denied 'access to quality information ... upon which to make informed decisions' (Ellis and McGovern, 2016, p 957).

Three recent studies (Ellis, 2020, 2021; Richardson, 2020) build on this work. Ellis (2020) explores what he terms the phenomenon of the 'social media test' or 'the evolution of social media into a legitimate measure of police performance' (Ellis, 2020, p 185). He argues that new technologies have enabled the 'sousveillance of public order policing – the watching from below' (Ellis, 2020, p 186) by ordinary citizens. Whereas in the past, the only way members of the public could bring video footage of police brutality to the attention of a wider audience was by handing that footage over to media outlets, digital platforms now allow members of the public to bypass the media and post footage themselves in real time on YouTube and Facebook. Ellis argues that, as a result, such footage 'can more readily test police truth claims of procedural fairness and accountability at unprecedented speed and to unprecedented numbers' and 'generate "teachable moments" that can deter and moderate police violence' (Ellis, 2020, p 186). Similarly, Richardson's (2020) study explores the concept of sousveillance or 'bearing witness while black' (Richardson, 2020, p xiv) to police brutality in the United States. She explores how African Americans have adopted Twitter as their social networking platform of choice for breaking news and to bypass legacy media outlets by capturing video evidence for each other and for wider, global audiences – and to create counternarratives to what they perceive to be '[p]ersistent news myths perpetuat[ing] the tendency to frame African Americans as inherently criminal, dismissively marginal, or simply "playing the race card" in a supposedly colorblind United States' (Richardson, 2020, p 71).

However, both Ellis (2020, 2021) and Richardson (2020) argue that the public's and media's ability to hold the police to account through these new technologies is limited. Ellis (2021) argues that bystander video footage of police brutality can be dismissed as a partial representation of events while new technologies such as body worn cameras afford the police, in turn, greater power of surveillance. Richardson (2020) also notes that '[t]he smartphone has been a gift and a curse for anti-police brutality activists' as 'the metadata they generate each time activists use them' have 'made it increasingly easy for federal and law enforcement authorities to track black witnesses' (Richardson, 2020, p 114).

To sum up, the last ten years have seen radical changes in relations between the police, the media and the public. New technologies have allowed the police to 'communicate with the public through modes previously unimaginable' (Lee and McGovern, 2014, p 114) and weakened the 'privileged position of journalists and media organizations as bridges between newsmakers and the public' (Boczkowski and Mitchelstein, 2017, p 23). But in the United Kingdom, the process of 'bridge decay' (Burt, 2002) had already begun, even before the widespread use of new technologies and digital platforms by the MPS.

Strategies of power: how the MPS use social media

As discussed at length in Chapter 2, police respondents who had been in post from the 1970s through to the late 2000s had a complex relationship with the press. While many studies have suggested that the relationship was essentially symbiotic, the chapter followed Ericson et al in suggesting that 'from the perspective of sources, the news media are ... in possession of key resources that frequently give them the upper hand' (Ericson et al, 1989, p 378). Police respondents in this study also shared this viewpoint, and discussed how journalists often took snippets from interviews to quote them out of context. But perhaps the biggest frustration expressed by both operational and press officers was the traditional press's emphasis on 'bad news'. As one press officer commented:

> 'We give them so many stories – real human interest stories of police officers committing acts of real heroism. If we're lucky, it might make a local paper. But if we cock up, it's front page news.'

However, it would appear that by establishing a virtual as well as a physical base with which to establish 'relations with … targets or threats' (De Certeau, 1984, p 36), the MPS and police in other jurisdictions (Lee and McGovern, 2014) have been able to redress this balance. By establishing a base, De Certeau argues that organisations are able to achieve the following key objectives: 'to capitalize acquired advantages, to prepare future expansions, and thus to give oneself a certain independence with respect to the variability of circumstances' (De Certeau, 1984, p 36).

The logics governing MPS use of social media

Writing in the late 1980s, Ericson et al (1989) argued that the two key reasons for police organisations to engage with the media were the release of relevant information to the public and institutional attempts to cast the police in a positive light. However, 30 years on, Lee and McGovern (2014) suggest that, with the expansion of police corporate communications globally, police departments are increasingly undertaking a range of activities above and beyond information dissemination and taking an increasingly proactive stance in their dealings with the media and with the public. Corroborating this, Ed Stearns, then Director of the Directorate of Media and Communication at Scotland Yard, responded in 2017 to a Freedom of Information Request by publishing the Metropolitan Police's Social Media Policy. The policy explains: 'Our social media accounts have been set up to assist in the prevention and detection of crime, as well as inform the public of Metropolitan Police related news, events, online facilities and major incidents across the Capital' (Stearns, 2017a, p 2).

Lee and McGovern (2014) argue in their study of police and media relations that there are three key logics of contemporary police engagement with the media. These are:

- the management of police image ('image work');
- the management of public risk and responsibilisation of the public; and
- attempts to increase confidence or trust in policing and the legitimacy of police organisations.

They argue that, while all three logics can be analysed as 'empirically discrete, in practice they inherently overlap, mutually reinforce and influence one another' (Lee and McGovern, 2014, p 40).

These logics are readily identifiable in the MPS's guidelines on the use of social media in official MPS accounts or those accounts run solely through the Directorate of Media and Communications. According to the MPS Social Media Policy, this includes:

- operational updates about the policing of events
- news about how the MPS is policing boroughs, major criminal investigations and prosecutions
- appeals for information and assistance from the public
- crime prevention advice or local community information relevant to participants of events
- advice about protecting yourself from crime
- news about online facilities from the MPS website and other policing related sources
- information from emergency services partners relevant to the safety and wellbeing of Londoners and visitors to the capital.

(Stearns, 2017a, pp 2–3)

The first two objectives fall under both the categories of image work and increasing trust in the legitimacy of the organisation. The sixth objective, leading citizens to the MPS's own news website, where press officers 'proactively promote positive stories' about MPS work (Stearns, 2017b, p 1), comes under the logic of image management. The remaining objectives fall under the logic of communicating risk and responsibilisation of the public.

Promoting the police image

Lee and McGovern argue that the management of image is the first key logic of police engagement with the media and includes 'attempts to filter and manage stories involving the police and the desire to present positive policing stories' (Lee and McGovern, 2014, p 47). Chapter 2 discussed how, in the 1990s and 2000s, as a result of the Wolff Olins report in 1988 highlighting the need for the MPS to improve its communication to the public, more resources were allocated to police corporate communications. In 1997, the then DPA had a staff of nearly 100 and a £9 million budget. However, as Bowling et al note, spending on the police, which had risen continuously since 1979, faced cuts from 2010, when the coalition Conservative/Liberal Democrat government came into power and 'resources and powers were reduced in the name of a tight public purse and austerity for the state agencies' (Bowling et al, 2019, p 13). These cuts also hit police corporate communications and, in 2015, the Directorate of Media and Communications announced that it was reducing staff from 55 'news roles' to 40 (Turvill, 2015).

Notwithstanding these cuts, in an interview with the *Press Gazette* in December 2015, Martin Fewell, then head of the Directorate, was more than optimistic about the future of the MPS's corporate communications. Shortly after the cuts in the Directorate's staff were announced, the Directorate launched a news website on the already existing digital site, the MyNewsDesk platform. As Martin Fewell explained:

What we're doing via the MyNewsDesk service that we use is what others would call a B2B service, business to business. It's providing the content in the best possible way for news organisations – because the bottom line is news organisations have the audience. We don't. Whether it's local or national, they've got the audience. So we're trying to deliver them the right content for their different audiences and get them to use as much of it as possible. (Fewell cited in Turvill, 2015)

In the same interview, Ed Stearns, the Directorate's then head of media, gave an example of this, describing how CCTV footage provided by the website, of a woman being punched on a bus, was taken up directly by the *Evening Standard*.

De Certeau suggests that one of the advantages for institutions in having an established base is being able to 'capitalize acquired advantages' (De Certeau, 1984, p 36). As discussed in Chapter 3, during the mid-2000s, the introduction of 24-hour rolling news, coupled with staff cuts across the news media industry, and the need to fill more space with fewer staff, as news outlets also developed online news sites, led to a greater dependence by journalists on police-produced press releases and other promotional material. In a climate of already restricted police/news media contact (Mawby, 2012; Colbran, 2017), the MPS have been able to capitalise on the crisis in the news industry, by providing more and more ready-made news stories and video footage for news organisations globally. MPS press officers acknowledged that such content still had to meet normative news values – as one commented, "if it's not visually exciting and impactful, they won't use it". Nevertheless, as Lee and McGovern comment, the fact that the police now have 'the capacity to film, edit and produce the story' means the police have greater capacity than ever before in dealing with the press to 'carry preferred images of the police' (Lee and McGovern, 2014, p 110).

Perhaps the biggest key advantage institutions have in establishing a base, according to De Certeau, is the ability to achieve 'a certain independence with respect to the variability of circumstances' (De Certeau, 1984, p 36). Although by 2012 social media had still not met with complete approval from some forces – with Colin Port, the Chief Constable of Avon and Somerset, expressing the concern that officers might spend 'more time tweeting than actually policing and we don't encourage officers per se to tweet' (Leveson, 2012a, p 826) – other witnesses in the Leveson Inquiry took a more favourable view of police use of social media. As Andy Trotter, then Chief Constable of British Transport Police and head of media for ACPO commented: 'Police forces can communicate instantly and can receive feedback without the filtering process of newspapers, television and radio. Public confidence in the tabloids is not always high therefore the police need to continue to develop means of direct communication' (Leveson, 2012a, p 829).

Until the end of the 20th century, as Lee and McGovern argue, 'the media primarily facilitated the police–public relationship through the reporting of police activities to the community' (Lee and McGovern, 2014, p 114). They comment, however, that the use of social media has 'fractured' that relationship and that, by establishing a virtual as well as a physical base, social media platforms are not only allowing the MPS and other police organisations around the world the ability to communicate more directly with the public than ever before, but also increasingly to bypass the traditional media and to achieve 'a certain independence' (De Certeau, 1984, p 36) from legacy outlets that would not hitherto have been possible.

One key problem for police organisations, including the MPS, in dealing with the media is that coverage for operations is not automatic; stories would only be deemed newsworthy if seen by the editor of an outlet to be of sufficient appeal to the demographic of their newspaper or broadcast outlet. Lee and McGovern note that, as a result, 'important stories are often ignored by journalists' and that 'the location and readership of a media outlet has a significant effect on whether a story is picked up' (Lee and McGovern, 2014, p 100). Similarly, MPS press officers commented:

> 'Papers want glamour, celebrity and one of the least glamorous things that we do stuff about is female genital mutilation, which is a big issue in certain communities. But newspapers don't want to write about that sort of thing. We've got a little coverage in certain places but mainstream, they're not going to write a page lead. Might write a page lead if we mucked up an investigation but that's the only way we'd get that out there.'

Yet, as Lee and Mc Govern (2014) observe, 'what does not make the news will almost certainly be disseminated through police social media' (Lee and McGovern, 2014, p 106). Platforms such as Twitter and Facebook afford the MPS independence from the traditional media by allowing press officers to promote 'good news' stories and stories of police valour.

An MPS press officer gave the following example:

> 'We put out a story about two police going into a burning building to rescue someone. Got one mention in a local paper and nothing anywhere else. We put it on social media and got a huge response and very positive response from the public.'

In the same vein, as part of the MPS Media Relations Standing Operating Procedures issued in 2006, the Directorate of Media and Communications also encouraged individual officers to send them stories of police success:

The 'Your News Box'

Despite the considerable amount of proactive work undertaken by the [Directorate] and the MPS generally, there are still many items of good news that are not reaching colleagues within the Service or – through the media – the wider public.

To enhance the gathering of positive news, for both an internal and external audience, an email account with the internal address ... has been set up. ... The Your News Box is designed to capture positive news and stories that may otherwise go unreported. (Fedorcio, 2012)

Thus, at a time of fiscal restraint, social media and digital platforms allow the MPS to promote the police image more effectively than ever before but, even more significantly, to bypass the news media by releasing stories – particularly ones of police success – that traditional news outlets might overlook or fail to publish.

Risk and responsibilisation

The second key logic of engagement with the media, according to Lee and McGovern (2014), is the management of public risk, or communication of threats or dangers to citizens, and the 'responsibilisation' of the public – a term which O'Malley explains as 'the process whereby subjects are rendered individually responsible for a task which previously would have been the duty of another – usually a state agency – or would not have been recognized as a responsibility at all' (O'Malley, 2009, p 277).

Bowling et al argue that, while order maintenance remains the core function of the police (Bowling et al, 2019), the police are one of a number of agents who are able to 'broker information about risks to public and private organisations concerned with the regulation of people and territories' – information which, Bowling et al argue, derives from their 'traditional patrolling and surveillance activities' and 'gives them uniquely privileged access to risk knowledge' (Bowling et al, 2019, p 121).

Although the term 'risk society' is a comparatively new concept, associated with the work of the German sociologist, Ulrich Beck, and referring to 'a systematic way of dealing with hazards and insecurities induced and introduced by modernisation itself' (Beck, 1992, p 21), Lee and McGovern (2014) suggest that this is not a new theme in policing. They argue that early policing models were also 'loosely risk based', involving 'the prevention of crime through intelligence-led policing and public information' but that, over recent decades, 'risk logics have expanded in importance ... along with the notion that the police cannot be seen as simply a crime-fighting instrumentality' (Lee and McGovern, 2014, p 44) – responsibility for crime control must be shared among government and non-state actors, a process that was evident in a Home Office Report published in 2004. The Report stated that the main thrust of reforms to improve police relations with communities must be 'to pass power from the political centre to local citizens and communities' (Home Office, 2004, p14); and that 'interaction with the public provides ... vital intelligence to help arrest criminals and tackle all levels of crime – from anti-social behaviour to serious organised crime' (Home Office, 2004, p 18).

De Certeau argues that an additional advantage for an organisation in establishing a base is 'a mastery of places through sight' (De Certeau, 1984, p 36). This 'makes possible a panoptic practice proceeding from a place whence the eye can transform foreign forces into objects that can be ... control[led]' (De Certeau, 1984, p 36). During and following the 2011 riots in the United Kingdom, police forces used social media platforms to allay public fears and concerns over safety. Similarly, Lee and McGovern report how, during two cyclones in Australia in late 2010 and early 2011, police used social media to inform the public about impending weather threats, safety measures and public transport closures, demonstrating how 'social media can play a vital role for police organizations in the dissemination of risk-related information' (Lee and McGovern, 2014, p 127).

Lee and McGovern (2014) argue that social media can also be used in enlisting more general help with policing. During the 2011 riots in the United Kingdom, a number of forces used Facebook to call for information, publish photographs and to name rioters who had been convicted of offences (HMIC, 2011; Denef et al, 2013; Procter et al, 2013; Williams et al, 2013). More recently, the MPS have been using social media to enlist the public's help with ongoing initiatives, such as the knife-crime campaign – and to reach new audiences, as one press officer commented:

> 'If you want to publicise a knife crime campaign, then you're not going to get 15- to 25- year-olds reading *The Guardian*. But they will look on social media. So we ran a campaign, offering knife amnesty boxes across Lewisham. We also ran testimonies of families who'd been directly affected by knife crime – so both sides of the story. We couldn't have done that through the old media and we couldn't have spoken as directly to the people involved in this kind of crime.'

A recent study by Ellis (2021), in an Australian context, sounds a note of caution. He argues that '[a]s diversified and "democratic" as social media can be, it reaches its limits when only reaching audiences that believe in what you have to say or find it useful in some way' (Ellis, 2021, p 35). However, Newman et al (2017) provide a counterbalance to this argument, suggesting that, on average, 'users of social media, aggregators, and search engines experience more diversity than non–users' (Newman et al, 2017, p 9) and that given young adults (18–24) are heavier users of social media platforms (Smith and Anderson, 2018) than older adults, there is some justification for supposing that the MPS's strategy may be reaching younger adults who would not necessarily engage with legacy media.

Nevertheless, it is clear that new digital technologies allow the police to communicate risk more directly than ever before to the public, to enlist public support for police initiatives more effectively than through the traditional news media and, at the same time, to increase their 'panoptic practice' (De Certeau, 1984, p 36) and capacity for social control.

Trust and legitimacy

The third key logic underpinning contemporary police/news media engagement, according to Lee and McGovern (2014), is the attempt to increase trust in policing and in the legitimacy of the police organisation. They note that, in 2010, a new customer service charter, informed partly by a public satisfaction agenda, was implemented by the NSW Police Force. In the United Kingdom, Myhill and Bradford (2012) comment that '[p]ublic opinions of the police have been a fixture at the top of the policy agenda in England and Wales in recent years, with successive governments stating they wish to see improvements in "trust and confidence"' (Myhill and Bradford, 2012, p 397).

Although several studies in the United Kingdom and in the United States have indicated that citizens' willingness to co-operate with the police is directly linked to the trust they place in the organisation and the legitimacy they grant it (Tyler, 1997; Sunshine and Tyler, 2003; Hough et al, 2010), international research has also shown that police encounters with the public have little or negative impact on public satisfaction (Skogan, 2006; Bradford et al, 2009). Nevertheless, Myhill and Bradford suggest that the police do have the capacity to enhance public confidence and argue that one way of doing so is 'showing interest in what people have to say and, fundamentally, creating the general impression that the police care' (Myhill and Bradford, 2012, p 417).

De Certeau (1984) argues that another key way in which institutions benefit from setting up a base is in acquiring the ability to 'prepare future expansions' (De Certeau, 1984, p 36). Whereas in the past, 'the notion of direct police-public communications [was] something that only occurred in personalized contexts such as "on the beat"' (Lee and McGovern, 2014, p 114), social media has allowed police officers at all levels to set up dialogue with the public, while circumventing the potentially problematic nature of direct police/citizen encounters (Skogan, 2006; Bradford et al, 2009). In the United Kingdom, the MPS communicates to Londoners through a variety of Twitter feeds. First, there is a corporate Twitter feed, which provides updates on news. The Twitter feed @MPSOnTheStreet is used by different officers to give insights into individual jobs or roles, while the Twitter account @CO11MetPolice is used for public order purposes, to give protesters advice and operational updates. In addition to those feeds, the Commissioner and other senior officers conduct regular web chats with Londoners, while officers are also encouraged to communicate directly with the public through social media, to promote the work that they do. These strategies are seen by the MPS as an important way of humanising the police and of 'reintroducing the police to their community' (Lee and McGovern, 2014, p 129). As one MPS press officer commented:

'Social media shows the public that policing really is a 24-hour service. We are there for them to get in touch any time of day or night and we want to hear their concerns and what we can do to address those concerns. Basically it's never been more easy for the public to get in touch.'

There is also an annual nationwide police award for 'best tweeting officer' and, in an article in the *Daily Telegraph*, the winner of the 2015 award, Sergeant Harry Tangye of Devon and Cornwall Police, was quoted describing social media as the 'new neighbourhood policing' (Jamieson, 2016). He explained that social media helped both to humanise and to demystify policing to the public and suggested that, through his Twitter feeds, use of social media was 'a way of making [the public] see how hard we work and that we are just normal people who want to do a good job and get home to our families' (Jamieson, 2016).

However, as Wood and McGovern (2020) observe in an article on the use of memes and other humour by NSW police on social media platforms, although such posts undoubtedly serve to 'humanis[e] the force' (Wood and McGovern, 2020, p 306), posts showing 'cute' pictures of police dogs or attempts at humour also serve as 'a tool of distraction' (Wood and McGovern, 2020, p 314). They suggest that such posts 'not only present a "sanitised" version of police work that is at odds with the reality of policing' but they also argue that the posts divert 'audience attention away from some of the more problematic and controversial aspects of policing, such as police brutality and violence' (Wood and McGovern, 2020, p 314). In a recent British study, Ralph (2021) suggested that officers themselves were often conflicted about the use of humour in social media, and while some officers saw it as an important way of humanising police work, some members of the public saw police use of social media as 'a waste of police resources' and 'argued that the police should either be tackling crime or engaging with people in physical spaces' (Ralph, 2021, p 10).

Overall, it would appear that the use of social media platforms has enabled the MPS to communicate more directly than ever before with the public, to promote the police image more positively than before and to increase their 'panoptic practice' (De Certeau, 1984, p 36).

Later stages of 'bridge decay' between the MPS and national crime reporters

While there have been numerous studies of the benefits to brokers in bridging structural holes (Burt, 1997, 2004, 2007; Mizruchi and Stearns, 2001; Seibert et al, 2001; Rodan and Galunic, 2004; Fleming et al, 2007; Soda and Bizzi, 2012), comparatively few studies have explored the issue of 'bridge decay' (Burt, 2002). The focus on the persistence and decay of brokerage opportunities began with Burt's (2002) four-year study of bankers' networks, showing that brokerage ties often decay quickly. Burt (2002) argues that because these ties are 'weak ties' (Granovetter, 1973) – ties to acquaintances rather than to friends, which are 'strong ties' – they need more effort to maintain and so 'show faster rates of decay over time than other kinds of relationships in a social network' (Boczkowski and Mitchelstein, 2017, p 22). Stovel and Shaw (2012) also suggest that the opportunity for a broker to extract excess gains through their privileged position may erode the confidence that alters have in the broker. Chapter 4 discussed how this situation arose when certain inner circle journalists, particularly those working for Murdoch-owned titles, appeared to enjoy a favoured relationship with some press officers, not least because of the immense power the organisation had in shaping public and political opinion.

A later study by Ryall and Sorenson also explored the issue of bridge decay. They argued that brokers can only be successful 'if they do not face substitutes … for the connections they offer' (Ryall and Sorenson, 2007, p 566). They suggest that two types of situations, and substitutions, might arise. On the one hand, a substitute might arise for the broker, in that another individual or organisation 'may have the connections necessary to enable completion of the project' (Ryall and Sorenson, 2007, p 572). Alternatively, they argue that 'a substitute may exist for the project that the broker can facilitate (i.e., the other actors may have available an equally attractive project that does not require the broker's connections' (Ryall and Sorenson, 2007, p 572).

Until the early 2010s, however troublesome relationships might be with individual journalists, the MPS did not have 'the option of not co-operating with journalists in general' (Ericson et al, 1989), due to one basic structural factor: 'it [was] difficult for most newsmakers to address the public directly' (Boczkowski and Mitchelstein, 2017, p 22). Social media changed that situation, enabling police organisations – including the MPS – to communicate more directly with the public than ever before, without the intervention of the media. New technologies also allowed the MPS to achieve its three key logics of engagement with the public – the management of its image; the management of public risk and responsibilisation of the public; and increasing confidence and trust in the organisation – more effectively than it had ever been able to do through the media.

Although scholars in both Australia and the United Kingdom (Lee and McGovern, 2014; Ellis and McGovern, 2016; Colbran, 2017, 2020) have also suggested that new technologies have enabled police organisations to bypass the media, officers interviewed for Lee and McGovern's study emphasised that social media was 'another strategy on top of police's traditional media activities' (Lee and McGovern, 2014, p 118). In other words, while the bridge between the police and the public had weakened considerably in other jurisdictions, the crime journalist nevertheless still held some importance for police organisations as a '*tertius gaudens*' (Simmel, 1950) mediating between the police and the public.

By contrast an MPS officer suggested that social media was rapidly becoming the most effective method of communicating with the public, and increasingly supplanting the news media in terms of importance and usefulness:

'The news media are no longer the only way of communicating with the public, they are just one of a number of ways – and not necessarily the most effective way for us to communicate with the biggest and most relevant audiences.'

As Lee and McGovern (2014) argue, however, any 'strategies of control that attempt to create some dialogue' must 'create within them the possibilities for their contestation' (Lee and McGovern, 2014, p 74). The next section explores how far journalists on legacy media outlets – and the public – are able to use 'tactics' of resistance (De Certeau, 1984) to resist the 'nets of discipline' (De Certeau, 1984) used by the MPS to control the flow of policing news in a climate of restricted police/news media contact.

Tactics of resistance: how journalists and the public use social media and new technologies to monitor the police

Police control over the flow of information

De Certeau argues that a key tactic of resistance is to 'make use of the cracks that particular conjunctions open in the surveillance of the proprietary powers' (De Certeau, 1984, p 37). Chapters 3 and 4 discussed how major stories about police corruption and malpractice had been leaked to the press from insider police contacts; and how, as a result of severe restrictions on police/news media relations, many crime correspondents feared that that channel was now closed to them.

Crime correspondents also argued that the advent of social media had enabled the MPS to exert even more control over the flow of policing information to the press. One crime journalist commented:

> 'Chats with the Commissioner may seem like the Met's being open but webchats do not open the Met up to scrutiny.'

In an article for the *Press Gazette* in May 2015, crime reporter Gareth Davies commented that:

> In my seven years as a reporter in Croydon the Met has never given the impression that it encourages officers to speak directly to the press. When it happens it is the exception rather than the rule, and it has become particularly infrequent following the breakdown in relations between the Met and the media in recent years. Most of the time an approach to a police officer will end in being directed to a press officer and, when you do get to speak to one, someone from the 'media team' is invariably present, either to check what is being said or even provide their own opinion. (Davies, 2015)

He went on to describe how, as a reporter for a local paper within the London area, he would approach the Press Bureau for significant events, such as terrorist attacks or murders, but for other incidents, would approach one of the Cluster or local press teams, covering respectively North, South, West and East London. However, as he explained, the South Cluster team for his area, no longer responded to 'reactive media enquiries' or 'inquiries into incidents which have taken place, RTC (road traffic collision), Twitter follow-ups etc.' but would only 'encompass "pro-active" good news releases' (Davies, 2015). He also suggested that, while crime incidents were being reported on the MPS's Twitter feed and news website, journalists were simply not being given background information to those reports or from the officers making those tweets:

> In many other stories our reporters have approached the Met press office and asked for basic information about incidents only to be told to go back to the officer who tweeted the information, and then failed to reply, in the first place. Even when we have received a response the stock answer from those officers has been to send us back to the press office. This is the Met that claims 'officers throughout London's boroughs are encouraged to speak directly to the media'. (Davies, 2015)

As a result, according to Davies, incidents of public interest were being reported with minimal information, or simply not being reported at all. As he commented: 'if you make it more difficult for journalists to verify and obtain information, then they produce less "bad" news' (Davies, 2015). In contrast, although Lee and McGovern (2014) reported that stories on the NSW police media website were similarly short, they noted that, unlike the Press Bureau, the NSW Police Media Unit have 'constant communications with journalists at which point follow-up information may be disseminated and interviews with relevant police might be organised' (Lee and McGovern, 2014, p 112).

Other crime correspondents suggested that the MPS were taking advantage of restricted press/police contact to present an unduly rosy picture of MPS successes. As one respondent explained:

'I went to this briefing and I knew off the record that this unit was in crisis. But this officer gave us all these success figures and we knew that they were glossing, but without officers within that unit prepared to speak to me, my hands are tied. And so we can't run that story and the public are left in the dark as to what's going on. It's bad for democracy but I think it's bad for the police to present themselves as this secretive force. That's what's happening and the public just haven't a clue.'

Most of the crime correspondents interviewed in this study in the period immediately following the Filkin and Leveson Reports (2012) were pessimistic about the future of crime reporting. However, a few younger respondents were more optimistic and argued that new technologies and digital platforms had opened new ways to research stories, to crowdsource relevant information for those stories and for the public to work with them in policing the police. One reporter described how a source had contacted him directly with mobile phone footage of police brutality:

'He told me that he was arrested and then when he was taken to the custody area of the police station he saw police officers beat another young Black boy. In the past, if an incident had happened, it was the police's word against the other person; now these days [the public] have the means to provide proof. And through social media, it's easier than ever for them to get in touch with the press to report these incidents.'

The same reporter suggested that social media had made it easier than ever to investigate stories and, in the process, changed the relationship of crime journalists with their readers or audience to a more collaborative process. As he explained:

'I was writing a story on Jimmy Mubenga,[1] the asylum seeker, and the circumstances surrounding his death on the flight to Luanda, and I was able to appeal immediately for witnesses through Twitter. Before social media, it would have been impossible for me to find those witnesses.'

Journalists' tactics of resistance

Lee and McGovern argue that, just as social media and new technologies have afforded the police more direct forms of communication with the public, as well as 'enhanced technologies of surveillance through recording and monitoring devices', the 'very same technologies and forums police are employing have also provided the public [and the press] with more sophisticated ways in which to monitor the police' (Lee and McGovern, 2014, p 174).

Two recent studies by Ellis (2021) and Richardson (2020) explore this concept of 'sousveillance', which Mann and Ferenbok have explained as 'watching from below' (Mann and Ferenbok, 2013, p 19). Bakir et al use the term 'hierarchical' sousveillance to describe a form of sousveillance that has 'political or legal intent targeted at the powerful', giving protestor use of smartphone videos and social media to monitor police at demonstrations as an example (Bakir et al, 2017, p 1). This is in contrast to surveillance or watching from above (Mann and Ferenbok, 2013).

Ellis's study focuses on the beating of a teenager, Jamie Jackson Reed, in 2013, by officers from the NSW police force and the effect on relationships between the NSW force and the local LGBTQI[2] community, following a bystander's uploading of the beating in real time to YouTube. This was a year in which other contentious cases of policing were exposed directly by bystanders through social media, in particular the video of the police shooting of 18-year-old Sammy Yatim in Toronto uploaded to YouTube (Schneider, 2016). 2013 was also the year in which the Black Lives Matter movement[3] was established in the US. His key argument is that the proliferation and diversification of digital platforms, notably social media networks, emphasise that institutional change is 'in constant dialogue with the demands of legitimacy' (Gilley, 2009, p 132) and that 'consent is continually renewed' (Beetham, 1991/2013, p 101, quoted in Ellis, 2021, p 2). Ellis explores the dynamic nature of police legitimacy through social media using a concept he terms the 'social media test' (Ellis, 2021, p 2) or 'the literal shift from the traditional "front page test", how one's actions would be construed under the scrutiny of front page exposure in a major newspaper ... to an evaluation of police performance through social media representations' (Ellis, 2021, p 2). Unlike in pre-digital days, when a story would surface for days or occasionally weeks to limited readerships, Ellis argues that the 'social media test' now increases the likelihood of 'exposure of police excessive force through bystander video distributed through social media in shorter timeframes to larger audiences' (Ellis, 2021, p 143). This 'amplified scrutiny' (Ellis, 2021, p 143) is not only prolonged through stories oscillating from social media platforms to mainstream media and back again, but such incidents of police brutality are also captured online in perpetuity.

Ellis argues that the capture of these individual incidents on video can have several effects. First, they can 'catalyse direct action, calibrate police practices and permanently shame police officers' (Ellis, 2021, p 143). Second, such videos can give context to the incident and, in the case of Jamie Jackson Reed, where one of the charges against him was offensive language, demonstrate to vulnerable communities 'how "trivial" gateway offences ... can escalate to more substantial charges' (Ellis, 2021, p 54). Third, he suggests that the capture of such incidents on video enables victims of excessive police force to compare their accounts with others and to evaluate the fairness of the outcomes they receive from criminal justice actors. Finally, he observes that such incidents challenge the 'hegemonic narratives' (Ellis, 2021, p 28) of 'primary definers' (Hall et al, 1978) – in this case, the police. Whereas in the pre-digital age, citizens had to hand footage of police brutality over to the press in order to for it to reach a wider audience, now members of the public can simply upload their footage themselves to social media in real time – pre-empting any official narratives by the police. As a result, Ellis also argues that Web 2.0 technology has 'diminished the role of mainstream media as "secondary definers" – news selectors and framers', which has 'elevated the role, but not always the credibility, of the bystander "unauthorized knower", whose precarious status is contingent on where they are, and not necessarily who they are' (Ellis, 2021, p 7).

Richardson (2020) takes this one step further in her study, suggesting that African American activists in the United States not only circumvent the media in order to publish video evidence of police brutality for each other as well as for a wider audience, but are also using social media platforms to create an alternative journalism. She argues that legacy media outlets are considered 'members of the "Fourth Estate", serving as elite watchdogs on high', while 'black witnesses report from below' (Richardson, 2020, p xiv).

Sousveillance for Richardson's respondents is not confined to the police but also to mainstream news outlets and she notes how African American activists interviewed for her study aimed 'to revise news narratives', with the Black Twitter community seeking to 'challenge racism, sensationalism or factual errors in legacy news reports' (Richardson, 2020, p 54). However, Ellis notes that the ability of vulnerable communities to hold the police to account is limited. Bystander video footage of police brutality can be dismissed as a 'partial' representation of events, while new technologies, such as body worn cameras, afford the police greater powers of surveillance in turn (Ellis, 2021, p 6). He also notes that the police can refuse to hand over footage (Ellis, 2021, p 97) or simply turn cameras off without consequence (Ellis, 2021, p 92). One crime journalist gave an example of this:

'So there were these armed robbers the coppers have been following. They knew they were planning a robbery on [X] and the coppers followed them on to the car park and waited till the point that they got out and they pulled their strike. And those robbers are pulled out and they are beaten to a pulp so badly that [one] loses his spleen. But the fuckers turned their dash cams off as they pulled up into the car park so you've just got the footage up to the point where the guy is leathered and the CS gas is used and it then stops.'

Another problem for citizens seeking redress for police brutality is the 'opacity over outcomes of police internal investigations' (Ellis, 2021, p 95) which, Ellis suggests, often denies closure to those who make formal complaints or take out civil cases against the police. The same crime journalist also observed that, in the United Kingdom, internal investigations of police conduct are also held in private, with civil actions that the police settle being subject to non-disclosure agreements (NDAs):

'So this guy who'd been beaten so badly he lost his spleen, goes to court and, on the day that he is due to take full proceedings out against this force, they settle and they settle with an NDA and the NDA covers the IPCC [Independent Police Complaints Commission][4] investigation into whether the amount of violence used was appropriate or not. And that's not made public, just all sorted out of court and swept under the carpet.'

In the opinion of this respondent, the opacity regarding internal police investigations often meant that the same mistakes are repeated again and again:

'So a couple of years before this case when the guy lost his spleen, a PC was killed during a training exercise – this was in another force, not the Met. And out of that PC's death came a series of recommendations which came from the IPCC and were kept secret and they were that you needed to have your dash cams on, you needed to be wearing body cams on all operations and they must stay on throughout the operation and CS gas cannot be used. It's fucking banned. So it then transpires within the IPCC report on the guy who lost his spleen but is again bound by a gagging order but I have a copy of it, that the same thing happened, body cams off, CS gas used and fast forward to another incident, a fatal shooting this time, three years later and the same thing happens. Did they have their dash cams on? No, they were switched off before he was shot and killed. Did they have their body cams on – they chose not to switch them on. So again at three points, they failed to follow guidance for a second time and yet these incidents have failed to result in a transparent investigation.'

Finally, Ellis (2020) comments that, in Australia, it may take years for cases 'to reach a "serious" enough threshold to be investigated by police oversight bodies' (Ellis, 2020, p 200). This appears also to be the case in the United Kingdom. In a recent article in *The Guardian*, Carla Cumberbatch – the sister of Darren Cumberbatch, who died in July 2017 after being punched repeatedly, sprayed with CS gas and Tasered by officers – said that she had been told that it could take three years for her to receive a full report from the Independent Office for Police Conduct,[5] even though at the inquest it was revealed that one officer 'admitted making incorrect statements on police notes after the event and copying another officer's notes word for word in his account of the incident' (Busby, 2021). The officer did not face disciplinary proceedings.

While new technologies still allow crime journalists to continue to infiltrate 'the space of the other' (De Certeau, 1984, p 37), it would seem that, in the United Kingdom, crime reporters' ability to hold the police to account or even to report routine crime stories has been impeded. Although new technologies also allow members of the public to hold the police to account, often circumventing the media when doing so, 'the "social media test" may pressure operational police and the police institution to account, but it can only go so far in holding the police to account' (Ellis, 2020, p 202). It would seem, in this respect, that social media platforms and new technologies have increased police control over flow of information and over the police image. However, as Goldsmith points out, 'the capacity to distort or mislead through the internet is immense' (Goldsmith, 2010, p 921). While it might seem that the balance of power in the police/news media relationship is skewed towards the police, the lack of accountability of content posted on digital platforms is a problem for both the MPS and the legacy media – and, as discussed in the next section, is exacerbated by the restrictions on contact between police and press.

The problems of social media

Ericson et al argue that 'all organizations – the police department, the family, the multinational corporation, the newspaper – need to keep some matters secret' (Ericson et al, 1989, p 379). In the case of the police, failure to control the press 'can mean loss of control over organizational life and serious harms' (Ericson et al, 1989, p 388). As a result, Ericson et al suggest that the easiest way for the police 'to overcome the ways in which they lose power in their relationships with reporters is to develop a spatial, social, and cultural system of relations that sustains a spirit of trust and reciprocity' (Ericson et al, 1989, p 126).

As both police and press respondents interviewed for this study acknowledged, that relationship of trust appears to have been lost, following the recommendations of the Filkin and Leveson Reports (2012) to restrict contact between the police and the news media. The advent of social media has also put new pressures on national crime journalists, already working to fill more space with fewer staff. Alejandro argues that journalists 'are forced to accelerate the traditional journalistic process because people now want real time information … to sit on a story until it is complete is to risk being out-scooped by competitors' (Alejandro, 2010, p 9). In the current media landscape, 'the fear of missing out on a story surfacing on social media can lead to the temptation to cover it before significant details are confirmed' (Beckett, 2016, p 33). For the crime reporter, there is an additional problem – severe restrictions on police contact, both official and unofficial, when trying to verify details of a breaking story. As one respondent explained:

'Take the Mark Duggan story. It was all over social media that a young man had been dragged from his car and shot point blank by police. But when I asked the press office, I just got no comment. And we couldn't take the risk of not printing in case it was true so we went ahead with the caveat that a witness reported that they had seen it.'

Rumours, conspiracy theories and fabricated information are far from new and, as Wardle and Derakhshan point out, 'the media has long disseminated misleading stories for their shock value' (Wardle and Derakhshan, 2017, p 10). Molina et al (2021) trace the concept of 'misinformation' back to the Spanish Civil War, arguing that it was then known as 'yellow journalism' or 'publishing content with no evidence and therefore factually incorrect, often for business purposes' (Molina et al, 2021, p 183). But while misinformation is not new, 'the emergence of the internet and social technology have brought about fundamental changes to the way information is produced, communicated and distributed' (Wardle and Derakhshan, 2017, p 11). Just as mobile phones and new digital technologies have allowed members of the public and the press to share information in real time, these same devices and platforms have also contributed to the spread of misinformation or 'fake news'. An example of this occurred during the 2016 presidential election in the United States, when a story published on a Macedonian website, *Conservative State*, falsely quoted Hillary Clinton as saying, 'I would like to see people like Donald Trump run for office; they're honest and can't be bought' (Silverman, 2016). The story generated over 481,000 engagements on Facebook. Wardle and Derakhshan make another important point: 'popular social networks make it difficult for people to judge the credibility of any message, because posts from publications as unlike as the *New York Times* and a conspiracy site look nearly identical' (Wardle and Derakhshan, 2017, p 12).

In this new media landscape, it would seem more imperative than ever for press officers to engage fully with crime reporters, to ensure fake news or inaccurate information is not reported in the public domain. However, the situation had deteriorated so badly that in 2013, following the beheading of Fusilier Lee Rigby by Michael Adebolajo and Michael Adebowale, the then chairman of the HAC, Keith Vaz, openly criticised the MPS's media policy, arguing that 'Scotland Yard should engage with the media and the public more openly if it wants to build community support in the battle against terrorism' (O'Neill, 2013).

Mr Vaz also suggested that the MPS's media strategy had compared poorly with that of the Boston Police Department, following terrorist bomb attacks at the Boston Marathon in April 2013. Police chiefs in Boston held regular live news conferences to update the public, and used social media networks such as Twitter to publicise developments and staunch rumours and incorrect speculation; in contrast, the 'Met Commissioner, Sir Bernard Hogan-Howe, has made only one televised statement since the murder of Drummer Lee Rigby, despite a huge anti-terror operation across London and in other parts of the country' (O'Neill, 2013). Mr Vaz was quoted as saying that he knew 'the police are very reluctant to give out confidential and sensitive information' but 'it is important that the press are kept informed and the public are kept engaged' (O'Neill, 2013).

The use of social media also poses problems for operational policing. As Beckett comments, the 'arrival of live video on social networks means that the citizen … can become a social network broadcaster' (Beckett, 2016, p 16) and, as a result, the risk of information or footage about an ongoing investigation being posted inadvertently by a bystander increases immeasurably. Beckett suggests that this is particularly relevant in the midst of a terrorist operation, where live video or pictures of a scene 'may endanger security forces or hamper their work' and comments that it is 'essential that, when the public is at risk, the news media works closely with security officials' (Beckett, 2016, p 20). One operational police officer saw this as a reason for relaxing relations with reporters:

'With social media, there is no control. And that's the big fear, that a journalist might get hold of footage, say of a building where we're deploying security forces, not wait to check – or worse, as I know there's blame on both sides, not get the guidance he or she needs from us – and that's the whole operation blown and people's lives put in danger.'

While the use of social media has undoubted benefits for the police, it also poses serious problems in terms of inaccurate reporting, obstruction of police work and the potential to compromise investigations.

Conclusion

In this chapter, I have explored how, at a time of already beleaguered relations between the MPS and the national news media, following the recommendations of the Filkin and Leveson Reports (2012), the advent of new digital technologies caused the 'bridge' between the MPS and national crime journalists to break down completely.

I argue that, through the use of social media platforms, the MPS have not only been able to communicate more directly than ever before with the public but, from the perspective of their press officers, to achieve many of their key aims in dealing with mainstream media – image work, the management of public risk and 'responsibilisation' of the public and attempts to increase public confidence and trust in the police. I highlight how, in the past, press officers often struggled to place stories of police courage or valour in the mainstream press, in part due to the latter's 'bad-news emphasis' (Ericson et al, 1989, p 378), whereas they are now able to place these stories on their own news website. In terms of the management of public risk, I argue that both police and press officers are able to use social platforms to allay public fears and concerns over safety and to enlist the public's support with ongoing initiatives as well as engaging in aspects of operational policing, such as appeals for witnesses and help with investigations. Finally, I suggest that MPS operational and press officers are using social media platforms as a way of 'humanising' the police, through the use of humour and through dialogue with members of the public with the aim of increasing trust and confidence in the organisation by this greater police visibility.

Moreover, I note that new digital technologies are increasingly enabling MPS press officers to bypass mainstream media altogether (Lee and McGovern, 2014). For many journalists, the advent of social media has appeared to enable the MPS to exert even more control over the flow of policing information to the press and to the public. It is true that new digital technologies have also provided both the public and the press with more sophisticated ways in which to monitor the police and publicly disseminate and circulate images and narratives of police brutality in real time – a recent example being the murder of George Floyd in Minneapolis in May 2020, which triggered worldwide demonstrations and protests. But although Ellis argues that such 'individual incidents can qualify hegemonic mainstream and police news media narratives ... and catalyse direct action' (Ellis, 2021, p 143), he also suggests that the police are not powerless in these situations. Bystander video footage of police brutality can be dismissed as a partial representation of events, while new technologies such as body worn cameras afford the police greater powers of surveillance.

The rise of the new investigative journalism start-ups

Introduction

In late 2018, I started preparing a proposal for a new book on police and media relations. I had nearly finished it when, scrolling through Twitter one afternoon, I noticed that there was a three-day event called 'Conspiracy' at the Centre for Investigative Journalism in South East London; according to the publicity note, its aim was to bring together 'investigative journalists, whistleblowers, hackers, artists and experts to challenge power and reinvigorate the field of investigative journalism'. I was in two minds whether to attend. On the one hand, as a qualitative researcher working in a rapidly changing field, there is always the temptation to do 'one more interview', just in case you have missed something crucial. On the other hand, there is also the knowledge that, however many interviews you carry out, ultimately all you can do is provide a snapshot of the field you are observing; by the time your book or article comes out, the world you are describing will almost certainly have changed.

I decided to attend the conference. I was very glad I did, as the initial session I attended ended up changing the scope of my research and the content of this book. That first session was called 'Who Pays The Piper' and centred around issues of funding for the new investigative non-profits. These non-profit organisations, as I found out, differed from traditional journalism outlets, in that they were funded by philanthropic foundations or member-donors and so were able to operate without the concern of debt, dividends and the need to make a profit. There were two speakers at this session: Rachel Oldroyd, the managing director of *The Bureau for Investigative Journalism*, one of the largest British non-profits; and Matt Kennard, a freelance investigative journalist. Both previously had considerable high-level experience in mainstream journalism: Rachel Oldroyd had worked for the *Mail on Sunday* for 13 years, where she ran the award winning 'Reportage' section in the *Mail*'s magazine supplement, *Live*; while Matt Kennard had written for *The New Statesman*, *The Guardian*, *The Financial Times*, *OpenDemocracy* and *Intercept*.

Before this session, I had never heard of the work being done by the non-profits; nor had I known what a non-profit was. The session was far-ranging – as well as covering the issues of funding on non-profits, the speakers described how new working practices were challenging journalistic norms. Both Oldroyd and Kennard seemed disillusioned with mainstream media and talked about how newsrooms no longer had the time or the money to fund investigative journalism and how, instead, editors were focused on how many 'hits' a story received online. Kennard related how, at a time of shrinking advertising revenue, editors were keener than ever to keep advertisers onside and how, on one occasion, he was forced to drop an investigation he had been working on for months because the editor feared a compromise of interests with one of the paper's advertisers. Although both were honest that the non-profit sector was not without its challenges – low pay, long hours and no guarantee of an outlet's longevity – both journalists conveyed a strong sense of passion about their work in this sector, describing how they finally had the freedom and time to pursue the kinds of investigation they believed should be reported. Equally, both made it clear that this was not a return to what they termed the 'campaign-led' journalism of the past. Rather, their aim was not merely to 'inform' the public but to engage with them, to discover the issues that mattered to them and to equip citizens with the information and knowledge they needed in order to make a change. As Oldroyd put it memorably, the non-profits had moved from transactional journalism, or journalism needing to make a profit, to transformational journalism, or journalism committed to bringing about social change on local, national and international levels.

Over the following 18 months, I spoke to several journalists on a number of non-profits, both in the United Kingdom and in other countries. I discovered how the non-profits were challenging journalistic norms – for example, I learned how *The Bristol Cable* was training members of the public to work alongside members of the organisation to research and report stories. I also discovered two further themes emerging from my interviews. First, rather than what one respondent termed the 'old' forms of crime journalism, the focus of respondents was on reporting 'systemic harm'. Second, they spoke about what they perceived to be the lack of diversity in mainstream media overall, and how another aim of their work was to give voice to marginalised and stigmatised communities in their reporting – particularly those communities that they believed had often been reported upon negatively.

In this chapter and in Chapter 7, I explore the impact on the field of crime and investigative journalism of the new investigative journalism start-ups in the United Kingdom. In this chapter, I explore the working processes on non-profits, how the non-profits are challenging journalistic 'norms' and expanding the Fourth Estate role of the investigative journalist. In Chapter 7, I argue that these new working practices have led in turn to a new form of crime and investigative journalism in the UK and broadened the traditional remit of crime news content. I focus on the work of three British investigative non-profits and projects, chosen to cover a range in terms of models of funding, the collaborations into which they enter and the ways in which they investigate stories. The three non-profits and projects selected are:

- *The Bureau for Investigative Journalism* – chosen as an example of collaborative working on a national and international level and of collaboratively working with legacy media organisations to share their stories with the aim of reaching as many citizens as possible.
- The *Bureau Local* – a project set up by *The Bureau for Investigative Journalism*, chosen as an example of collaboratively working on a local and national level, with a wider variety of non-traditional journalist actors involved in reporting, including local reporters, hyperlocal bloggers, technologists, community-minded citizens and specialist contributors.
- *The Bristol Cable* – chosen as an example of investigative journalism as activism, funded by over 2,000 members who all have a say and own an equal share in their media co-operative. As part of its mission, *The Bristol Cable* delivers free media training to members of the public so that 'Bristolians are equipped with the skills to report on important issues to them and have a platform to publish on' (taken from *The Bristol Cable*'s online mission statement).

In order to conceptualise the new ways in which journalists on these non-profits are collaborating with the public and with other non-profits and mainstream news organisations, I use Burt's (1992, 2002) work on structural holes but also draw upon Kim and Ball-Rokeach's work on communication infrastructure theory. Communication infrastructure theory, or CIT, is a 'theoretical framework that differentiates local communities in terms of whether they have communication resources that can be activated to construct community, thereby enabling collective action for common purpose' (Kim and Ball-Rokeach, 2006, p 174). I use this theory to explore how, at a time when mainstream crime journalists represent decaying 'bridges' between the police and the general public, journalists on non-profits are creating a network of new 'bridges' with members of the public, community groups and other news outlets to form what I describe as 'storytelling islands'; and creating a new form of crime journalism, through reporting with communities and not just about them.

I start my discussion with a brief summary of some of the key literature on non-profits to date, before moving on to how and why the investigative non-profit sector has developed over the last decade in the United Kingdom, how the non-profits are funded and how these new business models allow them to research and carry out investigative journalism in ways that are both innovative and, in terms of the content of crime news, transformative.

Investigative non-profits: a review of relevant literature

Journalism non-profits are not a new phenomenon; in the United States, they date back to the formation of the Associated Press in 1848. Birnbauer (2019) comments that, in the United States, non-profit organisations specifically dedicated to watchdog or investigative journalism have been operating for many decades, including *Mother Jones,*[1] *The Center for Investigative Reporting*[2] and, more recently, *ProPublica.*[3] In the United Kingdom, the broadsheet *The Guardian* also functions as a non-profit. *The Guardian* is part of Guardian Media Group, which was owned by the Scott Trust, created in 1936 by John Scott, the then editor and owner, to secure the financial and editorial independence of *The Guardian.* All profits made were reinvested into the paper to fund its journalism, rather than distributed to owners or shareholders as in commercial enterprises. In 2008, the Scott Trust's assets were transferred to a new limited company, Scott Trust Limited, but the purposes of the new company – to reinvest profits into the newspaper – remained the same.

However, over the last decade, there has been a rapid expansion in the non-profit investigative reporting sector. This has taken place against a background of huge change in the news industry. In the United States, in 2006, there were about 114,000 total newsroom employees – reporters, editors, photographers and videographers – in five industries that produce news: newspaper, radio, broadcast television, cable and other information services. By 2020, that number had declined to about 85,000, a loss of about 30,000 jobs (Walker, 2021). In the United Kingdom, the number of full-time journalists dropped from around 23,000 in 2007 to 17,000 in 2017 and, in the same period, over 300 local and regional newspaper titles were also lost (Mediatique, 2018).

In her study of American journalism non-profits, Konieczna notes that, over a similar period, these organisations have 'grown from a handful to hundreds since 2008, and from all-but-invisible to playing a serious role in the news ecologies in which they operate' (Konieczna, 2018, p 3). Part of the reason for this expansion has been, according to Deuze and Witschge (2020), '[t]he availability of a lot of (unemployed) journalistic talent ... a growing frustration with the lack of innovation in the ... news media landscape ... as well as the emergence of charismatic and media-savvy reporters' which 'cemented a path for journalism startups' (Deuze and Witschge, 2020, p vii). However, they also comment that in the Netherlands, where their study took place, it was 'a path partially paved ... by belonging to the dominant class of journalists ... (white, middle-class, male, well-educated, living in or near the capital)' (Deuze and Witschge, 2020, p vii). Similarly, Birnbauer (2019) notes that one of the key reasons for the expansion of investigative non-profits in the United States, following the financial crisis of 2007–8, was the transfer of senior for-profit journalists to this sector. Prior to this, Birnbauer (2019) suggests that mainstream outlets were averse to collaborating with bloggers and outside news organisations, worrying about 'the accuracy of the stories, the agendas of those writing them, the professionalism and ethics of the writers and the risk of legal action' (Birnbauer, 2019, p 13). By contrast, the new investigative non-profits, such as *The Center for Investigative Reporting* and *ProPublica*, were founded by journalists with years of experience in mainstream media. As a result, editors of mainstream outlets were, according to Birnbauer (2019), only too happy to work with these non-profits, and on occasion publish their stories, as 'their familiarity and standing dispelled many of the concerns held by legacy editors' (Birnbauer, 2019, p 15).

Oldroyd (2021) observes that, in the United States, in Germany and in the United Kingdom, non-profits often provide 'a bolster to public interest journalism' and that '[i]n these countries, organisations such as *ProPublica* in the United States, *The Bureau for Investigative Journalism* in the United Kingdom ... or *Correctiv* in Germany sit alongside the traditional media, often working with reporters from within larger newsrooms' (Oldroyd, 2021, p 102). Other models of non-profit journalism also exist; as Oldroyd notes, in countries where 'the news is predominately provided by government-backed outlets, mission-driven organisations relying on reader donations have set up as independent challenges to the status quo' (Oldroyd, 2021, p 103). These organisations include *Rappler* in the Philippines, founded by Nobel Prize winning journalist, Maria Ressa, and set up to hold the human rights abuses by President Duterte to account; and the *Daily Maverick* in South Africa, set up to provide independent reporting and to tackle stories not run by mainstream media (Oldroyd, 2021). Other models in the United States and in the United Kingdom aim to tackle local news, as many communities on both sides of the Atlantic have increasingly found themselves without local providers. In the United Kingdom, examples of these local non-profits include *The Ferret* based in Glasgow and *The Bristol Cable* based, unsurprisingly, in Bristol. News stories on these outlets are often sourced differently from the bigger non-profits, often including submissions from members of the public.

Most research on non-profits to date focuses on the United States, with the exception of Price's (2017) study of the Scottish investigative non-profit *The Ferret*, and Albeanu's (2016) study of *The Bristol Cable*. Studies have explored collaborative working practices on non-profits. Although peer collaboration in investigative journalism is not new, Stonbely (2017) argues that collaborative investigative journalism is entering a new phase as evidenced by three developments. The first is cross-border collaboration, the best-known example of this being the 'Panama Papers' story. This refers to the 11.5 million leaked encrypted documents that were the property of Mossack Fonseca, a Panama-based law firm. The documents were released in 2016, by the German newspaper *Sudetendeutsche Zeitung*, which dubbed them 'the Panama Papers'. The documents exposed the network of more than 214,000 tax havens involving people and companies from 200 different countries. The story was the result of a year-long investigation by over 100 teams of reporters, mostly working in traditional newsrooms but, as Oldroyd (2016) notes, coordinated by the non-profit, the *International Consortium of Investigative Journalists*.[4] The second development is the involvement of multiple and diverse partners, such as non-profits, commercial organisations, local news media and members of the public; and the third development is the use of big data or OSINT to research and tell stories (Usher, 2016; Baack, 2018), largely practised by the non-profits (Oldroyd, 2021).

Konieczna explores the practice of collaboration through 'news sharing' (Konieczna, 2018, p 5), both with other non-profits and also with traditional newsrooms. While she notes that respondents in her study from non-profits have suggested that they share news to improve the quality of journalism on mainstream outlets, Konieczna argues that '[s]haring forces the news nonprofits to produce content that mainstream journalists and editors might want to publish, which means their stories need to resemble stories that might appear in other publications' (Konieczna, 2018, p 186). She suggests that, as a result, 'although the nonprofits are being founded by people who seek to improve journalism in their communities, news sharing limits the organizations' ability to reform journalism' (Konieczna, 2018, p 187).

Wenzel (2020) explores the co-production of journalism by mainstream outlets, citizens and members of non-profits and takes a more optimistic standpoint than Konieczna (2018). She explores local journalism networks that are attempting to narrow the distance and create links between media, residents and other community stakeholders and, in particular, how some local journalism outlets are 'attempt[ing] to decenter journalistic power in order to share power with marginalized communities' (Wenzel, 2020, p 3). She argues that, by doing so, '[r]ather than a one-to-many model of news, [this genre] of journalism emphasize[s] participatory and multidirectional flows of media' (Wenzel, 2020, p 11). She also argues that this kind of journalistic intervention has two benefits. First, by engaging residents in the process of creating local news, she suggests that 'these interventions have the potential to offer shared spaces for dialogue and action on community issues' (Wenzel, 2020, p 4). Second, she suggests that community-based journalism projects, where journalists share power with citizens and 'make room for people to speak and be heard in ways that recognize difference and do not force conformity to journalism practices that are usually tied to norms of whiteness and class' (Wenzel, 2020, p 14), may be the first step in attempting to reverse the representational harms of mainstream journalism in the depicting of marginalised or stigmatised communities.

Deuze and Witschge (2020) have explored how journalism non-profits are 'deliberately stretch[ing] the ideological conceptualization of journalism'

(Deuze and Witschge, 2020, p 118). Traditionally, scholars have suggested that one of the key functions of journalism, is 'informing citizens in a way that enables them to act as citizens' (Costera Meijer, 2001, p 13). Similarly, Schudson (2008) sees journalism in terms of what it 'can do for democracy' (Schudson, 2008, p 11) – that it is meant to inform, investigate, provide multiple perspectives and a public forum. By contrast, Deuze and Witschge suggest that journalists on the new start-ups not only 'describe themselves as providing a much-needed alternative to legacy media' (Deuze and Witschge, 2020, p 118), but also believe that the function of journalism goes beyond merely 'informing' the public. As one of their respondents comments: 'To inform lacks several things that can make journalism relevant. It lacks the interaction with your audience, the assistance in situating issues – interpretation, involvement – why it is important' (respondent quoted in Deuze and Witschge, 2020, p 119). Nevertheless, Deuze and Witschge comment that it 'would be a mistake to assume that the types of journalism emerging inside and alongside legacy news organizations are necessarily different or oppositional to the core values, ideals, and practices of the profession' (Deuze and Witschge, 2020, p 20).

Finally, studies also explore the funding of the new non-profits. A study by Carvajal et al (2012) explored the funding of non-profit news organisations, either through crowdfunding or through grants from wealthy individuals. They argue that such practices placed 'the audience back at the heart of the journalistic mission' and that, in the process of donating to non-profit organisations, audiences were participating 'in the production of news and quality journalism in a broader sense than that of traditional media' (Carvajal et al, 2012, p 645). However, a more recent study by Benson (2018) of 15 non-profit news outlets showed that financial and business elites made up the bulk of their funders and warned that, as a result, philanthropic support risks replicating the interests of donors and may well end up creating news for small, elite and niche audiences. Similarly Usher (2021) argues that there are reasons for concern about the funding of non-profits in the United States; that 'wealthy donors and foundations tend to give to people and organizations they already know' (Usher, 2021, p 197) and that the 'kind of journalism that ends up getting supported can reflect the needs and interests of funders and not necessarily the needs and interests of local communities' (Usher, 2021, p 200).

It is clear from this albeit brief summary of literature on the non-profits that, while the majority of scholars see the emergence of the non-profits as a generally positive development in the field of journalism, they also raise important concerns. While respondents in Deuze and Witschge's (2020) study expressed a wish to represent marginalised and stigmatised groups more positively, Deuze and Witschge note that many of the journalists starting up these organisations are, nevertheless, White, male and privileged, like many of their counterparts in mainstream media and that, in terms of producing content, 'a new organization of newswork does not necessarily produce a different kind of news' (Deuze and Witschge, 2020, p 91). Usher (2021) raises the concern that one of the principal methods of funding for non-profits – donations from philanthropic funds – may mean that it is the foundation's agenda driving the stories being investigated; while Konieczna (2018) suggests that the practice of news sharing inevitably means that non-profits need to tailor their stories to the needs of mainstream outlets and that, as a result, the content of their stories may not be that radically different from the legacy outlets that her respondents often criticised for their lack of innovation. In the next three sections of this chapter, I explore how British investigative non-profits have sought to avoid these pitfalls.

The economics of non-profit journalism

In the United Kingdom, there are two main sources of funding for non-profit news start-ups: gifts from philanthropic foundations and/or wealthy individuals; and reader donations or membership.

The Bureau for Investigative Journalism was one of the first news non-profits in the United Kingdom, funded primarily by grant-makers and philanthropists. It was founded by David and Elaine Potter; the latter was a former *Sunday Times* journalist and 'had a good sense of what was being lost as the global financial downturn started to bite' (Oldroyd, 2016, p 318). As Birnbauer (2019) notes, 'investigative journalism looked particularly vulnerable: it was expensive to produce, was plagued by costly legal actions, it upset politicians and potential advertisers, and was unproductive in the number of stories it created' (Birnbauer, 2019, p 5). Nevertheless, a respondent from *The Bureau for Investigative Journalism* argued that, while funding by philanthropic foundations allows organisations relative freedom and autonomy to pursue stories those organisations believe to be important, such funding cannot be depended upon indefinitely and can often have a downside:

> 'The idea has always been that you can fund the journalistic remit and still be independent of advertiser influence and the influence of large corporate owners. But then you are still beholden to the objectives, if not the whims of philanthropic funders, but in some ways, that's probably less problematic than advertising or corporate ownership. But there are still problems, the philanthropic organisation may have its own agenda or it may simply find another cause it would rather support.'

In her study of American news non-profits, Konieczna argues that 'foundations can or do represent special interests and that they donate to journalistic projects in pursuit of an agenda beyond improving democracy'

(Konieczna, 2018, p 110). *The Bureau for Investigative Journalism*, and its project, the *Bureau Local* founded in 2017, have been able to avoid these problems by diversifying their revenue streams. In its annual report in 2019, *The Bureau for Investigative Journalism* reported funding from 18 organisations, including the Joseph Rowntree Charitable Trust, the Paul Hamlyn Foundation, Lankelly Chase, the Pears Foundation and the David and Elaine Potter Foundation. They also reported that just over 10 per cent of their funding came from individual donors. In the longer term, however, they are not averse to other revenue-generating approaches, but without compromising ideals, as a respondent from the *Bureau Local* explained:

'At the moment we have this idea the service journalism sits over here and profitable journalism sits over there. I think the two can sit together and I want to see, can we create a new brand of ethical journalism that serves communities, serves people, holds power to account, and get people to invest in that long-term?'

Konieczna (2018) comments that another key model of funding for news non-profits is that of reader-donors. She suggests that the main reasons for donors to fund non-profit journalism are, first, quality of the reporting and, second, a desire to offer general support for journalism, particularly investigative journalism. However, as Price (2017) and Hamada (2021) comment, a number of non-profits in the United Kingdom have chosen to operate as co-operatives, 'community owned and rooted in the places they serve' (Hamada, 2021, p 114). A respondent from *The Bristol Cable* explained why they and their co-founder had decided to set the organisation up as a co-operative:

'Now the reason we decided to set ourselves up as a co-op – we both wanted to create an organisation whose governance was democratic, was in the hands of the people, and not hedge funds or corporate shareholders. So, in that way we intended to create a member-owned organisation, in which member donations were our primary revenue stream alongside philanthropic funding. The corollary to that was that we were able to sidestep the advertising business model that was collapsing. We relied on people giving us money or donating but by doing so, to become part of that organisation, to become members and to participate in how the co-operative was run. And so, we were able to build a community in that way. And that was our aim.'

The same respondent noted that, on the surface, their model might look very similar to a membership or subscription model; but, as they explained, one of the main differences between a reader-donor led non-profit (Konieczna,

2018) and their model is that readers actively have a stake in the organisation and are consulted on key decisions:

'Firstly, we have a non-executive board of directors that is elected by and from our membership of now 2,800 members, but we also have an annual AGM where about 100 or 150 members come together and they participate in the big decisions like our direction. So for example like should we advertise on Facebook, should we be applying for funding from government. ... It would be possible to do that deep engagement without' being a co-operative, but there's something about that engagement being underpinned by our actual organisational structure lends it a credibility and means that we prioritise it.'

They also added:

'What we are aiming to do is to build a community. We want to do journalism differently and to really enhance levels of engagement and we're doing that by including the audience in every stage of the process, thinking of them as active users rather than passive recipients of news, and allowing them to participate in the work we produce, the governance of our organisation – basically, we want to be accountable to our community, not some media conglomerate.'

As Price notes in his study of the Scottish co-operative, *The Ferret*, this ethical dimension is 'an important consideration for many journalism start-ups, particularly those relying on public support and funding for their existence' as they need to 'demonstrate their credentials as a body worthy of being given such backing' (Price, 2017, p 1340). In their study of crowdfunded journalism, Porlezza and Splendore (2016) identified a range of ethical practices such start-ups might employ to engage audiences in an ethical way. These practices include publishing details of finances and including audiences in the news selection and production processes. As Porlezza and Splendore conclude, 'where journalists wear multiple hats between editorial content production and commercial interests, it is of vital importance that start-ups live up to ethical standards in order to build and maintain authority and credibility' (Porlezza and Splendore, 2016, p 212).

The Bureau for Investigative Journalism and *The Bristol Cable* publish annual accounts on their websites and, in both organisations, the managing editors or founders were equally as involved in the financial side as they were on the editorial side, in terms of constantly exploring new avenues of revenue. But as Price comments, in his study of *The Ferret*, its 'co-operative structure is not borne simply out of convenience but is integral to the nature of what it seeks to be and achieve' (Price, 2017, p 1340). In a study of Greek journalism co-operatives, Siapera and Papadopoulou (2016) argued that collaborative decision-making processes in these organisations significantly helped to build relationships between the organisations and their local communities and to restore lost trust in journalism.

In the same vein, a respondent from *The Bureau for Investigative Journalism* suggested:

> 'We're not trying to replicate the traditional media model. We are not driven by that transactional model; we are not doing our journalism to make money but, on the other hand, we're not doing it for free, there is an exchange here. The exchange is that we are transformational – that was the term we came up with. So we don't want money, but we do want transformation, we do want change. So it is thinking about journalism in completely different terms. And as a result, it has to be funded in a very different way.'

The next section explores how these new business models of journalism have given non-profits the time and space to carry out in-depth investigations in innovative ways.

Collaboration on non-profits

In terms of practices, there are two key differences between journalists on non-profits and their mainstream counterparts. The first is the practice of 'engaged journalism' or 'a range of practices that aim to build relationships between journalists and the public and involve the public in the process of cocreating journalism' (Wenzel, 2020, p 4). This extends to the process of collaboration and sharing of news stories with mainstream outlets, which Konieczna describes as 'repair[ing] the field of journalism' (Konieczna, 2018, p 5).

The second difference between journalism on non-profits and mainstream investigative journalism is in the practice of 'solutions journalism' or the practice of 'critically explor[ing] a response to a problem – looking at what is working or at how it works – including its limitations' (Wenzel, 2020, p 8). It is an approach, Wenzel suggests, that moves beyond the function of journalism as 'informing' citizens, to offer what she terms 'the whole story', that is to say, 'not only spotlighting social ills but also highlighting how they are being addressed' (Wenzel, 2020, p 8).

In the next three sections of this book, I argue that, through these two practices of engaged journalism and solutions journalism, the investigative non-profits in my study are changing the remit – and the content – of crime news in three important ways:

- Through working with marginalised and/or stigmatised communities, these interventions have the potential to challenge stereotyped and negative representations of these groups in mainstream media by offering alternative representations and narratives.
- Through taking on stories mainstream outlets no longer have the time or money to fund – and through investigating stories in new and innovative ways (big data, OSINT) – investigative non-profits are able to investigate stories traditionally under covered by legacy media (too time-consuming or impossible to research without inside sources).
- Through the practice of solutions journalism, non-profits are extending the traditional remit of watchdog journalism to explore social issues and to look at how problems are being addressed and what changes might be possible.

I start by exploring the practice of 'engaged journalism'; how non-profits are aiming to give voice to marginalised or stigmatised communities through this practice, and to start repairing what they perceive as the representational harms inflicted on these communities by mainstream reporting.

Engaged journalism: co-creating journalism with members of the public

The Bristol Cable

The concept of 'engaged journalism' is not a new one. Konieczna (2018) and Wenzel (2020) suggest its roots lie in what was termed the public or civic journalism movement of the 1990s, a movement which considered the role that citizens could play in the news-making process. One of the most notable proponents of this movement, Rosen (1999) called for journalists to 'address people as citizens, potential participants in public affairs, rather than victims or spectators'; to 'help the political community to act upon, rather than just learn about, its problems'; and to 'improve the climate of public discussion, rather than simply watching it deteriorate' (Rosen quoted in Wenzel, 2020, p 10).

As Wenzel also notes, throughout the 1990s, in the United States, there was 'a blossoming of a number of civic and public service journalism initiatives, with at least a fifth of all U.S. newspapers undertaking initiatives' (Wenzel, 2020, p 10). But as Wenzel (2020) and Anderson (2013) comment, the momentum behind this public/civic journalism movement in the United States had largely dissipated by the mid-2000s. In his study of the news ecosystem in Philadelphia, Anderson (2013) observed a mismatch between 'the rationalized production routines of news professionals and the routines (or non-routines) of journalistic amateurs' and that 'never knowing exactly when a blogger would post, whether that blog post would come in by deadline, and whether the content would be relevant' made it 'unlikely that amateur production could be easily integrated into professional newsroom routines' (Anderson, 2013, p 130). Although, as seen in Chapter 5, journalists on some legacy media outlets in the United Kingdom often used social media as a way of crowdsourcing help with investigations, they did not involve citizens further in the research or reporting of these cases.

The non-profits in this study have a very different relationship with their readers and with the general public. Key to that relationship is the concept of collaboration and the sharing of power between journalists and citizens. As one respondent from *The Bristol Cable* argued:

> 'It's not about telling the stories the journalist wants to tell or thinks should be told, it's about asking people what do you want, what do you need. And for us to work with them, to build those stories, those investigations.'

In her study of community-centred journalism in the United States, Wenzel (2020) uses CIT to understand the network of relationships she observed between the local media, citizens and local community groups coming together to report on issues in their town or county (see Figure 6.1).

In this model, the journalist is no longer the privileged *tertius gaudens*, occupying a bridging position (Burt, 1992) between news sources and the public. Instead, drawing on Ball-Rokeach et al's (2001) work on CIT, Wenzel argues that, in community based reporting, the journalist is only one actor in a larger network where other actors, such as local citizens and community groups, have agency. In this kind of reporting, there is a multi-participatory flow of information through a network of 'bridges' between residents, local community organisations and local media who are all 'storytelling actors' involved in circulating stories about their community.

One of the key aims of *The Bristol Cable* is to engage members of the public – or what they term 'communities' – in the process of researching and investigating stories.

Figure 6.1: Communication infrastructure theory network

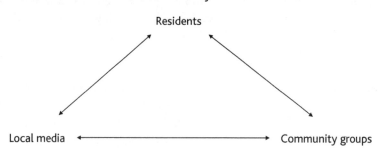

The term 'community' is one that is used a great deal by journalists on non-profits and, as such, it may be useful to explore further the sense in which they might be using it. Interestingly, the term 'community' is one that, Mulligan (2015) argues, has 'agonized and polarized western sociologists since the academic discipline began to take shape towards the end of the 19th century' (Mulligan, 2015, p 340). Mulligan notes that Durkheim effectively began his sociological writing by strongly criticising ideas about community life in urban society and suggested that urbanisation would make the concept of community outdated. However, interest in the possibility of community persists to this day, with Delanty (2003) suggesting that the idea of community 'offers people what neither society nor the state can offer, namely a sense of belonging in an insecure world' (Delanty, 2003, p 195). Other scholars have noted a darker side to the idea of community. Mulligan argues that '[a] projection of community will commonly create a sense of there being "insiders" and "outsiders" and this inevitably causes resentment on the part of the excluded' (Mulligan, 2015, p 347). However, he also notes that in the wake of natural disasters such as the 2004 tsunami in Sri Lanka, politicians, the media and citizens often evoke 'the need to "rebuild" affected communities' (Mulligan, 2015, p, 341) alongside the need to restore damage done to buildings and land. This last sense of 'rebuilding' might be the most fruitful to explore in terms of what 'community' means to journalists on non-profits, given the importance to respondents of 'repairing' (Konieczna, 2018).

As a respondent from *The Bristol Cable* explained, one of the reasons the co-operative was founded was to "do journalism in a different way", which, in turn, made the founders reconsider their positioning of themselves as reporters in their community. One of the most important issues to the founders was that they wanted to "report with their communities not about communities". As the same respondent explained, their background had been in activism and this, in turn, informed how they saw their role as founder and reporter on *The Bristol Cable*:

'I was at university, involved in all sorts of social justice campaigns, but realising that activism wasn't the be-all and end-all; you often end up preaching to the converted, shouting down a megaphone that only echoes with people who are familiar with the issues that you are talking about. And you're not really involving people who might be a bit more removed, who may not frankly have the time to read up on the way in which ... migrant populations are affected by Home Office policies at a local level. So what we wanted to do was to produce journalism with a community for a community and to share our power, whatever that might be, with that community.'

Early studies of journalists' perceptions of their audiences suggested that journalists generally underestimated their audiences (Atkin et al, 1983) and had an unflattering and patronising view of them. Groot Kormelink and Costera Meijer (2018) argue that this has changed in the digital age and they suggest that, with a decreasing revenue from advertising and a greater dependence on audience subscriptions for news, news organisations now take audiences much more seriously, However, Robinson (2019) comments that, although '[t]he conventional wisdom of the digital era is that journalists can now know their audiences in far more intimate detail than at any other time in the history of the profession' (Robinson, 2019), the journalists he interviewed for his study 'recognize their obligations to reach an audience, but they are wary of allowing readers to dictate what is newsworthy' (Robinson, 2019). He concludes that '[d]espite the increasing availability of digital audience tools, this research suggests that personal proximity is a critical factor in influencing one's audience perceptions' (Robinson, 2019) – in other words, even in a post-digital age, Robinson suggests that journalists' conceptions of their audience or readership are still influenced very much by how they imagine their peers and, in particular, their colleagues will respond.

It would appear that what the journalists on *The Bristol Cable* are doing is somewhat different (see Figure 6.2). Journalists on this non-profit are actively engaging with their readership by asking them to take part in the running of the organisation and to co-create stories – though, inevitably, such members of the co-operative will only represent a subset of the entire readership/membership of *The Bristol Cable*. By setting up this three-way loop of storytelling, *The Bristol Cable* are creating conditions for citizens to work with them to advocate change or to access local policy and power structures, in contrast to mainstream crime reporting practices, where citizens are involved in crowdsourcing stories and helping with research, but are not active stakeholders and do not participate in the framing and reporting of stories.

The Bristol Cable's practice of engaged journalism is important for another reason. One of the key aims of many start-ups – including *The Bristol Cable* – is

Figure 6.2: Model of storytelling network on *The Bristol Cable*

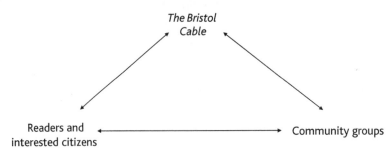

to 'give voice to lesser-represented groups' (Deuze and Witschge, 2020, p 120). Following the death of George Floyd in 2020 and the global awareness of the Black Lives Matter social movement, lack of diversity in mainstream newsrooms 'became part of the larger public discourse around racial inequity' (Usher, 2021, p 55). In the United Kingdom, a report on Diversity in Journalism, based on the 2020 Labour Force Survey data, compared the characteristics of all in employment in the UK with those of journalists. In terms of ethnicity, 8 per cent of all journalists came from non White ethnic groups, as opposed to 12 per cent of all British workers (Spilsbury, 2021).

Many journalism scholars (Callison and Young, 2020; Richardson, 2020; Wenzel, 2020; Usher, 2021) have argued that this lack of diversity leads to a disconnect between journalists and their audiences. In turn, they argue, this leads to a lack of trust in the media from some sections of the general public. Although Callison and Young suggest that '[j]ournalists have responded to the shifting and increasingly technological landscape by attempting to diversify how they know what they know and do what they do' (Callison and Young, 2020, p 202) through a variety of practices, including the use of social media, they suggest that these 'attempts have been internal to the field and often in a way that reinforces existing power relations' (Callison and Young, 2020, p 202) and they call for 'alternate modes of operating as a journalist' (Callison and Young, 2020, p 202). Richardson (2020) argues that the livestreaming of civil rights abuses is a response to a mainstream media that has not made spaces for the voices and experiences of Black people, while Usher argues that, although it would be ridiculous to imagine that journalists are 'crafting stories with an explicitly racialized intention like "this will appeal to the white people that live up in the suburbs"', there are nevertheless 'issues that white people will simply not spot because of the privilege that being white affords' (Usher, 2021, pp 61–2).

More broadly, Usher (2021) suggests that the problem of a disconnect between journalists and their audiences is not just down to a lack of diversity in newsrooms but also to what she terms a problem of 'place': the 'place' of the journalist, the 'place' of audiences and the 'place' where journalists carry out their work. On the first, she argues that '[c]ultural proximity affects the way news is produced and the news that citizens read and use to learn about the world' (Usher, 2021, p 64); if 'journalists are supposed to speak truth to power without really understanding the place of those who are disempowered, their mission is hampered from the outset' (Usher, 2021, p 64). Thus, according to Usher, the first consideration of 'place' that narrows the 'news aperture' (Ericson et al, 1987, p 9) is the fact that many mainstream journalists may be White and privileged and possibly 'miss[ing] important stories that they may not even know to ask about' (Usher, 2021, p 60).

The second consideration is the 'place' of the audience. Usher argues that, for most mainstream outlets, the aim is to attract a 'quality audience', 'those who can and will pay, especially for digital subscriptions and those who are worth enough to advertisers as a demographic group to cut individual deals with newspapers' (Usher, 2021, p 53). Usher notes how, in a 1991 study, Kaniss argued that local news outlets set the news agenda in ways that favoured those with higher socioeconomic status and marginalised the poor and people of colour. A more recent study by Napoli et al (2015) showed, in a comparison of three New Jersey 'news ecosystems', that the wealthy suburb of Morristown got 23 times more news stories per capita than Newark, one of the poorest cities in the survey (although Newark is New Jersey's largest city by population).

The third aspect of 'place' affecting lack of diversity and lack of representation of marginalised communities is where journalists work. As both Usher (2021) and Wenzel (2020) comment, the loss of jobs and of local newspapers in the United States – and, as discussed in this chapter, in the United Kingdom – means that local journalism, where it exists, is often carried out at a distance from the readership it serves. Hamada (2021) observes that, in the United Kingdom, the weekly circulation of local newspapers dropped from 63 million in 2007 to 31 million in 2017 (Mediatique, 2018). As she comments: 'Sometimes newspaper offices in smaller towns and rural areas have been closed by newspaper groups and events in those places covered by writers sat at desks tens of miles away or more, often unaware of local dynamics' (Hamada, 2021, p 112).

In her study of community-centred journalism, Wenzel (2020) argues that one reason for negative media coverage of certain neighbourhoods was because there were often very weak links between communities and local media. She argues that such 'narratives tended to be told by "parachuting" outsiders reporting on moments of crisis' and that '[s]uch disconnects reinforced inequitable power structures by continuing to circulate stigmatizing narratives that contributed to the marginalization of communities' (Wenzel, 2020, p 27). Usher (2021) argues that, when journalists are 'out of place' or working at a long distance from the communities they are writing about, 'they do not know what they are missing because they are not *there*, physically, culturally or cognitively' (Usher, 2021, p 68, emphasis in original).

Robinson (2018) adds another factor to the mix and suggests that many of the 'norms' of journalism preclude the inclusion of Black and other marginalised voices. These 'norms' include reports from 'experts' who, Robinson notes, have been historically White; but also the discouraging of anonymous sources, to ensure accountability and avoid potential hidden agendas. As she notes, these 'norms' excluded those who are 'uneducated, non-credentialed ... as well as those who are scared to speak out' (Robinson, 2018, p 87). Like Usher, she argues that there is often a 'structural chasm' between reporters and the communities they report upon, and notes that, in her study, most of the reporters she interviewed were White, came from higher income families and had few African American friends. She describes how, as a result, the reporters she interviewed depended on the same Black or Brown sources for quotes, and how one reporter suggested that he would always make a beeline for Black or Brown community leaders in public meetings, rather than seeking sources in neighbourhoods: 'You went to these people because you knew you could trust that they would go on camera in a timely reliable way. If I go into neighourhoods, I cannot reliably and quickly find someone truly engaged in the issue who would also be willing to speak publicly on TV' (respondent quoted in Robinson, 2018, p 123). She explores in more detail how what she terms these 'disconnects' (Robinson, 2018, p 89) between reporters and Black communities, in particular, lead to 'superficial coverage' of issues concerning these communities. She describes in her study an incident when a national network, NBC, contacted a Black community leader, Michael Johnson, CEO of the Boys and Girls Club of Dane County in Madison. A report had been published suggesting that Dane County was the 'worst in the country for racial disparities' (Robinson, 2018, p 89) and NBC were looking for a comment from Michael Johnson. Johnson demanded a pre-interview with the producers and a written note outlining the intent of the story before he would speak to them. The news organisation declined to do this, and Johnson posted about the situation on Facebook, saying that he could not be 'part of a blind story' (Robinson, 2018, p 90). Robinson notes that a reporter from NBC answered, suggesting that, if it had agreed to Johnson's requests, the network would have put itself in 'a position of having to stick with a pre-defined narrative which isn't good for you, Madison, or them' (reporter quoted in Robinson, 2018, p 90). She argues that these exchanges showed a 'structural chasm' between the NBC reporters and Johnson and his community and that 'how journalists perceived the ground rules of public information production conflicted with how activists and those in the Black community understood the goal of the content' (Robinson, 2018, p 90). For the reporters, Robinson argues that 'the process of creating an objective ... story trumps the community's concerns; for Johnson and his supporters, unknown journalists must first earn some trust that the story will help the community' (Robinson, 2018, p 90). As a result, Robinson shows how Johnson and his community were excluded from the story because they did not 'play by the rules of the journalistic field' (Robinson, 2018, p 90).

The founders of *The Bristol Cable* believe that one way in which they are changing narratives about marginalised and stigmatised communities is by changing working practices and challenging journalistic norms. While not all of the founders are White and middle-class, they are all university educated and aware of that privilege, acknowledging that, as a result, they may be unaware of certain issues or problems facing certain social groups in Bristol simply because they do not have contacts in those groups. Robinson

(2018) and Wenzel (2020) argue that, in order to access Black and Brown voices, journalists first need to show that they are worthy of trust from those communities. Similarly, the founders of *The Bristol Cable* argued that, first, they had to go into those communities and others across the city, talk to them and find out what were the stories members of the public thought they should be covering; and, second, establish trust by sharing their journalistic power with the members joining their co-operative.

'We went to speak to academics, local representatives of various different community groups, spoke to people in the street, went to speak to students … it was very much about aggregating people's thoughts on what a new media model could look like. This way of building community via media was almost unheard of and we got a lot of feedback. We organised a lot of public meetings for people to come forward and share their views on a proposal that we put forward with regard to what we envisaged a media organisation to look like.'

The respondent argued that, as a result, *The Bristol Cable* not only started to build an engaged community, but also realised that, had they set up their organisation in a more traditional way, they would potentially not only be maintaining the status quo in terms of inequality of access for certain communities, but also they would be missing out on key stories:

'I think we did two things by setting up the *Cable* in this way. One is to feed information to mainstream journalists who might not be aware of what is going on across the city. The other was being able to draw on community members to source story ideas and investigation leads. And to work on story ideas with people who either had experience because they were involved in different sectors professionally or they were facing issues in their day-to-day lives so they could contribute information to the production of journalism on the one hand in terms of sourcing but also in terms of impact – in terms of what they wanted to happen next. And these were stories we might not – if it had just been us – have chosen to tell.'

The Bristol Cable are also addressing potential power imbalances between journalists and communities – and challenging journalistic norms – in another way, through training community members to take on aspects of reporting alongside the main team:

'We organised a series of workshops that enabled people to come and learn how to produce media of different kinds. One was the ABC of writing articles, there was also a class on how to do photojournalism. Also one on how to do reporting via your smartphone. There was also a session on the ethics of journalism in order not to slander or to get involved in defamation – all of that to get people to realise that, even though they may not have received journalistic training, either through schools of journalism or at universities or other funded institutions, people could still be involved in producing reports of quality that could be considered journalism.'

As the same respondent noted, if *The Bristol Cable* was going to tell stories in a different way, it needed a more diverse group of people to carry out that reporting:

'It was also our aim to democratise the production process. Obviously, one of the things that was at issue here was there weren't enough journalists out there, because local papers had closed, but also those journalists reporting in newsrooms were of a particular kind – it's often said "pale, male and stale". But that was our aim, if we were going to work with communities and tell stories about them, then those citizens needed the skills to tell the stories alongside us.'

Such an initiative presents, as Wenzel notes, challenges to existing journalistic norms and practices by questioning 'who gets to provide community news and information' (Wenzel, 2020, p 151). What also seems to be clear from these accounts is that, by sharing power with communities, *The Bristol Cable* is significantly opening the 'news aperture' (Ericson et al, 1987, p 9) through its change in positioning the organisation in relation to the communities it serves. In the past, mainstream news outlets have traditionally privileged the views of experts or 'primary definers' (Hall et al, 1978), thus 'enacting a view of the world partial to particular sources and their versions of reality' (Ericson et al, 1987, p 9) and either excluding the perspectives of marginalised or less powerful individuals or organisations or affording them a 'less significant status' (Ericson et al, 1987, p 9). By contrast, *The Bristol Cable* has involved under-represented communities in every stage of the production process, including story selection and reporting, and enabled other voices and other perspectives to contribute to the news process. As one respondent commented:

'You realise by not involving communities, by not giving them a voice or a platform for debate, how many stories you would miss, just because you wouldn't know where to look for them, or even to think that they might be important or worth telling. And there is of course always more work to be done on this front.'

Robinson (2018) argues that one of the causes of what she and other scholars perceive to be an increasing disconnect between journalists working for mainstream media outlets and certain communities are reporters' working practices. She comments that '[a]sking reporters to be less reliant on officials or more inclusive of people not necessarily in traditional power structures is often fruitless' (Robinson, 2018, p 88) – that do so would be seeking to alter the field of journalism substantially. But what can be seen here is a shift in that field – from the journalist as the privileged 'bridge' spanning the structural holes between sources and the public, to the journalist as part of a network, sharing power with members of the public and other community organisations, and setting up instead what I term a 'storytelling island'. In this model, the journalist is a co-creator of news, the flow of information is multi-participatory and mainstream journalistic 'norms', such as the need to privilege experts, have given way to a more inclusive form of story creation.

Engaged journalism: sharing the news

The Bureau for Investigative Journalism

The Bureau for Investigative Journalism is also committed to a more inclusive method of researching and reporting their stories, by building networks with communities and collaborators. However, unlike *The Bristol Cable* where the aim is to create a network of equal partners – residents, community groups and editorial staff – who are all involved in every stage of the reporting process, the model of storytelling on *The Bureau for Investigative Journalism* is more akin to the traditional pre-internet model; the traditional 'bridge' (Burt, 1992), with journalists firmly at the centre of the network and with stories originated within the team (see Figure 6.3).

As a member of *The Bureau for Investigative Journalism* team explained:

> 'Most of our stories originate in house to be honest. ... We do sometimes get stories from whistleblowers but we're not their first stop. And I think that type of reporting happens more in the commercial sector than in the non-profit. Does a member of the public know who the BIJ [*The Bureau for Investigative Journalism*] are? Unlikely. Do they know who *The Guardian* is? Yes, So that's where they are more likely to go.'

However, where *The Bureau for Investigative Journalism* does differ from its mainstream counterparts is in its process of collaboration with other journalists and media organisations. Stories are developed to be shared on their website but also with larger outlets, both nationally and internationally, to maximise audience reach. These outlets include the *New York Times*, *Al Jazeera* and *Newsweek*, and many other national and international titles and broadcasters have featured their work.

While the goal of *The Bristol Cable* could be broadly categorised as focusing on community-centred journalism, the goal of *The Bureau for Investigative*

Figure 6.3: Model of storytelling network on *The Bureau for Investigative Journalism*

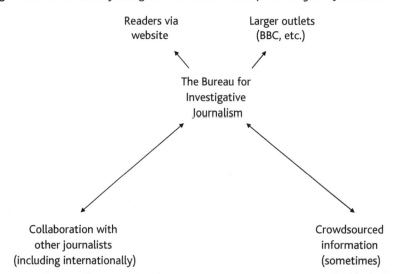

Journalism could be seen as being more akin to what Konieczna describes as 'repair[ing] the field of journalism' (Konieczna, 2018, p 5). Unlike *The Bristol Cable*, the managing editor and other reporters on *The Bureau for Investigative Journalism* largely come from traditional news organisations and bring with them the norms and practices of traditional journalism as well as the concern 'that traditional journalism ... once worked better than it does now' (Konieczna, 2018, p 5). In Konieczna's study, one of the ways in which non-profits hope to 'repair the field of journalism' is by 'collaborating and sharing in the process of news production' and, through this process, 'injecting quality news reporting' (Konieczna, 2018, p 5).

Konieczna argues, however, that non-profits that engage heavily in sharing content with for-profit organisations effectively have to produce content for two audiences – 'readers but also members of the news media: editors at other organizations who are tasked with deciding whether to publish their stories, and reporters who might decide to reference the centers' work' (Konieczna, 2018, p 187). As a result, Konieczna raises the concern that:

> Sharing forces the news nonprofits to produce content that mainstream journalists and editors might want to publish, which means their stories need to resemble stories that might appear in other publications. In other words, although the nonprofits are being founded by people who seek to improve journalism in their communities, news sharing limits the organizations' ability to reform journalism. All of this raises a particular tension for the news nonprofits: are they able to

act as oppositional even though they feed back into the mainstream organizations they aim to improve upon? (Konieczna, 2018, pp 186–7)

Although, as one respondent acknowledged, the model of storytelling on *The Bureau for Investigative Journalism* is "not innovative and … we constantly have conversations as to how we can be more innovative", they nevertheless break new ground through reporting on crimes that are often under-reported by the legacy media and through their use of public data and open source intelligence to research their stories. Computer-assisted reporting has been a feature of investigative journalism since the 1960s (Lewis and Usher, 2014). However, in the last decade, as Lewis and Usher (2014) comment, more and more newsrooms have been hiring individuals 'who know how to write software code … typically through roles such as developer, data scientist, or "programmer-journalist" for specialized newsroom teams that build news applications, data visualizations, and related interactive features' (Lewis and Usher, 2014, p 383).

As far as audiences are concerned, Oldroyd (2021) suggests that one of the key features of this new style of reporting is the way in which infographics let 'people discover for themselves the revelations discovered by the reporters' (Oldroyd, 2021, p 105). She describes how reporters at *The Bureau for Investigative Journalism* built a database listing all the public-owned assets that had been sold off by local authorities who had become desperate to raise funds. The team wanted 'to let local people see how the policy was affecting facilities so that they could better do something about it' and the investigation by the team, which was called SoldFromUnderYou, included 'an interactive map that let the public see what properties had been sold in their area' (Oldroyd, 2021, p 105).

More crucially, in terms of crime and investigative reporting, the use of big data in its reporting allows *The Bureau for Investigative Journalism* to investigate stories that are often under-reported by mainstream media such as 'accidents at work, pollution of the environment, much white collar crime, corporate corruption, state violence and governments' denial or abuse of human rights' (Jewkes, 2011, p 59). As Oldroyd argues, these crimes are rarely reported by legacy media outlets; as such work is 'time consuming and painstaking' – '[r]eporters can literally spend months building and analysing datasets, developing whistleblowers' and 'collecting realms of testimony' (Oldroyd, 2021, p 107). Additionally, as noted at the start of the chapter, proprietorial bias or the desire to keep advertisers onside, can also constrain the kinds of stories being told – or lead to them being dropped (Clifford and White, 2017).

Over the last ten years, the advent of companies such as OpenCorporates has allowed organisations such as *The Bureau for Investigative Journalism*, and its project, the *Bureau Local*, to carry out investigations into these 'invisible' crimes of the powerful, such as money-laundering, organised crime and corruption. OpenCorporates is based in the United Kingdom and is the largest open database of companies in the world. As a former member of staff explained:

'Basically the driving force behind the company is the relationship between money and power, and the company was set up to enable journalists and others to carry out collaborative data-driven investigations. With our data, journalists can search and co-reference records to trace criminal connections and patterns.'

The use of large data sets has informed many of *The Bureau for Investigative Journalism*'s major investigations on a national and international scale. A recent year-long investigation into global corruption, entitled 'The Enablers', explored how UK business executives, lawyers and political advisors have been enabling oligarchs, dictators and criminals around the world 'to open political doors, lobby against sanctions, to fight legal battles and launder money and reputations' (taken from the website of *The Bureau for Investigative Journalism*).

The Bureau Local

The *Bureau Local* is a project set up by *The Bureau for Investigative Journalism* in 2017. Like *The Bureau for Investigative Journalism*, reporters on the *Bureau Local* also use large datasets in their work, particularly in the reporting of crimes of the powerful and crimes of social harm. However, unlike *The Bureau for Investigative Journalism*, the aim of the *Bureau Local* is to concentrate on local stories, collaborating 'to build databases that reveal systemic problems about the country they live in and provide specific local stories that allow people to relate to the problem' (Oldroyd, 2021, p 108). In order to carry out these investigations, the *Bureau Local* has a network of almost 1,000 people across the United Kingdom, including journalists, technologists, academics, lawyers, community organisers and activists, who work together on investigations. As Hamada describes:

Whoever is interested comes together to work on each specific story, and a dataset is usually compiled – sometimes from the top down through Freedom of Information requests, or sometimes from the bottom up through networked grassroots data gathering. This data is used for storytelling at a national, regional and local level, and partners work together to publish on the same date. (Hamada, 2021, p 115)

Like *The Bureau for Investigative Journalism*, the *Bureau Local* also aims to increase its audience reach by sharing its stories with larger news outlets.

Although one of the reasons it was set up was to fill the resulting news gap left by the demise of so many local newspapers in the United Kingdom, the aim of the *Bureau Local* is to provide stories that can be used not only at a local but national level:

> 'Part of the beauty of the project is that issues can be reported from a macro systemic level, down to a micro, granular level, creating multiple points of engagement and potential impact. For example, a domestic violence story could be reported on BBC News and picked up by a parliamentary committee, applying political pressure at a government level. Meanwhile, it could be reported on by the local newspaper … reaching the communities directly affected and equipping them with evidence, but also applying pressure to MPS and local politicians who want to be seen to be responsive to their voters.'

However, unlike *The Bureau for Investigative Journalism*, where stories generally originate from within the core team of reporters, the *Bureau Local*'s team actively ask for story suggestions from their network, but also from the general public via social media. The storytelling model could be seen then as a hybrid of those of *The Bureau for Investigative Journalism* and *The Bristol Cable* (see Figure 6.4).

At the heart of the storytelling network is the CIT structure, with the *Bureau Local* working with both citizens and wider communities to find stories and to report on them with the aid of these groups, and with a multi-directional flow of information between all three parties, forming a 'storytelling island' in the same way as the founders of *The Bristol Cable*. Unlike *The Bristol Cable*, those stories are then shared with larger legacy

Figure 6.4: Model of storytelling network on the *Bureau Local*

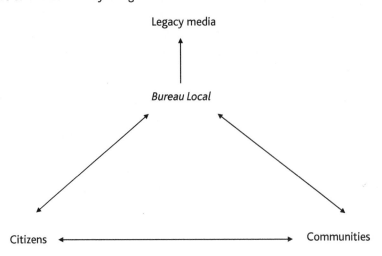

media outlets, which serve as a 'bridge' between the *Bureau Local's* CIT network and source of stories and the traditional audience.

Like *The Bristol Cable*, the *Bureau Local* is committed to giving voices to under-represented communities and allowing a variety of perspectives to be featured in its reporting; and by sharing news that does not rely solely upon the perspectives of accredited experts, it is most certainly contributing to field repair (Konieczna, 2018). Second, both *The Bureau for Investigative Journalism* and the *Bureau Local* are expanding the remit of 'crime news' by reporting on what both organisations term 'systemic harms' or, as I shall discuss in Chapter 7, crimes of 'social harm'. As a respondent from the *Bureau Local* commented:

'I think what makes a *Bureau Local* story is that, first and foremost, we are also looking at systemic issues, under-reported issues, the stories the mainstream media aren't telling.'

But while *The Bureau for Investigative Journalism* use big data and collaboration with other journalists to research and report their stories, the *Bureau Local* work with communities to understand the issues that concern them. Some of the key members of the *Bureau Local* team, in terms of forming these connections with members and organising events where community reporters working on *Bureau Local* stories can check-in and brainstorm, are the community organisers, who are all trained journalists with many years of mainstream media experience between them. One of the community organisers explained his role at the *Bureau Local*:

'Every day at work is very much an experiment, as we don't know what works, we're trying to figure it out. But I think it's about trust, the more we can co-create this stuff, the more we can be closer to and more in line with the audience, the better the journalism is going to be. The more our interests align, the better. So a big part of that is finding out what the interests of our audience are.'

By working with communities to understand the issues that concern them – and creating a 'storytelling island' with them – the *Bureau Local* is able to expand the remit of crime news and to help 'repair' the field of crime and investigative journalism through sharing this content with those communities. Recent stories have included reports on homelessness; the impact of funding cuts to refuges for victims of domestic violence; and a data-led investigation into the current government funding crisis and its impact on communities. This last investigation used data to reveal which local authorities were heading for financial collapse; the public spaces such as libraries and community centres being sold off; and the increasingly risky methods to which councils have turned in order to generate extra revenue, including billion pound investments in property.

In the final section of this chapter, I explore how non-profits are not only expanding the remit of crime news but also how they are challenging and extending the traditional watchdog Fourth Estate role of the investigative journalist through the practice of solutions journalism.

Solutions journalism: telling 'the whole story'

Solutions journalism, like engaged journalism, has its roots in the civic journalism movement in the United States during the 1990s, although Wenzel (2020) argues that its origins can be traced back even further to the work of Galtung (1986) and the concept of 'peace journalism'. Galtung (1986) suggested that, rather than drawing on a conflict-oriented frame in reporting on war-torn areas, journalists should instead draw from a frame 'more common in health reporting, where journalists are encouraged to examine causes of disease as well as strategies for their prevention' (Wenzel, 2020, p 10). However, like the concept of engaged journalism, this intervention met with resistance from many legacy media outlets and largely faded from journalism discourse by the early 2000s (Wenzel, 2020).

The concept of solutions journalism was revived in 2013, by two *New York Times* journalists, David Bernstein and Tina Rosenberg, who joined forces to create the Solutions Journalism Network – an organisation set up to train journalists in the principles of this intervention, and to support organisations practising solutions journalism around the world. In their mission statement, they challenge the 'theory of change of watchdog journalism' (Wenzel, 2020, p 9) and the idea that, by exposing social ills and harms to the public, change and reform will inevitably follow:

> Solutions journalism heightens accountability by reporting on where and how people are doing better against a problem – removing excuses and setting a bar for what citizens should expect from institutions or governments. It offers a more comprehensive and representative view of the world. And it circulates timely knowledge to help society self-correct, spotlighting adaptive responses that people and communities can learn from. (Taken from website of Solutions Journalism Network)

The goal of solutions journalism is 'not to advocate for a particular solution but rather to critically explore a response to a problem – looking at what is working or at how it works – including its limitations' (Wenzel, 2020, p 8). In her study, Wenzel gives the example of solutions journalism reporting being carried out by the *Cleveland Plain Dealer* on lead poisoning. In their series, 'Toxic Neglect', the reporters 'broke down the dimensions of the problem, but rather than stopping there, they also reported on how other cities had responded to the challenge' (Wenzel, 2020, p 9). This coverage was subsequently followed by a number of reforms in Cleveland, including new home inspection policies, and posting of warning signs.

The non-profits in this study are advocates of this method of journalistic intervention. As a respondent from *The Bureau for Investigative Journalism* commented:

'It is thinking about journalism in completely different terms. Good newspaper editors and good programme editors will always think about the impact of their work, and how that work changes things, and that's how they went forward, and that's how the public service side of journalism is embedded within journalism, per se. But to actually embrace that and to say *that* public service, *that* transformation, *that* change – that's the living, breathing core of what we do.'

In an investigation called 'Locked Out', the *Bureau Local* used data to 'highlight the inadequacies of Local Housing Allowance' and 'collected evidence to show the ineffectiveness of recent homelessness reduction legislation in England' (Hamada, 2021, p 118). Members of the team set up 'story circle' meetings to talk to citizens who had been personally affected by these issues, in order to give context to the data and evidence collected, and fed back findings to policymakers and politicians. Similarly, *The Bristol Cable*'s citizen-led investigation 'The Ice Cream Slavery Case' – into the practices of the Lopresti ice-cream and property business in Bristol over a five-year period, with claims of immigrant workers in the ice cream business being kept 'in slave-like conditions' (Cantwell-Corn and Aviram, 2019) – led eventually to a criminal case being made against the owner of the two businesses, Salvatore Lopresti.

Finally, one of the criticisms the Solutions Journalism Network has of traditional watchdog investigative journalism is that it focuses on reporting and uncovering social harm or corruption but 'omits critical information necessary for society to create change' (Wenzel, 2020, p 9). By highlighting how problems are being addressed or not addressed in the case of both the *Bureau Local* and *The Bristol Cable* investigations described in this chapter, 'solutions journalism removes the excuses used by authorities who claim a problem is intractable' (Wenzel, 2020, p 9). Solutions journalism also challenges traditional watchdog journalism in two other ways – it stretches 'the ideological conceptualization of journalism, which presumes that journalism is there to "inform" the public' (Deuze and Witschge, 2020, p 118), but it also shifts the narrative by focusing on solutions to social harms from one of blame to one of collective efficacy on the part of journalists and communities (Wenzel, 2020).

Conclusion

In this chapter, I have explored how *The Bristol Cable*, *The Bureau for Investigative Journalism* and the *Bureau Local* are challenging journalistic norms and, although they do not set out to cover 'traditional' crime stories, are nevertheless changing the remit of crime news through new and very different working practices. While the traditional working model of mainstream journalism positions the journalist as a bridge between news sources and the public, I argue that *The Bristol Cable* have adopted a new form of storytelling and co-creation of journalism through working with members of the public and community groups. I argue that such a practice can be conceptualised in terms of CIT, or communication infrastructure theory, where the journalist is one of a number of actors with agency and there is a multi-way and multi-participatory flow of information between journalists, citizens and their communities. I argue that this method of creating journalism can also be conceptualised as a 'storytelling island'. In particular, I suggest that by working in this way, journalists are able to give voice to under-represented and marginalised groups and, instead of privileging the views of experts, are able to include a greater variety of perspectives in their reporting.

Although its working processes are more akin to the traditional model of journalist as bridge, I argue that *The Bureau for Investigative Journalism* are nevertheless challenging conventional journalistic norms, through their collaborations with other journalists and other outlets and through the extensive use of big data and OSINT in their research and investigations. As a result, I suggest they are able to expand the remit of crime news by tackling crimes that are often under-investigated by mainstream media, such as white-collar crimes and other financial crimes.

I argue that working methods on the *Bureau Local* are a hybrid of these two models. In creating stories, the *Bureau Local*, like *The Bristol Cable*, adopt a CIT mode of working, or the establishment of a 'storytelling island', where journalists share their power with citizens and story ideas are sourced from their readership or the wider community. I argue that by creating journalism in this way, the *Bureau Local* are also expanding the remit of crime news by reporting on crimes that rarely receive media attention – because they occur in the private sphere, such as domestic violence, or are not subject to public scrutiny, such as white-collar crime or crimes that could be broadly described as social harms. While Konieczna's (2018) study suggested that the practice of news sharing with larger outlets by non-profits meant that news content was not radically different from that produced by legacy media, I suggest that the very different working practices adopted by these new outlets have led to a new form of investigative journalism in the United Kingdom.

Finally, I argue that through solutions journalism interventions, these non-profits challenge the traditional Fourth Estate role of watchdog journalism, that the journalist's role is to 'inform' citizens. Instead, I suggest that the aim of these non-profits is to produce 'transformational' journalism, working with citizens to bring what they term the societal or systemic harms they are reporting upon to wider societal attention, with the aim of sparking societal change and amelioration of these harms.

7

The changing face of crime news

Introduction

In this chapter, I focus on how non-profits are expanding the remit of crime 'newsworthiness'. The chapter begins by exploring definitions of crime and 'social harm'. It then draws upon the considerable body of news media criminology that has developed in the United Kingdom since the 1990s (Greer, 2010a), to give a brief overview of how stories about crime and justice are constructed according to particular cultural assumptions and ideologies (Chibnall, 1977; Jewkes, 2004). I then explore how specific working practices, particularly the giving of 'preferred readings to the ideological messages of particular source organizations' (Ericson et al, 1987, p 9), mean that other voices are often excluded or given less status. I also explore how these practices largely precludes any meaningful discussion of causes or effects of crime in crime news reporting. By contrast, I suggest that the innovative working practices and production processes of the new non-profits, as described in Chapter 6, have helped to 'repair' (Konieczna, 2018) the field of crime and investigative journalism in three key ways: the reporting of crime as 'social harm' (Hillyard and Tombs, 2005); the reporting of causes and effects of crime; and a conscious attempt to diminish representational harm to stigmatised and marginalised communities through more inclusive forms of reporting.

What is crime and what is social harm?

Before embarking on a discussion of differences between the content of crime stories and investigative narratives published in legacy media outlets and in the non-profits in this study, it may be helpful briefly to discuss the evolution of the concept of social harm within the discipline of criminology as a way of widening the ways in which crime is visualised and constructed.

Muncie argues that the most common and frequently applied definition of crime is an act that 'violates the prevailing legal code of the jurisdiction in which it occurs' (Muncie, 2001, p 10). However, as Zedner (2004) argues, crime may be both a criminal and a civil wrong simultaneously. She argues that '[t]o think about crime, as some criminal law textbooks still do, as comprising discrete, autonomous legal categories remote from the social world, is to engage in an absorbing but esoteric intellectual activity' (Zedner, 2004, p 61). As Newburn (2007) notes, '[a]t its most extreme, a crude legalistic approach to crime implies that if there were no criminal law, then there would be no crime' and that '[i]n its more extreme version, it also suggests that no matter what acts someone may have committed, if they are not subject to criminal sanctions, then they cannot be considered criminal' (Newburn, 2007, p 8).

As Newburn (2007) also comments, much of 'criminology, though aware of some of the problems inherent in legal definitions, nevertheless proceeds on the basis of precisely such an approach to defining crime' (Newburn, 2007, p 8); and that '[m]uch of what criminologists do uses categories derived from the criminal law' (Newburn, 2007, p 8). Criminologists have long struggled with the 'inherent limitations of a state-based definition of crime' (Hillyard and Tombs, 2017, p 285). Sutherland's (1949) research into unethical practices among corporate managers in the United States suggested that such practices were often considered non-criminal; as violations of civil, rather than criminal, law. He argued that crime should be defined not on the basis of criminal law, but on the more abstract notions of 'social injury' and 'social harm'. Schwendinger and Schwendinger (1970) promoted a definition of crime based on a conception of the denial of basic human rights, and suggested that if 'the terms imperialism, racism, sexism and poverty are abbreviated signs for theories of social relationships or social systems which cause the systematic abrogation of basic rights, then imperialism, racism, sexism and poverty can be called crimes' (Schwendinger and Schwendinger, 1970, p 148). More recently, Tifft and Sullivan proposed to extend the definition of crime to include 'social conditions, social arrangements, or actions of intent or indifference that interfere with the fulfilment of fundamental needs' (Tifft and Sullivan, 2001, p 191).

As Hillyard and Tombs note, in the 1990s, a number of criminologists 'began to think in a more concentrated way about how a concept of social harm could be more progressively developed as an alternative to crime' (Hillyard and Tombs, 2017, p 285). This approach aimed to 'encompass the detrimental activities of local and national states and of corporations upon the welfare of individuals, whether this be lack of wholesome food, inadequate housing or heating, low income, exposure to various forms of danger, violations of basic human rights, and victimisation to various forms of crime' (Hillyard and Tombs, 2005, p 14). They suggested such harms might fall into four categories – physical, financial, psychological and sexual – and argued that such an approach would encompass 'a far wider range of the deleterious harms to people's welfare throughout their life' (Hillyard and Tombs, 2017, p 289). Additionally, they suggested that 'a focus on harm allows a much wider investigation into who might be responsible unrestricted by individualistic notions of responsibility' and creates 'the opportunity to consider a range of policy responses to reduce harm beyond the dominant, relatively easy, but ineffective response of criminalization' (Hillyard and Tombs, 2017, p 289).

Later in this chapter, I return to this concept of 'social harm' and suggest that these concepts – extending the reach of crime to encompass social harm, to investigate who might be responsible 'unrestricted by individualistic notions of responsibility' and to consider policy responses to reduce harm – inform the new approach to crime and investigative reporting by the non-profits in this study. In the next section, however, I provide a necessarily brief overview of the existing research into the content of media representations of crime and some of the concerns about that content raised by media criminologists.

Media representations of crime

Greer (2010a) argues that crime news has always been and probably always will be a significant feature of news media content. He suggests that this is because 'crime news serves particular social, cultural, political, moral and economic purposes, the reading of which may vary considerably depending on the theoretical approach adopted' (Greer, 2010a, p 201). For example, he argues that for Durkheimian functionalists, 'crime reporting can help to reinforce moral boundaries and promote moral cohesion' (Greer, 2010a, p 201). For Marxists, crime reporting can be seen to strengthen 'the legitimacy of "law-and-order" and the authoritarian state, helping to manufacture mass political consent around the interests of a powerful minority'. For feminists, Greer suggests that crime news can contribute to the 'wider subjugation of women ... by reinforcing gender stereotypes that maintain unequal power relations' (Greer, 2010a, p 201). He concludes that what all these approaches have in common is that 'media representations of crime and criminal justice are a crucial, yet highly selective and unrepresentative, source of information about crime, control and social order' (Greer, 2010a, p 201).

Since the early 1990s, a number of studies have developed a qualitative approach towards the study of media representations of crime, offenders and victims, suggesting that such representations are constructed according to particular cultural assumptions and ideologies (Chibnall, 1977; Jewkes, 2004). These studies include: work by feminist criminologists, arguing that crime is a gendered concept in news discourse (Gelsthorpe and Morris, 1990; Heidensohn, 2000; Wykes, 2001; Morrisey, 2003; Jewkes, 2011); the depiction of 'otherness' in the media (Greer and Jewkes, 2005); and the increasingly adversarial stance taken by the British press (Greer and McLaughlin, 2017). The following is a brief overview of key themes emerging from that work.

Wykes (2001) argues that, by the early 1990s, second-wave feminism had 'worked for over 20 years to empower women to resist subordination in social relations and organisation' (Wykes, 2001, p 139). However, change was slow and women 'remained significantly disadvantaged in many areas, even after considerable legislation' (Wykes, 2001, p 139). Feminist criminologists on both sides of the Atlantic, concerned with 'both apparent injustices to women criminals and the high incidences of violence against women' (Wykes, 2001, p 140), suggested that representation of women in the media was a contributory factor (Heidensohn, 1985; Allen, 1987; Carlen, 1988; Young, 1988; Faludi, 1992).

Although media analysts were still influenced by the work of Chibnall (1977) and Hall et al (1978), suggesting that the values of the press were likely to be 'commensurate with the interests of contemporary capitalism' (Wykes, 2001, p 141), feminist criminologists argued that attention should also be paid to the fact that the journalists who wrote and edited the news, and the owners of newspapers, were overwhelmingly male (Christmas, 1997); and that '[a]ny concern with relations between representation and reality necessitates some close attention to issues of power, ideology and knowledge about the world' (Wykes, 2001, p 142). Feminist scholars (Heidensohn, 1985; Young, 1990) argued that media texts portrayed a divide between 'good' and 'bad' women. 'Good' women were 'pure, passive, caring, maternal, monogamous, house-proud, dependent'– qualities that related closely to the 'socio-economic needs of Victorian capital and patriarchy' (Wykes, 2001, p 138). By contrast, women who did not conform to that model 'attract labels outside of the range available for "good" women and are thereby defined as deviant, often mad or bad' (Wykes, 2001, p 136).

In her study of crime reporting in the United Kingdom in the 1980s and 1990s, Wykes (2001) argues that the reporting of gendered violence posed a problem for the press. Violence of all kinds fits in with news values (Chibnall, 1977; Jewkes, 2004); sex and violence 'attract large audiences and boost sales' (Wykes, 2001, p 141). At the same time, she argues that gendered violence could be seen 'as not only breaking the law, but also the sanctity of heterosexual relations, which are central to patriarchal power' (Wykes, 2001, pp 141–2). She charts how press accounts negotiated that conflict through six case studies of intimate killing featured in the press – John Perry, John Tanner, Joseph McGrail, Linda Calvey, Pam Sainsbury and Sara Thornton – and suggests that the press accounts she collected reported cases of violent men and women very differently. Of the women Wykes studied, Linda Calvey was described as ruthless and cold-blooded and a gangster's moll, while newspaper reports on Sara Thornton described her abortions, dislike of underwear and marijuana. By contrast, Joseph McGrail's murdered wife was a 'bullying alcoholic woman' and McGrail 'finally cracked ... when he came home from work to find her drunk and demanding yet more drink' (*Daily Telegraph*, 1 August 1991, quoted in Wykes, 2001, p 149).

Wykes also explores the ways in which news reports reinforced particular ideological responses to race, poverty and class, as well as gender, arguing that crime news reports obscured issues of poverty, inequality and racism, and instead concentrated on apportioning blame, singling certain groups out, such as the homeless, as being personally responsible for their situation through 'bad luck, irresponsibility and incompetence, sudden financial crisis, relationship breakdown or just wilfulness' (Booth, 1989, p 47). Wykes argues that a 'kind of middle-classness of family life and values was evident in this reporting of the homeless' and that '[c]lass ideology added to journalistic ideology directed selections and representations in the media towards the interests of those producing the news and creating the policy' (Wykes, 2001, p 130).

Scholars have also suggested that this 'middle-classness of family life and values' in crime reporting extends to issues of race. In an exploration of the reporting of the 1993 racist murder in South London of Black teenager Stephen Lawrence, McLaughlin (2005) argues that the right-wing newspaper, the *Daily Mail* constructed a 'psychopathological version of whiteness that made the racist murder comprehensible to the ethnoracial imaginary of Middle England' (McLaughlin, 2005, p 165). Normally known for its 'knee jerk framing of young black men as "muggers" and "yardies"' (McLaughlin, 2005, p 179), the *Daily Mail* described Stephen Lawrence as 'a devout Christian and a hard-working sixth-former who wanted to train as an architect' (McLaughlin, 2005, p 169). His parents were described as 'decent, moderate people who ... had brought their son up to respect the law and not to see colour as an issue' (McLaughlin, 2005, p 169), while his murderers were described as 'the gang of evil killers' that 'threatened all that Middle England stood for' (McLaughlin, 2005, p 171). McLaughlin argues that, in the course of the *Daily Mail's* 'attempt to invest the campaign with universal human interest and the moral claim to "one of us" sameness a process of erasure occurs' – that '"race" is made to matter less and less' (McLaughlin, 2005, p 179). He notes that, in the process of distancing the Lawrences from the paper's 'dominant discourse of "problematic blackness"', hard-hitting statements by Doreen Lawrence, 'that the murder was the inevitable result of decades of racial discrimination and the failure of the authorities to act against racist violence' (McLaughlin, 2005, p 180), were disregarded by the newspaper. Similarly, McLaughlin argues that, while it acknowledged the racial aspect of the actual killing, the newspaper linked the suspects to a 'well-established discourse that blamed many of Britain's ills' on a minority 'lawless white underclass masculinity' – in other words, that 'white racism' was an 'exceptional ... rather than routine or commonplace experience for a significant section of the population' (McLaughlin, 2005, p 180).

A study by Greer and Jewkes (2005) further explores this concept of 'otherness' in the media. They argue that '[o]ne of the most prevalent messages – imparted with various degrees of subtlety across much of the U.K.'s contemporary media, but with particular vigor in the conservative press – is that people commit crimes because "they" are not like "us"' (Greer and Jewkes, 2005, p 20). Saeed (2007) discusses this concept of 'otherness' in terms of representations of British Muslims in the UK press and how these representations have forged links 'between race, nationhood, patriotism and nationalism' (Saeed, 2007, p 445) to define British Muslims as an 'alien other' (Saeed, 2007, p 443) and a threat to a British national culture 'ethically pure and homogeneous in its whiteness' (Saeed, 2007, p 445). Elliott-Cooper's (2021) study also explores the 'othering' of Black people in the media and traces these representations back to the 18th and 19th centuries when he argues 'imperial cultures and discourses were popularised through media that included government reports, journalism, fiction and philosophy' (Elliott-Cooper, 2021, pp 90–1).

More recently, Greer and McLaughlin (2011a, 2011b, 2012, 2013, 2015, 2016, 2017) have identified two new practices in crime news reporting, which they describe as 'trial by media' and 'scandal hunting' (Greer and McLaughlin, 2017, p 261). They describe 'trial by media' as 'a form of populist justice in which individuals and institutions are judged in the intermediatized "court of public opinion"' (Greer and McLaughlin, 2017, p 268). They argue that the development of 'trial by media' can be traced to the newspaper investigative campaign, which they suggest 'was re-energized and restructured in the 1990s to establish market distinction and demonstrate newspapers' growing sense of power' (Greer and McLaughlin, 2017, p 269); and they describe how, through a series of high-profile campaigns, newspapers began pressurising governments to take responsibility for institutional failures in the criminal justice system. These included a campaign by the *News of the World*, after the murder and abduction of eight-year-old Sarah Payne, to pass a 'Sarah's Law', giving parents the right to know if paedophiles were living in their community. The *News of the World*'s stance was that the lack of such a law had cost Sarah's life.

The practice of scandal-hunting focuses more on 'high-profile individuals or institutions whose official position carries the expectation of upholding clearly defined moral or ethical principles' (Greer and McLaughlin, 2017, p 277). Examples of scandal-hunting include the politicians' expenses scandal in 2009, and the revelations of institutional child abuse, following the death of Sir Jimmy Savile in 2011, when several high-profile celebrities and public figures were accused of this crime. As Greer and McLaughlin comment, '[o]nly some were convicted, but all were subjected to a shaming intermediatized trial by media' (Greer and McLaughlin, 2017, pp 279–80).

Two key points arise from this brief summary of crime news content over the last 30 years that are particularly relevant to this discussion. First, as Ericson et al argue, journalists can be seen 'as a kind of "deviance-defining élite," using the news media to provide an ongoing articulation of the proper bounds to behaviour in all organized spheres of life' (Ericson et al, 1987, p 1). As already discussed, by 'marking the outer edges of group life' and by supplying 'the framework within which the people of the group develop an orderly sense of their own cultural identity' (Erikson, 1966, p 13), some crime journalists may focus on and 'reinforce cultural fears of "otherness"' (Greer and Jewkes, 2005, p 20). Second, as Wykes (2001) has noted, by reinforcing particular ideological responses to race, poverty, class and gender, issues of poverty, inequality and racism are obscured. News reports are about specific crimes rather than 'trends, causes or remedies' (Reiner, 2010, p 180).

Production processes and working practices on legacy media outlets

Why traditional crime news leaves so much out of the frame

In his book, *Telling About Society*, Becker (2007) recounts how, when he lived in San Francisco, a regular sight from his window were groups of tourists consulting their maps and then looking disconsolately at the large hills that stood between them and their destination. At first he was puzzled, then began to realise the problem – that on the maps the tourists were consulting, the map's straight line looked like a pleasant walk through a residential neighbourhood instead of a steep hill climb – and that the maps were made originally for motorists, for whom hills are less of a consideration than walkers. He argues, however, that the maps and the networks of people who use them, exemplify a more general problem: 'representations of social reality ... give a picture that is only partial but nevertheless adequate for some purpose. All of them arise in organizational settings, which constrain what can be done and define the purposes the work will have to satisfy' (Becker, 2007, p 3).

One of the main themes of this book has been the exploration of the ways in which systemic relations between journalists and their sources shape crime news; and how, like all representations of reality arising in organisational settings, crime news is only a partial picture. This suggests a number of interesting and relevant questions. What is the function of crime news? And why, as media criminologists have suggested, are crucial aspects of knowledge about crime and policing left out of the picture? What other factors contribute to these omissions in crime news content?

On the first question, Ericson et al (1991) suggest that the 'aggregate product of [the] activity' of crime newswork is the representation of order – 'morality, procedural form, and social hierarchy – in ways that help people to order their daily lives' (Ericson et al, 1991, pp 3–4). They comment that:

> In terms of their ability to choose what to convey, and the huge audiences to whom they convey it, journalists possibly have more

influence in designating deviance and in contributing to control than do some of the more obvious agents of control. In effect, journalists join with other agents of control as a kind of 'deviance-defining élite', using the news media to provide an ongoing articulation of the proper bounds to behaviour in all organized spheres of life. (Ericson et al, 1987, p 3)

Discussing in more detail the significance of crime news in society, they argue that: 'News of crime, law and justice delineates the order of things, the procedures by which that order is accomplished, the organizational arrangements through which the procedures are invoked, the specific legal and policing provisions for reproduction of social order, and the identity of the human agents of this reproduction' (Ericson et al, 1991, p 74). As a result, Ericson et al (1991) argue that, by working with institutions they are reporting upon, such as the police, to classify an event or crime and how it is dealt with, journalists 'help to give shape to moral order and its articulation with social order' and that, in reporting on crime, they are not providing an account of what happened but a 'morality play of how what happened fits into the order of things' (Ericson et al, 1991, p 74).

Ericson et al (1987) argue that it is in this process of drawing 'the contours of the moral boundaries of society ... of who and what are in and out of bounds' that we can 'locate the significance of journalism' (Ericson et al, 1987, pp 6–7). Crime news is a 'daily "common-sense" articulation of deviance and control processes' (Ericson et al, 1987, p 7) and as central agents in drawing the 'contours of the moral boundaries of society', they draw upon key spokespersons in the 'hierarchy of credibility' (Becker, 1967) to publicise what they think are the most significant problems in terms of deviance and control and what should be done about them. In terms of crime news, what the police define as 'crime' and the solutions to that problem are the definitions generally found in media narratives – not as the result of 'a conspiracy but of routine social practices and firmly held cultural beliefs ... specific to the organizations involved' (Ericson et al, 1987, p 23). But this in turn leads to a very specific kind of narrative about crime that omits certain elements – elements of cause or effect or solution – from the story.

Why crime news rarely explores causes and effects of crime

Ericson et al suggest that news sources such as the police often wish 'to eschew causal explanation, especially in terms of the structure and process of their own organizations' and that when sources do offer explanations, 'it is typically in pursuit of their own legitimacy' (Ericson et al, 1991, p 268). They also comment that news imperatives limit explanations of causes and effects of crime. First, the focus is on present-time events and the individuals involved in those events. Second, the focus on dramatisation in news storytelling reinforces the emphasis on present-time storytelling. As Chibnall notes, '[a] violent act is more amenable to dramatization than are the conditions and processes which shape its development. ... The causes of violence are more complex and intractable, less open to instant empathetic understanding' (Chibnall, 1977, p 79).

Journalists interviewed for this study – particularly those working for broadsheets – were also critical of what they perceived to be the limited scope of crime reporting; but they acknowledged that news imperatives, such as the need to make stories dramatic, militated against more in-depth reporting or discussion of causes or effects of crime. As one reporter commented, "you have to play the game to get your stories printed". The same reporter gave an example of how, on one occasion, they had managed to write such a story and get it published:

'So I was in the Old Bailey, just hanging about. There was a case, a typical scuzzy gangland killing. And I happened to run into the detective who was running the case and, as we were chatting, he told me that the gun had been used for seven shootings. And he showed me all the pictures, all the evidence, and I thought, if I tell it one way, it's just another gangland story. But if I tell it another way, the history of a gun, it becomes something else, a story about gun culture and it was actually a really tragic story that was all about this cycle of violence ... how people become tangled up in that world and can't get out.'

Nevertheless, they noted that the story had been "a very hard sell" to their editor and that it had been a "very unusual story" for the paper to run.

Negative representation of people of colour and other marginalised communities

Another key area of concern for media criminologists, in terms of the content of crime news, is the way in which certain marginalised or stigmatised communities are represented negatively in the media. Following the murder of George Floyd in 2020, the representation of people of colour in the media came under the spotlight, with journalists and media scholars calling for radical change in mainstream newsrooms. Criticisms largely centred around two issues – the practice of objectivity in newsrooms and the lack of diversity among journalists on mainstream outlets in terms of race, class and gender.

Ward (2010) traces the practice of objectivity back to the early 18th century in the United States and the creation of a news press for the masses, as opposed to what had previously been largely an opinion press for elites. The primary business of newspapers changed from providing opinion to providing news and the initial 'penny press' in major US cities expanded into the large newspaper organisations of press barons such as Hearst and Pulitzer. Ward argues that the effect on journalism's norms was dramatic: '[p]apers that emphasized news displayed a "veneration of the fact" and stressed the virtues of accuracy, brevity, and timeliness' (Ward, 2010, p 140). In 1866, Lawrence Gobright of the Associated Press in Washington, DC, voiced an early commitment to what would become the journalistic norm: 'My business is merely to communicate facts. My instructions do not allow me to make any comments upon the facts which I communicate' (quoted in Ward, 2010, p 140). By the beginning of the First World War, Ward suggests that the practice of objectivity was widely espoused by most editors and journalists. According to Ward, traditional objectivity could be characterised in the following way: '[A] report is objective if and only if it is an accurate recording of an event. It reports only the facts, and eliminates comment, interpretation, and speculation by the reporter. The report is neutral between rival views on an issue' (Ward, 2010, p 141).

Nevertheless, objectivity had its critics. Ward notes how '[i]n the 1960s, an "adversarial culture" that criticized institutions and fought for civil rights was skeptical of objective experts and detached journalism' while '[o]ther journalists practiced a subjective personal journalism that looked to literature for its inspiration' (Ward, 2010, p 144). By the end of the 20th century, new media technology allowed almost anyone with a computer to publish their commentary or photos online, giving, as Ward (2010) argues, further support to the rise of opinion journalism. But as Ward and other scholars note, over the last two decades, there have been further attacks on the practice of objectivity – that it is undesirable, because it forces writers to use restricted formats, encouraging a superficial reporting of official facts; while, as Meyers (2020) notes, 'a strict adherence to balance – in the sense of giving equal weight and credence to all sides on a contentious issue – can mislead more than inform', as in 'coverage of climate change in which equal space is also given to deniers'.

Similarly, Canella (2021) argues that, at a time when 'search and social media algorithms filter content based on users' preferences, blurring the boundaries between journalism, activism, advertising, and entertainment … placing credible news next to conspiracy theories, and making it harder for audiences to distinguish the difference' (Canella, 2021, p 4), the concept of objectivity is used as a selling point by news organisations 'to legitimize their authority and cater to a perceived audience' (Canella, 2021, p 10). For journalists to maintain their positions as 'truth tellers' (Canella, 2021, p 4), the public need to view them and the organisations that employ them as being credible. But as he also argues, 'journalism is a cultural institution that is never neutral, truths are never disinterested, and journalists' truth claims and editorial practices are influenced by the power dynamics embedded in the sociopolitical and historical contexts in which they work' (Canella, 2021, p 2). Canella (2021) suggests that story selection and the choice of news sources all reveal journalists' and their news organisations' orientation to power. Similarly, Usher (2021) argues that one of the key problems arising from lack of diversity in newsrooms is that in 'White-majority newsrooms … journalists stand to miss important stories that they may not even know to ask about' (Usher, 2021, p 60).

As I discussed in Chapter 6, one of the key aims of many of the journalists working on non-profits and interviewed for this study was to include a wider range of perspectives in their reporting and, in particular, to give voice to communities often represented negatively or excluded from crime news narratives. As one respondent commented:

'We talk about lack of diversity being a problem in terms of police recruitment and how they serve their communities, but I think it's also a problem in our industry and how we represent those communities.'

Another respondent commented on their perceptions of the practice of objectivity in the national newsrooms in which they had worked:

'I think the idea of objectivity belongs to another era, when there were no women, no Black people, no immigrants or trans people working for these supposedly neutral outlets. And I think it's a practice that is supposed to promote fairness and balance but in reality means certain people just don't get a seat at the table and certain stories are not being told.'

However, as I have discussed in Chapter 6, lack of diversity in newsrooms is not the only reason why certain voices and perspectives are privileged over others in crime reporting. Another key factor is lack of trust in the media by marginalised or stigmatised communities, particularly those who believe their communities have been unfairly or negatively represented in the news. As a result, as Robinson (2018) argues in her study of community networks, many of the journalists she interviewed found it difficult to find people of colour who were willing to talk to them either on or off record. In the sample of journalists she studied, only two reporters ventured into neighbourhoods or community centres with the sole purpose of networking and building relationships, although almost all the journalists she spoke to wanted to extend their networks. This in turn meant that the journalists' networks 'recreate[d] a local community's dominant hierarchies' and that they tended to use 'official sources that tend to be White or regular contacts that tend to be outspoken at meetings or confident in approaching reporters' (Robinson, 2018, p 131). She also notes that '[d]eadline pressures and declining resources in the newsroom mean that reporters have little time to develop the necessary relationships in communities of color, and become frustrated after repeated rejections from people who don't know them or who have had poor experiences with media' (Robinson, 2018, p 131). Accordingly, many of the Black parents she spoke to rarely watched or read local mainstream journalism because they did 'not see issues relevant to them or people who look like them' (Robinson, 2018, p 134).

Robinson (2018) argues that part of the reason so few people of colour see themselves represented in the media is through what she terms 'missed connections' (Robinson, 2018, p 128). She argues that there is often a clash between journalistic norms and practices – the need to meet deadlines, to have sources prepared to speak on the record and so on – and the needs and perceptions of the communities she studied, as illustrated by the example of NBC and Michael Johnson that was discussed in Chapter 6. As Robinson (2018) concludes, such journalistic norms are meant to protect journalists' professionalism but they also 'perpetuate absences in the media' (Robinson, 2018, p 158).

To sum up then, many of the concerns about media representations in crime news are undoubtedly tied up with lack of diversity in newsrooms. But it would be fair to say that journalistic norms and practices on mainstream outlets also play a part in narrowing the 'crime aperture' (Ericson et al, 1987, p 9). The practice by journalists of using key spokespersons in the 'hierarchy of credibility' (Becker, 1967) to define social problems and their solutions often militates against meaningful discussion of causes and effects of crime; the practice of objectivity and the need to have statements by sources on the record often prevent the voices of people of colour being heard, for fear of being represented negatively; and the frequent structural disconnects between journalists and the communities they report upon – working at a distance from those communities, relying on the same sources within those communities, and not extending networks – can lead to coverage that, at best, is superficial and, at worst, is negative and harmful.

Changing the narrative: 'crime news' content on non-profits

In their study of news start-ups, Deuze and Witschge argue that, 'in terms of producing content', the start-ups they studied 'did not necessarily differ all that much from what their colleagues elsewhere made' (Deuze and Witschge, 2020, p 91). I argue, however, that the non-profits in this study are in fact offering very different content in terms of crime and investigative reporting to that of legacy media outlets. I suggest that this content differs in three important ways: giving a voice to communities generally portrayed negatively in legacy media; reporting on systemic and social harm rather than crime as a specific event, and, through the practice of transparency and publication of data used to research stories, allowing causes and effects of crime also to be brought into the crime news discourse.

Repairing representational harm on The Bristol Cable

One of the first initiatives to give voice to communities generally portrayed negatively in legacy media was *The Bristol Cable*'s series of stories about the Traveller community in Bristol – an initiative which started in 2015 and is ongoing to this day. Like 'welfare cheats' or immigrants, Travellers are often portrayed in the media as the enemy of Middle England or 'of the "normal" settled community' (Richardson and O'Neill, 2012, p 170). Richardson and O'Neill (2012) cite an example of this coverage from an article in *The Sun* published in 2005 as part of a campaign run by the newspaper, entitled Stamp on the Camps:

> The rule of law is flouted daily by people who don't pay taxes, give nothing to society and yet expect to be treated as untouchables. ... The villain of the piece is the Human Rights Act, which our judges have limply interpreted to mean that these wandering tribes have a right to family life and respect for their homes which outweighs any harm they might do to the environment or rural communities. (*The Sun*, 9 March 2005, cited in Richardson and O'Neill, 2012, p 172)

Morris (2000) notes that those 'who write and speak of Gypsies and Travellers often do not know them, and therefore do not often present a complete or balanced picture' (Morris, 2000, p 214). She comments that Travellers experience both direct and indirect exclusion from this process of reporting, 'by not being involved in the creation of stories about them either as interviewees or as journalists' (Morris, 2000, p 214).

The Bristol Cable started its series on prejudice against Traveller communities in their city in 2015. Right from the start, reporters on the *Cable* were clear that their aim was to challenge existing legacy media narratives about Travellers and to allow Travellers themselves to become involved in the reporting of issues that were having an impact on their lives. As one of the reporters, Hannah Vickers, explained:

> Firstly, as press coverage of these communities is so overwhelmingly negative and has such a narrow focus, there is zero public interest needed to provide more of the same. ... There are so many articles about Travellers, but very few where the people being written about get to say anything. These populations are massively misserved by the media. How many articles have you read where an angry resident is

interviewed about mess or noise or blocking the field? And how many of those articles included quotes from people on the encampments?

... [S]econdly, one of the Cable's editorial policies is to highlight injustices and give a voice to marginalised people, and these populations are among the most marginalised and socially deprived ethnicities in the UK.

Our job and responsibility as journalists is to cover the under-reported voices, study the facts and context, and avoid shock headlines. It makes for a less sensationalised, exciting story, but a more accurate, balanced one. ... This is what the other papers should be doing. If there was more responsible journalism about these populations, people wouldn't have such a skewed narrative about Gypsies, Roma and Travellers. (Vickers, 2020)

Chapter 6 described how non-profits such as *The Bristol Cable* were engaging in both the practice of engaged and solutions journalism. Engaged journalism refers to a range of practices that aim to build relationships between journalists and the public and involve the public in the process of co-creating journalism; while solutions journalism suggests 'that a journalist's role is not only to report on problems but also to rigorously report on "responses to social problems"' (Wenzel, 2020, p 4). However, Wenzel also argues that such practices will not 'build trust with marginalized communities unless they are reflexive about journalistic norms ... that reinforce hierarchies of race, class and geography' (Wenzel, 2020, p 4).

As already noted, journalists in Robinson's (2018) study of community networks expressed the desire to network and build relationships with marginalised communities, with the aim of creating a more inclusive form of reporting, but were constrained in doing so by the need to meet deadlines and have sources willing to talk at short notice, and by the general mistrust of the media by Black and Brown people in those communities. At the same time, Robinson (2018) notes that the White reporters she interviewed 'were keenly aware of their white skin as they covered stories about racial disparities – so much so, they felt their difference prevented them from truly being able to get at the core of the story' (Robinson, 2018, p 131). As a result, Robinson notes that stories that dealt with racial inequalities or 'challenges to institutional authority' were rarely covered during her period of observation (Robinson, 2018, p 132).

All respondents from non-profits interviewed for this study flagged up the need to be aware of their own journalistic 'blind spots' (Usher, 2021, p 39). As a respondent from *The Bristol Cable* explained:

'I think it's important to be open about the fact that, as individual journalists, we are going to have worldviews which inform which stories we decide to take on and which we don't and how we tell stories. So that's why, right from the start, we knew that we had to have the broadest church of views within our editorial team – and by sharing power with our readers, our communities, to find out from them what stories we needed to tell, and how we should be telling them.'

As Usher (2021) argues, although lack of diversity in newsrooms is certainly one factor in lack of inclusiveness in news reporting, another key factor is the issue of 'place' and that '[w]here journalists are located, where they work, whom they speak to each day – their *place* – affects what they know, what they value, and what they come to see as important' (Usher, 2021, p 68). In Chapter 6, I discussed how, particularly on a local level, cuts in staff and the closing of many local news outlets mean that journalists are often working at a distance from the communities they cover, leading to a disconnect between them, their organisations and their readership or audience.

By contrast, as described in Chapter 6, journalists on *The Bristol Cable* believe they are very much part of their community. Also, because they are not part of a regular daily publishing cycle, their focus is not on producing a story by a set date, but on gathering all the evidence they need to stand up a story and to spend time forging relationships with hard-to-reach communities. This approach means that the *Cable* spends time with members of a particular community to source stories and collaborate with them during the newsgathering process. As Alon Aviram, one of the founders of the *Cable*, explained:

We will often sit with someone who has no prior experience in producing journalism and work with them to produce a piece of content. That could take a couple of days just online or it could be a person comes into our office over a period of a couple of months and researches and develops a piece. Because our journalism is slower, we have the space to be able to really nurture people's development. (Aviram quoted in Albeanu, 2016, p 330)

By adopting these practices, *The Bristol Cable* is able to produce a more inclusive form of reporting but also an approach that is grounded in what Ward (2010) describes as 'pragmatic objectivity' (Ward, 2010, p 145). Although, as I noted, some respondents were critical of the practice of traditional objectivity in mainstream newsrooms, pragmatic objectivity, according to Ward (2010), is characterised by transparency and an acknowledgement that journalism is an 'active, interpretive, cultural activity' (Ward, 2010, p 146). He suggests that this practice:

allows the reporter to draw conclusions, especially as these relate to a commitment to truth and the public interest, so long as such conclusions are well evidenced. Rather than avoid judgment, journalists should strengthen how they research and test their claims. Rather than fudge the fact that journalists select sources, facts, and angles, journalists should justify their selections. (Ward, 2010, p 149)

In her reporting on issues affecting the Traveller community in Bristol, Vickers (2020) notes that she is an 'ally' but not 'a cheerleader'. Although a number of her reports set out directly to redress the 'skewed narrative', including articles showing the positive contributions Travellers have made to their local community, including the donation of food to local food banks, in other reports, Vickers is careful to give space to both the perspectives of Travellers and of local politicians and the wider community. An example of this was her coverage of the tensions unauthorised encampments can create, which included opinions from unhappy local residents as well as from Bristol councillors who wanted to bring in tougher legislation. At the same time, Vickers and the *Cable* are careful to give Travellers the chance to tell their own stories – to report with the Traveller communities, rather than on them. In a story on the Gypsies and Travellers Communities Bill, put forward by Conservative MP Andrew Selous, which proposed turning Traveller sites into land for housing and moving all Gypsies and Travellers into houses 'to help them integrate', the *Cable* explored at length the impact of the Bill on Travellers' lives, drawing from a series of interviews with named members of the community. One Traveller, Luke Wenman, argued that: 'It's an excuse for cultural cleansing. There are two ways people tackle Travellers. One, they force you to continue being on the move, or two, they force you to assimilate' (Wenman quoted in Vickers, 2019). He also commented about Selous: 'It's as if we aren't his constituents. We are the local community. Where else are we from? Who else do we get to vote for? We shouldn't be othered' (Wenman quoted in Vickers, 2019). By contrast, a report in the *Daily Mail* in November 2019, outlining proposals by the Home Secretary to enable police to remove 'unwelcome visitors', did not include any interviews with Travellers, stressing instead that trespass was currently 'a civil matter meaning landowners face a long and expensive legal battle to remove offenders' (Webber, 2019).

In terms of news content, in many respects, *The Bristol Cable* is taking a very different approach to that of mainstream outlets: funding by reader donations and the lack of a fixed publishing cycle mean that journalists are able to spend time making connections with communities, which in turn leads to a greater diversity and range of perspectives in its reporting. Although, as one of the respondents from *The Bristol Cable* explained, editorial judgement is still needed to determine whether something is a good story, and whether data has been reliably collected, this is very much applied with a 'light touch'. But it should also be noted that, unlike the *Bureau Local* or *The Bureau for Investigative Journalism*, *The Bristol Cable* does not generally share its stories with mainstream outlets and its primary focus is on local news. What matters to the *Cable* are regular readers – and donors – not one-off hits that come from writing sensationalist stories. Thus, while in the bulk of its reporting about marginalised communities such as Travellers, the *Cable* sets out deliberately to redress representational harms by giving voice to those groups, it also has the freedom, because it does not share its news, to run stories that deal with issues specific to Travellers that might be difficult to place with mainstream outlets.

Taking a 'social harm' approach to crime reporting on the Bureau Local

Another way in which investigative reporters on non-profits are aiming to change narratives is by reporting on what they term systemic harms, rather than reporting on crime as specific events. As Hillyard and Tombs argue, '[m]any events and incidents which cause serious harm are either not part of the criminal law or, if they could be dealt with by it, are either ignored or handled outside of it' (Hillyard and Tombs, 2005, p 9).

The project 'Dying Homeless' was started by the *Bureau Local* in 2018. Prompted by the death of a homeless man found outside the Houses of Parliament, the *Bureau Local* decided to investigate how many people were dying homeless in the United Kingdom but then came to the realisation that no one was collating this data (Hamada, 2021). As Hamada, who is also a reporter on the *Bureau Local*, notes, '[p]eople were dying unacknowledged, without lessons being learnt and without commemoration' (Hamada, 2021, p 116). In an interview with the Global Investigative Journalism Network (GIJN), the *Bureau Local* reporter leading the investigation, Maeve McClenaghan, described how she 'devised a simple Google form for network members to fill out, with details of homeless deaths they encountered' (Coogans, 2021). *The Bureau for Investigative Journalism* advertised the form on Twitter and put it on their website, hoping to reach as many people as possible.

At the same time, McClenaghan and the rest of the team also traveled across the UK, visiting soup kitchens and homeless shelters to meet sources and understand the issue through first-hand accounts, again setting up 'storytelling islands' by working directly with these communities to co-create stories. They looked at local press reports, gathered details from police and coroners' reports, as well as speaking to doctors and others working with homeless people, to ensure they had as full a picture as possible. McClenaghan described 'the process as a "part-crowdsourced, part-jigsaw puzzle investigation"' (McClenaghan quoted in Coogans, 2021). However, while a key aspect of the project was identifying how many people died homeless in Britain, 'the project also sought to go beyond numbers by capturing and memorializing individual stories of the deceased' (Coogans, 2021).

The *Bureau Local*'s reporting set out to 'show the real people behind the numbers and the things that might have led to their often-premature deaths' (Hamada, 2021, p 117). Hamada (2021) comments: 'One man who died was not yet 40 – he had been a successful sailor and had also regularly volunteered, including building schools and helping in a homeless kitchen. However, he lost two children in succession and this sent him to rock bottom' (Hamada, 2021, p 117). By focusing on personal stories as well as statistics, the *Bureau Local* team also discovered that '[s]weeping cuts to mental health provision and drug and alcohol services, coupled with a benefit cap, increased rental costs, and lack of housing ha[d] created the perfect storm' (Coogans, 2021). In her interview with GIJN, McClenaghan argued that understanding the stories behind the statistics was essential in order to capture the causes and effects of homelessness in the United Kingdom and highlighting what needs to change. She commented: 'I think it was only through really going deep into those stories that you understand, there are moments when interventions could have helped, and they weren't there, and here's how we learn lessons to prevent this from happening again' (McClenaghan quoted in Coogans, 2021).

Like *The Bristol Cable*, one of the key aims of the *Bureau Local* is to give voice to under-represented communities and to work with those communities. But there are nevertheless some significant differences in their reporting and content. First, unlike the *Cable*, while the *Bureau Local* engages with its readers and communities to find story ideas and, on occasion, through its numerous open online events, to ask readers or other interested citizens for a steer on its investigations, stories are reported solely by the *Bureau Local* team. This may in part be due to their very different origins – *The Bristol Cable* was founded by a group of friends without prior formal journalistic training, who had come from a background of activist politics at university, while the *Bureau Local*'s staff all have extensive journalistic experience, though from a variety of outlets, including other non-profits.

Second, as noted earlier, *The Bristol Cable* does not share its stories generally whereas the *Bureau Local* and *The Bureau for Investigative Journalism* frequently pair with large outlets nationally and internationally to extend the reach of their work. But while Konieczna suggests that this practice 'limits what the news nonprofits are able to do, because it has them forever looking to their counterparts in commercial journalism' (Konieczna, 2018, p 206), this is not necessarily the case for the *Bureau Local* and *The Bureau for Investigative Journalism*. Although the editors are mindful as to where they might publish their work more widely, the focus of their stories is radically different to most mainstream organisations.

The Death of the Homeless project is a case in point. Instead of reporting on a single case, the *Bureau Local* are focusing on what they would term 'a systemic wrong' or a crime of social harm – a radical change in the remit of what is generally considered to be crime news; in that respect, they are 'repairing' the field by producing very different content for mainstream outlets. Also, as I argue in the next section, through their practice of transparency, they are not only enabling other journalists and citizens to carry out further investigations, but enabling causes, effects and possible avenues for change to be part of the journalistic conversation.

Transparency and exploring the causes and effects of crimes of social harm

Over the last 20 years, researchers have increasingly suggested transparency in journalism as a way to improve journalism and form a stronger relationship with audiences. One of the earliest studies by Kovach and Rosenstiel (2001) argued that transparency in journalism could take two forms: dialogue with the public, and telling and showing the public how journalism is done. Other researchers have built on this research and suggested that transparency can be linked to increased trust, trustworthiness, accountability and authenticity (Singer, 2007; Karlsson, 2010, 2011; Phillips, 2010); that a more transparent journalism requires new practices and skillsets among journalists (Bivens, 2008); and that transparency can be seen as a defensive move to preserve journalistic authority (Karlsson, 2010). I also suggest that transparency, as practised by the non-profits in this study, can be linked to the practice of solutions journalism, described in Chapter 6; or as Wenzel (2020) describes it, offering ' "the whole story" – not only spotlighting social ills but highlighting how they are being addressed' (Wenzel, 2020, p 8). This is an aspect of crime reporting that scholars (Jewkes, 2004; Reiner, 2010) argue is often omitted from the discourse.

In their work, the *Bureau Local* employ both methods of transparency: engaging with the public to receive input on stories they are investigating, but also documenting how they research and tell their stories. This latter practice is not generally employed in mainstream crime or investigative journalism. In an opinion piece for the MediaShift website on transparency versus objectivity, media scholar and former journalist, Gabriel Kahn, recounts how, when he worked at the *Wall Street Journal* in the 2000s, 'editors could sometimes be so thorough in picking apart the assertions in my reporting that it felt like I had been run over by a truck' (Kahn, 2017). But he also notes that 'few ever prodded me to let my readers in on all the work involved collecting the facts, holding them up to the light, and actively seeking out information that might debunk a central premise of a story' (Kahn, 2017). He concludes that, at a time of declining trust in the media as an institution, '[a]uthority and trust will only return if reporters share some of the messy sausage-making process with the audience' (Kahn, 2017). Similarly, a respondent from the *Bureau Local* argued:

> 'What is key to us is transparency, radical transparency. We need to be much clearer about how we are getting information, and when we don't know something, say we don't know rather than making something up.'

For each investigation undertaken by the *Bureau Local*, open data is published on its website, showing the 'workings behind our investigations and guides for taking our stories further' (from the *Bureau Local* website). The aim of the *Bureau Local* is to make the investigative process accessible to local reporters wanting to report on issues covered by the *Bureau Local*, but also to the general public. There are four resources available for each investigation undertaken by the *Bureau Local*: data, or evidence behind each investigation; a 'reporting recipe' or a how-to guide to use the data and develop the story for reporters; code or technological tools to interrogate or visualise data; and other resources used as part of the investigation.

For the 'Dying Homeless' project, these resources include a collaborative database of deaths in England and Northern Ireland from 2017 onwards; a reporting recipe explaining how the *Bureau Local* have used that data, and including key quotes and extracts from individuals involved in the project; and a description of the methodology used by the *Bureau Local*.

One of the key issues for the *Bureau Local* in investigating this story was to find out if local councils had carried out a Safeguarding Adults Review (SAR) after the death of each homeless person. A SAR 'is a multi-agency process that considers whether or not serious harm experienced by an adult, or group of adults, at risk of abuse or neglect, could have been predicted or prevented' (taken from the Staffordshire and Stoke-on-Trent Safeguarding Partnership Board website). The resources give an overview of findings by the *Bureau Local*; an explanation of the data collated on SARs carried out by relevant local authorities; and the methodology used to collect this data, in this case Freedom of Information requests sent to all local authorities responsible for protecting adults. The template of the request sent to local authorities is included as well as key questions asked – in this case, how many SARs were undertaken over a period of six years and how many reviews were undertaken for both people who were statutory homeless and people who were statutory homeless who died?

The website explains how the team analysed their findings and gives suggestions as to how members of the public can contribute to the project. These suggestions include: checking in the *Bureau*'s database for local deaths of homeless people; checking if the relevant council has undertaken a review of the death; if not, asking councils if they will undertake reviews in the future; and contacting homelessness charities to interview them about these issues. More specifically, it is also noted on the website that the reporters had not collated information about inquests into deaths of the homeless, and members of the public are asked for their assistance with this: to find out if there have been deaths in their area and to contact their local coroner's office to find out if inquests have been carried out. Finally, long extracts from interviews carried out by the *Bureau Local* are also included for the use of local reporters wishing to report on this issue in their area.

We have already seen how a number of news imperatives militate against discussion of the effects and causes of crime – the need to meet deadlines, the focus on the 'present-time, specific events, the individuals involved in those events, and the contingencies of the events' (Ericson et al, 1989, p 268) and the privileging of accredited 'experts', who typically offer explanations only 'in pursuit of their own legitimacy' (Ericson et al, 1991, p 268). Quoting Pfohl (1985), Ericson et al (1991) comment that:

> By focusing on events involving exercises of lawful authority in institutional settings, news augments the thrust of legal control. News joins with the law in excluding the deviant because it too 'produces the appearance (or collective representation) that troublesome persons rather than troublesome social structure are at fault. This mystifies the social roots of trouble in a society that is structurally unequal'. (Pfohl, 1985, p 353, quoted in Ericson et al, 1991, p 278)

By contrast, the non-profits in this study have moved away from an approach of crime as a discrete event to one of social harm. Through the practice of transparency and, linked with it, the practice of solutions journalism, they have also moved towards what Wenzel (2020) calls an alternative form of accountability journalism – the goal being not to advocate for a particular solution but to critically explore a response to a problem, looking at what works or what does not work – but also enabling citizens and other journalists to take action by using the *Bureau Local*'s data to carry out further investigations of their own. As Wenzel (2020) also notes, solutions journalism shifts the narrative from one of 'Who's to blame' to 'What can we do?'

However, one topic the non-profits in this study have not covered extensively to date is that of policing. *The Bureau for Investigative Journalism* ran a number of early investigations into the broader field of criminal justice – including stories on the handling of rape cases by the Metropolitan Police; deaths in police custody; joint enterprise; and the impact of cuts on police and courts – but over the last five years, have concentrated more on investigations of social harms. Respondents from *The Bristol Cable* commented that policing stories were "mainly the preserve of mainstream news" and that unless a story arose which they considered to be of interest to their local community, it was not an area they would explore in the future. Conversely, the *Bureau Local* suggested that they might run more stories on policing and the criminal justice system in the future if it aligned with their aims.

Conclusion

In this chapter, I have explored how the non-profits are changing the remit of crime news in their reporting. As Becker (2007) notes: 'Reports on society ... make most sense when you see them in organizational context, as activities, as ways some people tell what they think they know to other people who want to know it, as organized activities shaped by the joint efforts of everyone involved' (Becker, 2007, p 15). In previous chapters I have explored how social and cultural relations between the MPS and journalists, and between journalists on the non-profits, members of the public and other news sources, all shape the content of crime news – and what is omitted from the picture. In this chapter, I focus on three aspects of crime reporting that have received particular attention over the years in qualitative criminological research – the 'othering' of marginalised or stigmatised communities; the under-reporting of certain crimes, particularly crimes of social harm; and the concentration on crime as a discrete event, without discussion of causes or effects.

Although many scholars have rightly suggested that lack of diversity in newsrooms is a contributory factor, I also follow Usher (2021) in suggesting that 'place' plays a part. With the closing of many local news outlets over the last 20 years, journalists are often reporting at some distance from the communities they are covering and that contributes, in turn, to a disconnect between journalists and their public, leading to superficial reporting at best and harmful reporting at worst. Mistrust of the media, particularly in communities often represented negatively, and the need to have reliable dependable sources willing to talk at short notice, and on the record, often precludes more diverse voices being included in traditional crime reporting.

I suggest that the very different working practices on the non-profits have addressed many of these problems – that by not needing to meet the demands of a daily publishing cycle, non-profit journalists are able to spend time forging meaningful relationships with marginalised and hard-to-reach communities and ensure a greater range of perspectives are included in their reporting. I also argue that, while some scholars (Konieczna, 2018) have suggested that the practice of news sharing by some non-profits limits their ability to provide an alternative form of reporting to the mainstream outlets, the non-profits in this study that do engage in this practice are radically changing the content of crime news in two respects: through a focus on crime as systemic harm rather than crime as a discrete event; and, coupled with that, a move towards exploring the causes and effects of the social harm through the emphasis on evidence and data sharing as part of their reports on their websites.

8

How does the Fourth Estate work now in crime and investigative reporting?

Introduction

The murder of George Floyd in May 2020 brought about calls to defund the police on both sides of the Atlantic. But it also brought about calls to radically overhaul the content of crime reporting; that it was racist, classist and sexist and created harms for marginalised and stigmatised communities through its coverage of them. The last two chapters have discussed how *The Bristol Cable*, the *Bureau Local* and *The Bureau for Investigative Journalism* have attempted to address the misrepresentation of stigmatised or marginalised communities through working with these communities in the reporting of their stories. But in the United Kingdom, there is another problem facing legacy crime journalists – the breakdown of relationships between the national press and the MPS.

This chapter begins by summarising the key findings of this study. It then moves on to a final discussion of the future of crime and investigative reporting in the United Kingdom; what lessons can be learned by legacy media from the work of the non-profits; and why this breakdown in police/news media relations is not only harmful for the press and the public, but also for the MPS.

In 2019, eight years after the original phone-hacking scandal and seven years after the publication of the Leveson and Filkin Reports (2012), I attended another conference run by the Centre for Investigative Journalism at Goldsmiths College, University of London. One of the talks was entitled 'A Life in Crime'; it featured Fiona Hamilton, Crime and Security Editor at *The Times*, and freelance journalist, Michael Gillard, being interviewed by author and crime journalist, Duncan Campbell.

Hamilton started her talk by describing what she termed the 'Golden Age of Crime Reporting', an era predating the Leveson and Filkin Reports (2012), in which police officers were happy to help crime journalists, particularly when reporting on sensitive issues such as terrorism; and when there were, according to Hamilton, monthly briefings by the MPS Commissioners. She claimed that relations between the police and the press had deteriorated over the intervening seven years to such an extent that, while she was covering a murder case at the Old Bailey, a senior police officer – with whom she had formerly been on good speaking terms – hid behind a pillar rather than speak to her, so great was his fear of being labelled a whistleblower if seen talking to a member of the press.

Hamilton talked of how she and her colleagues had to rely on Freedom of Information requests in order to find out any information on whether or not MPS departments were operating efficiently; and that, more often than not, repeated requests had to be made. She described how victims and witnesses of crime were being explicitly warned against speaking to the press by the MPS and told that 'their words would be twisted'. She also commented that, even when she and her colleagues were informed of crimes, it was almost impossible to obtain further background information from the Directorate; as a result, she feared that many crimes were simply being buried by the MPS. While she could see the MPS benefiting from this impasse in relations – that senior officers were more easily able to cover up botched investigations, internal abuses of power and corruption – she and her colleagues were severely impaired in their ability to hold the police to account.

The last ten years have seen what Beckett (2018) terms a paradox of power for journalism. Organisations such as *The Bristol Cable* and *The Bureau for Investigative Journalism* are changing journalistic norms and changing the nature of crime news. Although these organisations are still comparative newcomers to the field of journalism, they have not only produced important investigative journalism at the local and national level (and, in the case of *The Bureau for Investigative Journalism*, at international level) but have also helped to stimulate positive social change, as in the *Bureau Local*'s investigation into the death of homeless people.

Nevertheless, one area in which the non-profits are not speaking 'truth to power' is that of policing. This is a conscious move on their part, as described in the last chapter, as their belief is that this remains the domain of legacy media. In terms of crime reporting, however, as argued throughout this study, traditional crime reporters' ability to fulfil their Fourth Estate role has been greatly diminished by technological changes, the global crisis in the news industry and, in the United Kingdom, the impact of the Leveson and Filkin Reports (2012) on police/news media relations.

The non-profits may be transforming crime and investigative reporting but one key source – the police – increasingly controls the flow of policing news to the press and the public. If knowledge is power, the question of who controls the production and distribution of information is more important than ever in an era of fake news and disinformation. The Fourth Estate has transformed radically over the last ten years, allowing '[p]rofessionals, amateurs, and hybrid variations of such identities, many institutions, many technologies' to become involved 'in the production of journalism across diverse channels and platforms' (Deuze and Witschge, 2020, p 2). Yet in the case of the police in the United Kingdom, the Fourth Estate has never been so hamstrung in its ability to carry out its watchdog role.

Key findings from this study

This book seeks to make three primary contributions to the field of police/ news media relations and to research on crime and investigative news reporting. These are:

- a re-evaluation of classic criminological texts from the 1970s, 1980s and 1990s, suggesting that police/media/public relations might be even more complex than previously imagined, and expanding the discussion to explore police/news media relations in the first decade of the 2000s;
- an exploration of the subsequent impact of the Leveson and Filkin Reports and the advent of social media on police/media/public relations; and
- to advance understanding of the role that digital start-ups are playing in expanding the remit of crime news.

Throughout this study, I have drawn on three theoretical frameworks to conceptualise how police/media/public relationships – and the role of the crime journalist – have changed over the last 40 years.

First, I follow Lee and McGovern in drawing on the work of De Certeau (1984) on the strategies and tactics of everyday life throughout Chapters 2 to 5, to understand the strategies used by the police – both before and after the widescale use of the internet – to control the ways in which the organisation and its work are represented in the media and the tactics used by the press and the public to resist that control and, through new technologies, to hold the police to account.

The second framework I use to understand the changing role of the crime journalist draws from Burt's (1992, 2002) work on structural holes and bridge decay. This is a concept derived from social network analysis research, which is more frequently used in sociology, economics and computer science. In Chapters 2 and 3, I suggest that, before the advent of the internet, the crime journalist was a bridge between two unconnected worlds – the world of the police and the general public. Because they were spanning the distance between these otherwise separate worlds, crime journalists could be described as bridging a 'structural' hole (Burt, 1992). By controlling the information flow between sources and their audiences, I argue that crime journalists were very powerful and possibly even more powerful than the classic studies of the 1970s and 1980s suggest. In Chapters 4 and 5, I draw on Burt's (2002) work on bridge decay to explore how two factors – the severe restrictions on police and media contact following the recommendations of the Filkin and Leveson Reports (2012), and the advent of social media – led to the decay of the 'bridge' between the police and the mainstream media.

Finally, in Chapters 6 and 7, I draw on the work of the media scholar, Ball-Rokeach, and her concept of CIT. This framework was originally used to explore multilevel storytelling networks in local communities, specifically links between citizens, communities and their local media organisations. I use this framework in a similar way to explore how, over the last ten years, journalists on investigative non-profits have been setting up new patterns of working or networks of bridges with local communities. I argue that, in this frame, journalists are not the sole bridge but only one member of the storytelling network – and that citizens, local community groups, charities and other organisations all have agency in creating crime news.

Re-evaluating the classic criminological texts from the 1970s, 1980s and 1990s: the journalist as 'bridge' between the police and the public

The orthodox view of police–media relations in early studies (Chibnall, 1977, 1979; Hall et al, 1978) was that power was asymmetrical in favour of the police. However, I argue in this study that, in terms of power relations between the police and the media during this period, the media may have been even more powerful than these early studies suggest.

First, I argue that crime journalists held a very privileged position in the pre-internet age. They formed a 'bridge' between the police and the public, spanning a structural hole or an empty space between two clusters or networks of connections. According to Burt, structural holes are 'an opportunity to broker the flow of *information* between people, and *control* the projects that bring together people from opposite sides of the hole' (Burt, 2002, p 337, emphasis in original). The person who brings these two worlds together is known as the *'tertius gaudens'* or the one who benefits, by controlling a flow of 'accurate, ambiguous or distorted information' (Burt, 2002, p 338). The press were very powerful during this period, not least because they were the only channel through which the police could communicate with the public, to ask for help with investigations, to call for witnesses or to publicise police success. While press officers had the ability to 'withdraw' or initiate 'bridge decay' with individual reporters, they were, at the same time, acutely aware that journalists always had the ability to find alternative sources. Access was not automatically guaranteed, details of crimes released by police press officers had to fit normative news values and, as I discuss in Chapter 2, on occasion key investigations were not publicised as they were not deemed sufficiently newsworthy by the press.

I argue that, from both press officers' and operational officers' responses, the relationship was always multilayered, complex and contingent; it involved a whole network of interactions between the MPS and the press at many levels, and at every rank – both officially and unofficially. I explore some of the strategies used by police press officers to control the flow of information to the press and to protect the police image, including the pre-emptive release of bad news to avoid inaccurate or unduly hostile reporting and allowing journalists to accompany operational officers on sensitive investigations to avoid damaging leaks which might jeopardise the operation as well as endanger police officers and members of the public.

While press officers suggested that relationships were generally based on reciprocity and trust, senior police officers argued that, from their perspective, the media held powerful resources – they held no illusion that they could control the news agenda. This may also have been due to the fact that, as the 'public face of the force' in dealing with the media, police officers often believed themselves to be personally attacked and beleaguered by the press, when investigations did not turn out as planned, or evidence of police malpractice or abuses of power were revealed.

I also follow Ericson et al (1989) in suggesting that there were two cultures of crime reporters in the United Kingdom: the inner circle, who had close affinities with police officers and often worked on tabloids that gave considerable play to the reporting of crime incidents; and the outer circle, who were either freelances or worked for alternative or broadsheet outlets, whose relations with the police were broadly but not exclusively marked by conflict and tension.

Early studies (Chibnall, 1977; Hall et al, 1978; Schlesinger and Tumber, 1994) suggest that the police were the primary sources of stories for crime reporters. However, I argue that, while this was the case for inner circle journalists, most outer circle journalists suggested that the police were rarely a primary source of stories for them. Most outer circle respondents suggested that this was due to the fact that either they, or the organisations they worked for, took an anti-police stance in their reporting. However, some outer circle journalists acknowledged that they did use unofficial police sources on occasion but were careful not to make them public, for fear of alienating their sources, who were, as one outer circle journalist described, "members of the public, victims, witnesses, relatives of people in prison, solicitors and barristers".

Similarly, inner circle journalists acknowledged that they would like to have a wider circle of contacts than they did, but were fearful of alienating the main source of what they termed "bread and butter work" from the police. I suggest that there was some tension at times between inner and outer circle journalists with the latter criticising the former for "too cosy relationships". I also suggest that, at times, the price of 'exclusive scoops' from their contact led to inner circle journalists turning a blind eye to police malpractice or abuse of power.

I explore the different kinds of 'leaks' made by individual police officers and suggest that these disclosures varied as to whether they were made to inner or outer circle journalists. I suggest that inner circle journalists were often used by individual police officers to leak information that might damage or even end a colleague's career. I argue that this was a particular problem in the MPS and was seen less in other forces – mainly because of the large number of senior officers in the MPS, all with their own personal political agenda and the desire to move up the career ladder. By contrast, outer circle journalists were often used by police officers to leak stories of police corruption, stories that would otherwise have gone unreported. However, I also suggest that these relationships could often bring benefits to both reporters and to senior officers, with outer circle journalists sometimes being able to provide MPS officers with tip-offs and valuable insider information gleaned from their underworld contacts.

While both inner and outer circle journalists were in a powerful position as the bridge or *tertius* between the police and the press, it could be argued that the negotiating power of inner circle journalists was weaker than that of their outer circle counterparts, because they were more dependent on police sources for their day-to-day crime reporting. Outer circle journalists did not have that dependence and thus, on occasion, were able to negotiate deals. In Chapter 3, I explore how these tactics of resistance were used by the press, giving an example where an outer circle journalist bartered with a senior officer, agreeing to drop a story with damaging content about the senior officer for a bigger 'scoop' and confidential information about another officer's investigation.

I extend my analysis in Chapter 4 to explore relationships between the MPS and the news media in the 1990s, 2000s and 2010s. Although a number of studies (Mawby, 2002a; Cooke and Sturges, 2009) have also examined police/news media relations in this period, this analysis is the first to date to explore in-depth the impacts of the Leveson and Filkin Reports.

First, I suggest that in the late 1990s, early 2000s and 2010s, a number of other factors further complicated the relationship between the police and the news media in the United Kingdom. These were the introduction of 24-hour rolling news and the advent of the internet. By the end of the 2000s, online websites were viewed as essential for all newspapers, major broadcasters and news agencies. At the same time, a fall in advertising revenues forced newspapers to cut back on staff. Pressures in newsrooms to produce more articles to fill more space in print and online editions led to fewer journalists gathering stories outside the office and, in its place, the rise of 'churnalism' (Davies, 2008) – journalism based on the reuse of material obtained from sources such as press releases or syndicated news reports, rather than original research. As a result, Mawby argued that these changes had weakened the ability of crime reporters 'to act as the prime conduit of policing news and to hold the police to account' (Mawby, 2010, p 1066).

I argue that another factor affected the relationship between the MPS and some sections of the national press – the continuing rise of the Murdoch-owned newspaper industry, including such titles as *The Times*, *The Sun* and the *News of the World*. Central to this, and of particular salience to MPS senior officers, was the emergence of a practice by many of these titles which Greer and McLaughlin term 'trial by media'; they describe this as a 'news media-led process by which individuals – who may or may not be publicly known – are tried and sentenced in the "court of public opinion"' (Greer and McLaughlin, 2011b, p 138). Both Silverman (2012) and Greer and McLaughlin (2011b) explore how former MPS Commissioner, Sir Ian Blair, was subjected to this process, most notably for his handling of events surrounding the killing of Jean Charles de Menezes, shot dead by firearms officers as part of the investigation into the 7/7 terrorist attacks in London in 2005.

This study extends Greer and McLaughlin's work by noting that, during this period, many respondents described how there was overt favouritism by certain officers in the Press Bureau towards journalists working for Murdoch-owned titles. Whereas in the past, inner circle journalists working for tabloid papers with a pro-police stance were rewarded by 'scoops' or 'exclusive information', these were increasingly only given to reporters working for outlets owned by News International. Journalists in post at this time suggested that MPS press officers were aware of the power of the Murdoch empire to cause reputational damage to both individual officers and to the organisation and thus gave their journalists favoured treatment to ensure positive coverage.

To sum up, while it would be true to say that the balance of power between the police and the news media obviously changed over time, with different Commissioners and press officers in post, from the point of view of police respondents interviewed for this study, the press were perhaps more powerful and in possession of more key resources than earlier studies have suggested; and that, certainly during the 1990s and 2000s, inner circle journalists working for Murdoch-owned titles were very powerful indeed.

The effect of Leveson and the advent of social media on police/media/public relations: 'bridge decay' between mainstream crime reporters and the MPS

In Chapters 4 and 5, I explore how and why the 'bridge' between the mainstream media and the Metropolitan Police collapsed. Burt argues that there are two key ways in which a relationship brokered by a *'tertius'* between two unconnected worlds can break down: a contact or network of contacts can withdraw from the relationship, or a contact can turn to 'an arbitrator ... to settle disputes' (Burt, 1992, p 234). I argue that in the aftermath of the phone-hacking scandal of 2011 and revelations of improper relations between senior MPS officers and the national press, the relationship between police and press was turned over to three separate arbitrators – namely, the inquiries headed by HMIC (HMIC, 2011), Elizabeth Filkin (Filkin, 2012) and Lord Leveson (Leveson, 2012a, 2012b). As a result of these 'arbitrations', recommending restrictions on all police contact with the press, both official and unofficial, the 'bridge' between the MPS and the press effectively 'decayed' (Burt, 2002) almost overnight.

I suggest that inner circle journalists were hardest hit by these restrictions. A number of inner circle respondents suggested that they were no longer receiving even routine stories and that, even if they were given 'exclusive' information by one of their police contacts, they would not be able to publish for fear of compromising them. I also note how both inner and outer circle journalists were called by a police officer from Scotland Yard, asking for a list of their police contacts. Some outer circle journalists believed that their ability to carry out their Fourth Estate role had been severely compromised; whereas, in the past, the majority of stories about police malpractice or corruption had come from within the organisation, these journalists believed that this channel was now firmly closed to them and that control over the flow of information to the public and to the press was very much in police hands. However, not all outer circle journalists were of the same opinion, and I note how one outer circle journalist welcomed the changes in relations between the MPS and the press, suggesting that relations between the police and some journalists were too close and needed to be regulated.

I also explore operational and press officers' perspectives on the recommendations made by the Leveson and Filkin Reports (2012). I argue that a number of press officers were unhappy about the restrictions on police/news media relations and that they had not been consulted during the Inquiries as to how they thought the police/news media relationship should be regulated. One press officer commented that the reviews in both cases had been carried out by operational staff who had no "understanding of the complexities of the police/media relationship and the benefits to both parties", and that they had not been aware of the consequences of their recommendations. A key problem for both operational and press officers was the clampdown on unofficial contact with the media. As described in Chapter 2, these off-the-record meetings were of particular importance to officers working on sensitive operations, where disclosure of information about an operation at too early a stage might jeopardise that investigation. Another concern for operational and press officers was that, as a result of these restrictions, more and more inaccurate reporting might find its way into the press. Press officers also believed that the new restrictions had made their job harder: that in a climate in which colleagues had been investigated for having a coffee with a press contact, using discretion to decide what could or could not be given as background to a journalist was a luxury they could no longer afford. Finally, police respondents expressed concern that this breakdown in communication would seriously damage police and media relations in the long term.

The second factor to hasten the decay of the bridge between the police and the press was the advent of new digital technologies and their effect on relations between the police, the public and the press. If the revelations of improper relations between the police and the media had exposed the 'rot' in the bridge between the two, I argue that the police uptake of social media led to its total collapse.

In Chapter 5, I suggest that initial uptake of social media was slow on the part of the police, but that the nationwide riots in the United Kingdom in 2011 were a turning point, as the MPS used social media not only to reassure the public but also to call for witnesses and information about the rioting. As in Chapters 2 and 3, I draw on De Certeau's work to explore the strategies of power the police are using in this new digital environment. I follow Lee and McGovern (2014) to suggest that, over the last 15 years, three key objectives have informed the MPS's official relationship with the press: promoting the public image; management of risk; and increasing trust in the organisation. I argue, as do they, that the use of social media has enabled the police to pursue all these aims more effectively than ever before. First, social media and digital platforms allow the MPS to promote the police image more effectively than ever before by releasing stories – particularly ones of police success – that traditional news outlets might overlook or fail to publish. Second, new digital technologies allow the police to communicate risks, such as weather threats or public disturbances, more directly than ever before to the public, to enlist public support for police initiatives more effectively than through the traditional news media, and to reach audiences, particularly younger people, who are more likely to engage with social media platforms. Third, I suggest that social media is used by the MPS – individual officers as well as press officers – to 'humanise' the police, though humorous posts and through regular webchats hosted by the MPS Commissioner and other senior officers.

While these platforms are allowing the MPS to communicate more directly with the public than ever before, I also argue that new digital technologies are allowing the police increasingly to bypass mainstream media and traditional crime reporters. Crime reporters reported that while crime incidents were being reported on the MPS's Twitter feed and news website, journalists were simply not being given background information to those reports, or from the officers making those tweets; and that, as a result, incidents of public interest were being reported with minimal information, or simply not being reported at all. Other crime correspondents suggested that the MPS were taking advantage of restricted press/police contact to present an unduly rosy picture of MPS successes. However, a few younger respondents were more optimistic, arguing that new technologies and digital platforms had opened new ways to research stories, to crowdsource relevant information for those stories and for the public to work with them in policing the police.

In Chapter 5, I explore the tactics of resistance used by the press, and increasingly by members of the public, to hold the police to account. An early study by Greer and McLaughlin (2010) explored how new technologies could enable members of the public to produce information that challenged 'official' police narratives. They discuss how mobile phone footage, passed to a journalist on *The Guardian* by a member of the public, showed that the death of a newspaper vendor, Ian Tomlinson, was due to police brutality rather than natural causes – the version of events given to the press by the MPS – and how, as a result, the 'news media focus at G20' changed 'from "protestor violence" to "police violence"' (Greer and McLaughlin, 2010, p 1041). The widespread use of social media platforms such as YouTube and Instagram means that members of the public can now bypass the media as well, posting real-time footage of police brutality to these platforms and pre-empting any attempts at a counter-narrative by the police or by some sections of the media. The murder of George Floyd in 2020 is a case in point. However, I follow Ellis (2021) and Richardson (2020) in arguing that the public's – and the media's – ability to hold the police to account is limited and that bystander footage of police brutality can often be dismissed as a partial representation of events. Moreover, new technologies such as body worn cameras afford the police, in turn, greater power of surveillance.

I also suggest that the lack of accountability of content posted on digital platforms is a problem for both the MPS and the legacy media and, in the United Kingdom, is exacerbated by the restrictions on contact between the police and the media. Just as mobile phones and new digital technologies have allowed members of the public and the press to share information in real time, these same devices and platforms have also contributed to the spread of misinformation or 'fake news'. I discuss how, in the aftermath of the shooting of Mark Duggan in London in 2011, rumours spread rapidly on social media about the manner of his death, including speculation about how he had been dragged from his car and shot at point blank range by a MPS officer. A journalist interviewed for this study recalled how he called the Press Bureau for guidance on how to report the story but was given no assistance and, as a result, an initial report was printed with erroneous information. The use of social media also poses problems for operational policing, with the ever-present risk that information or footage concerning an ongoing investigation, posted inadvertently by a member of the public, may compromise the investigation or even endanger officers' and citizens' lives.

To sum up, at a time of already strained relations between the police and the media in the United Kingdom, the advent of social media and digital technologies led to almost complete 'bridge decay' between the MPS and mainstream crime journalists – and I argue that new digital technologies are increasingly enabling MPS press officers to bypass mainstream media altogether (Lee and McGovern, 2014). I also suggest that for many mainstream journalists, the advent of social media has appeared to enable the MPS to exert even more control over the flow of policing information to the press and to the public. Nevertheless, I argue that the advent of new digital technologies has had some positive impact upon the field of crime and investigative journalism. One example is the citizen journalism community, *Bellingcat*, which uses video footage and other data freely available on the internet, or OSINT, to carry out major investigations. One example of *Bellingcat*'s work was the evidence they provided through OSINT to prove that Malaysian Airline Flight 17 had been brought down by Russian missiles. Another example of their work was the identification of the Russian spies who attempted the assassination of Sergei Skripal, a former Russian military officer and double agent for the British intelligence agencies, and his daughter, Yulia Skripal, in the city of Salisbury, England in 2018.

The rise of the investigative non-profits: new networks of bridges between journalists, news sources and the public

In Chapters 6 and 7, I examine the impact of three investigative non-profits and projects, *The Bristol Cable*, the *Bureau Local* and *The Bureau for Investigative Journalism*, on the field of crime and investigative reporting. I argue that, at a time when crime reporters on legacy media outlets believe they can no longer speak to truth to power as effectively as they once could, or fulfil their public service mission, the non-profits are taking on many stories the legacy media no longer have time or money to fund and, in the process, starting to transform the content of crime news.

In the United Kingdom, there are two main sources of funding for non-profit investigative news organisations: gifts from philanthropic foundations and/or wealthy individuals, and reader donations. I explore how these very different models of funding – and the fact that these non-profits are not tied in, as are many of their mainstream counterparts, to daily publishing cycles – mean that non-profits are able to carry out investigations in innovative ways. In turn, this has changed the relationship of journalists on these non-profits with their sources and with their audiences – and the nature of their storytelling.

Although they do not set out to cover 'traditional' crime stories, I argue that non-profits are nevertheless changing crime news in four respects: through a conscious attempt to give voice to under-represented or stigmatised communities and to attempt to reverse negative stereotyping of these communities often found in mainstream news; to move away from a focus on crime as discrete event to crimes of 'social harm'; a move towards discussion of causes and effects of crimes, particularly crimes of 'social harm'; and an attempt to bring about social change through their practice of 'solutions journalism'.

I argue that there are three key practices in relation to which journalists on non-profits broadly differ from their mainstream counterparts. The first is the practice of 'engaged journalism' or 'a range of practices that aim to build relationships between journalists and the public and involve the public in the process of cocreating journalism' (Wenzel, 2020, p 4). This also extends to the process of collaboration and sharing of news stories with mainstream outlets. The second is through the practice of transparency, or the publication of data and information on sources used in the course of investigations, enabling the public not only to understand reporters' methodologies, but also to use these resources to contribute themselves to investigations. The third way in which journalists on non-profits broadly differ from mainstream investigative journalism is through the practice of 'solutions journalism' or the practice of 'critically explor[ing] a response to a problem – looking at what is working or at how it works – including its limitations' (Wenzel, 2020, p 8). It is an approach that, Wenzel (2020) suggests, moves beyond the function of journalism as 'informing' citizens, to offer what she terms 'the whole story', that is to say, 'not only spotlighting social ills but also highlighting how they are being addressed' (Wenzel, 2020, p 8).

A more inclusive form of reporting and repairing representational harm

On *The Bristol Cable*, instead of being a 'bridge' between news sources and the public, the journalist is only one actor in a larger network where other actors, such as local citizens and community groups, have agency. In this kind of reporting, there is a multi-participatory flow of information through a network of 'bridges' between residents, local community organisations and local media who are all 'storytelling actors' involved in circulating stories about their community. In this study, journalists from *The Bristol Cable* aim to engage communities in the 'process of reimagining local news and information', offering 'shared spaces for dialogue and action on community issues' (Wenzel, 2020, p 4). Such a practice is known as 'engaged journalism' or 'a range of practices that aim to build relationships between journalists and the public and involve the public in the process of circuiting journalism' (Wenzel, 2020, p 4).

I argue that a key aim for *The Bristol Cable*, and one of the key ways in which it is changing the content of crime and investigative news reporting, is to give a voice to under-represented and marginalised communities that are frequently negatively portrayed in the legacy media. I suggest that *The Bristol Cable* achieves this aim in a number of ways: by talking to members of the public and holding open meetings with various community groups, to find out what issues concern them most and which stories are not being told, but also by sharing their journalistic power with members of the public and involving them at every stage of the process – thus creating 'storytelling islands'. As I have noted in Chapter 7, one reason for negative media coverage of certain neighbourhoods was because there were often weak links between communities and local media; that in some areas, where local newspapers had been closed down, stories were often told by 'parachuting' outsiders 'reporting on moments of crisis' and that such disconnects 'reinforced inequitable power structures by continuing to circulate stigmatizing narratives that contributed to the marginalization of communities' (Wenzel, 2020, p 27). In addition, journalists rarely had the time to forge relationships with residents and instead continued to rely on the same, often privileged sources. By contrast I explore how, by not being tied into a daily publishing cycle or creating journalism for-profit, journalists on *The Bristol Cable* have been able to take time to build relationships of trust and open up their storytelling to feature a wider range of perspectives, as in their coverage of the Traveller community. Stories included chronic lack of sites for Travellers, health and education inequalities, racist profiling of communities by the police and instances of hate crime directed at Travellers in Bristol – and their own criticisms of media representation of these communities.

Crimes of 'social harm'

I suggest that the storytelling model is very different on *The Bureau for Investigative Journalism*; unlike the *Cable*, which was started by a group of friends involved in activism and without prior journalistic experience, most of the journalists on both *The Bureau for Investigative Journalism* and the *Bureau Local* have extensive high-level journalistic backgrounds and left those jobs to set up or work on these non-profits. On *The Bureau for Investigative Journalism*, the journalist is still a 'bridge' between news sources and the public and the majority of stories originate within the *Bureau*'s team, although the public are often involved when journalists need to crowdsource information. On the *Bureau Local*, the model of storytelling is a cross between that of *The Bristol Cable* and *The Bureau for Investigative Journalism* – some stories come from within the team, others from regular 'open' newsroom sessions with members of the public. However, unlike *The Bristol Cable*, the *Bureau Local* does not involve members of the public in the actual reporting of stories. Additionally, while *The Bristol Cable* mainly produces stories for its own site and for a predominantly local audience, both *The Bureau of Investigative Journalism* and the *Bureau Local* produce news to be shared with other outlets, to increase the reach of their stories. These outlets include the *New York Times*, *Al Jazeera* and *Newsweek*, and many other national and international titles and broadcasters have featured their work.

While Konieczna (2018) suggests that the practice of news-sharing 'limits what the news nonprofits are able to do, because it has them forever looking to their counterparts in commercial journalism' (Konieczna, 2018, p 206), I argue that this is not necessarily the case for the *Bureau Local* and *The Bureau for Investigative Journalism*. I suggest that, while the editors obviously are mindful as to where they might publish their work more widely, the focus of their stories is radically different to most mainstream organisations. Unlike traditional crime reporters, whose primary source for stories is the police, leading to a focus on crime as a violation of the law or crime as a specific event, I argue that *The Bureau for Investigative Journalism* and the *Bureau Local* do not use the police as a primary source and instead have taken a conscious stance to focus on what they term 'systemic harms' or crimes of 'social harm' (Hillyard and Tombs, 2005). Their aim is to investigate stories that rarely receive attention from mainstream media, such as work accidents, pollution of the environment, white-collar crime, corporate crime and abuse of human rights, through the use of big data and OSINT. I argue that these crimes were traditionally difficult to research – that, in the case of corporate crime and white collar crime, reporters were dependent on inside information, developing whistleblowers and collecting testimonies. Such work was painstaking and time consuming and, as a result, these crimes are often under-reported by legacy media (Ericson et al, 1991). However, over the last ten years, the advent of companies such as OpenCorporates – the largest open database of companies in the world – has allowed organisations such as *The Bureau for Investigative Journalism* to carry out investigations into 'invisible' crimes of the powerful, such as money-laundering, organised crime and corruption.

Causes and effects of crimes

I argue that the practice of transparency – the sharing of data and information on sources used in the course of investigations – also allows a discussion of causes and effects of crime in the reporting by *The Bureau for Investigative Journalism* and the *Bureau Local*. For the *Bureau Local*'s 'Dying Homeless' project, these resources included a collaborative database of deaths in England and Northern Ireland from 2017 onwards; a 'reporting recipe' (or a how-to guide) explaining how the *Bureau Local* have used that data, including key quotes and extracts from individuals involved in the project; and a description of the methodology used by the *Bureau Local*. The website explains how the team analysed their findings and gives suggestions as to how members of the public can contribute to the project. I discuss how these suggestions include: checking in the Bureau's database for local deaths of homeless people; checking if the relevant council has undertaken a review of the death; if not, asking councils if they will undertake reviews in the future;

and contacting homelessness charities to interview them about these issues. Such a practice sets up multiple flows of information between journalists at the *Bureau Local*, reporters for other media organisations, community organisations, charities and members of the public, and moves beyond traditional models of campaigning journalism.

Solutions journalism

I argue that the final way that the non-profits are changing the remit of crime news is through their practice of solutions journalism. The goal of solutions journalism is 'not to advocate for a particular solution but rather to critically explore a response to a problem – looking at what is working or at how it works – including its limitations' (Wenzel, 2020, p 8). The practice challenges the 'theory of change of watchdog journalism' (Wenzel, 2020, p 9) and the idea that by exposing social ills and harms to the public, change and reform will inevitably follow. I argue that the final aim of the non-profits in this study is not merely to inform the public but to bring about social change and explore this through a case study of the *Bureau Local*'s investigations, 'Dying Homeless', on deaths of homeless people in the United Kingdom, and 'Locked Out', the follow-up investigation into affordable rental properties in the United Kingdom for those on low salaries or in receipt of housing benefit.

I discuss how, in both investigations, the *Bureau Local* worked with individuals directly affected by these social problems to feed back their findings to policymakers and politicians. In the case of the 'Dying Homeless' investigation, significant changes were made: the Office of National Statistics and the National Records of Scotland began to record data of deaths of homeless people, to highlight where these problems were most acute.

Although Konieczna (2018) and Deuze and Witschge (2020) both share concerns that, despite different working models, the content of non-profits' reporting is not vastly different to that produced by their legacy media counterparts, I suggest that this is not the case for the non-profits included in this study. I argue that, particularly in the cases of the *Bureau Local* and *The Bureau for Investigative Journalism*, non-profits are 'repairing' (Konieczna, 2018) the field of crime journalism by sharing their work with bigger outlets and feeding these very different types of crime narrative back into the legacy media. In November 2021, *The Bureau for Investigative Journalism* was nominated for outstanding reporting in several categories at the forthcoming British Journalism Awards, alongside more established organisations such as the BBC, *The Guardian*, *The Telegraph* and *The Sun*, demonstrating not only the esteem in which the *Bureau*'s work is held by its peers but also how the *Bureau* is increasingly being seen as an important player in journalism more generally. Even, if at this stage, *The Bureau for Investigative Journalism* and the

Bureau Local are not well known by the general public, the chances are high that many people have read their work in more mainstream outlets. In short, this study suggests that crime and investigative journalism is not on its way out but is being 'reimagined and creatively and passionately practiced in lots of different ways' (Deuze and Witschge, 2020, p 16) by these non-profits.

Looking to the future

This book has been a study of crime and investigative journalism's relationship with power – it has explored how crime and investigative journalists come to know what they do; whose perspectives are privileged, whose are omitted and why; what kinds of stories are they telling and for whom; who benefits from these narratives; and what kind of role should journalists play in society.

The book has been written at a time when, as Callison and Young note in their study of journalism's long-standing representational harms, 'the practice of journalism increasingly confronts wide and sustained criticism – and its crisis' (Callison and Young, 2020, p 200). They argue that the criticism and/ or perceived crisis in journalism have been largely centred around failing economic models, the advent of digital technologies and competition with newer and larger media platforms such as Facebook and Google. Yet they suggest that, by and large, journalism studies have not to date tackled issues of 'journalism's founding ideals and methods related to who can speak for whom, how and why' (Callison and Young, 2020, p 201) and representational harms of under-represented and/or stigmatised communities. They suggest that most of the current work in journalism studies, particularly on the crisis in the field and on new entrants such as the non-profits featured in this book, instead 'reflects the ways in which journalists have been negotiating with professional norms and practices, experimenting and inventing new ways of responding to and contending with these multiple reckonings facing journalism' (Callison and Young, 2020, p 201).

These representational harms, the dominance of frames in crime reporting that ignore, criticise or blame minority communities (Wykes, 2001; Jewkes, 2004, 2011; Greer and Jewkes, 2005), and the ways in which crime stories reinforce structural inequities and identities such as gendered or racist stereotypes, have long been the concern of media criminologists. This book aims to make a meaningful contribution to both media criminology and journalism studies, in that it seeks to understand the power relations between journalists and sources, and how production processes, personal ideologies and journalistic practices such as the practice of objectivity shape these stories. It also seeks to explore how non-profits, through their very different working practices and the very different ideologies of those working in these organisations, have helped to shape very different crime narratives – an area which has not yet been explored in media criminology.

Although there is much to be optimistic about in terms of the future of crime and investigative reporting, and the ways in which non-profits are changing the remit of crime news, there remains a major concern. The non-profits are indeed speaking truth to power to many organisations and government bodies, with the aim of sparking societal change, but they are not speaking truth to power to the police – and nor are legacy media outlets.

In 2017, I wrote an article which was published in *The British Journal of Criminology*, discussing the breakdown in relations between the MPS and the national news media. In it, I suggested that there needed to be a return to former relations of trust and reciprocity between the two parties, enabling national crime reporters once more to carry out their Fourth Estate role. Further research for this book has convinced me that that this is an incomplete and too simplistic view of the situation.

Although former relations between the police and the press brought undoubted benefits to both sides, these relations also descended, as I have described, into unorthodox and, at times, bordering on criminal behaviour. At the time of the Filkin and Leveson Reports (2012), the press argued that a free flow of information was essential for them to carry out their watchdog role, and that many stories of police abuses, corruption and botched investigations had come from unofficial sources. Yet, it is also true to say that, at times, police officers used the press for more nefarious reasons, such as to air grievances or to bring about the downfall of certain colleagues.

The problem was – and is – not all on the police side. Legacy crime reporting is in many respects seriously flawed. Callison and Young comment that journalism 'legitimizes, amplifies, and reinforces some experts, views, and perceptions of events and problems in the world – and their potential range of solutions – over *other* experts, views, and perceptions even while they obscure how it is they arrived at their own perceptions' (Callison and Young, 2020, p 11). Through these practices, we have seen how crime journalists not only produce news that focuses on the sensational and the violent, without questioning causes, effects or solutions; but also represent certain marginalised communities in ways that often maintain and reinforce existing power relations.

The non-profits have shown that there are other ways of reporting, of positioning themselves as journalists in relations to the communities they are reporting upon, and other ways of telling stories that are less harmful to marginalised communities. Legacy crime journalists need to be more critical of the systems they are operating within, the kinds of experts they are using, as well as what kinds of expertise they are deploying. They also need to be more critical – now, more than ever, with limited access to sources – of police accounts. Sometimes such reports are seriously flawed and sometimes they reveal serious bias.

In March 2021, a number of demonstrations took place around the country in response to the proposed Police, Crime, Sentencing and Courts Bill. One of the proposals in this Bill gives police forces broad authority to place restrictions on protests and public assembly. Under this Bill, police forces will be allowed to criminalise protests they believe constitute a 'public nuisance', including imposing starting and finishing times and noise limits, and will be able to consider actions by one individual as 'protests' under provisions of the Bill (Casciani, 2021). While a riot taking place on Sunday 21 March resulted in clashes between the police and demonstrators, Matty Edwards from *The Bristol Cable* reported in *The Guardian* on Sunday 28 March that the subsequent demonstrations on Tuesday 23 March and Friday 26 March, reported by the national press very much in the same vein, in fact 'were very different events' (Edwards, 2021). As an eyewitness, along with other colleagues from *The Bristol Cable*, he suggested that protestors on both nights were determined to 'make the demonstration peaceful' (Edwards, 2021). On the Friday night, he noted that: 'At around 10pm, however, police forcefully advanced into the sitting crowd, hitting them with riot shields and batons. My colleagues filmed protesters being struck repeatedly by riot shields and knocked to the ground. A number of protesters suffered head wounds' (Edwards, 2021). Edwards reports Bristol's Labour mayor, Marvin Rees, as stating 'that the actions of some protesters on Friday had been "politically illiterate and strategically inept", and [he] declined to condemn the police's tactics' (Edwards, 2021); but Edwards suggests that 'a 10-minute scan of excellent reporting from multiple media sources in Bristol would have given any national journalist a more complete picture of what happened' (Edwards, 2021) and that incomplete coverage runs the risk of misleading the national public.

More openness between the police and the media seems to be essential – for journalists, so that they can carry out their jobs more efficiently, with fewer mistakes in reporting; for the public, so that they are better and more accurately informed; but also for the police themselves.

In 1989, Ericson et al suggested that 'most sources do not have the option of not co-operating with journalists in general' (Ericson et al, 1989, p 381). In a post-internet age, this is no longer true and the police no longer need to rely on the press to communicate effectively with the public or to convey news about their work. But as Ericson et al also note, a source 'that is expected to engage the public conversation but fails to do so sows the seeds of long-term hostile relations with journalists, and sometimes with members of other source organizations' (Ericson et al, 1989, p 381).

I would add the general public to that list. By keeping journalists at bay, the MPS is not only hindering the press in acting as 'the eyes and ears of the public' (Leveson, 2012b, p 20), but creating a perception that it is an organisation with much to hide and an organisation that thrives on secrecy. Improvements in communication between the police and the press are sorely needed – but sadly, at the present time, there seems little evidence to suggest that they will be forthcoming.

Notes

Chapter 1

1   *Bellingcat* is a Netherlands-based investigative journalism website that specialises in fact-checking and open-source intelligence. It was founded by British journalist and former blogger Eliot Higgins in July 2014.

Chapter 2

1   The Flying Squad is a specialist branch of the Metropolitan Police that investigates armed and organised crime.

2   Counter Terrorism is a Specialist Operations branch of London's Metropolitan Police Service, formed to respond to terrorist activities within the capital and the surrounding areas.

3   The Brixton riot of 1985 started on 28 September in Lambeth in South London. It was sparked by the accidental shooting of Dorothy 'Cherry' Groce by the Metropolitan Police, while they sought her 21-year-old son Michael Groce in relation to a robbery and suspected firearms offence; they believed Michael Groce was hiding in his mother's home.

4   Muriel McKay (1914–70) was an Australian woman who was kidnapped on 29 December 1969 and presumed murdered in the first few days of 1970.

5   Keith Rupert Murdoch AC KCSG is an Australian born American billionaire businessman, media tycoon and investor. Through his company News Corp, he is the owner of hundreds of local, national and international publishing outlets around the world, including in the UK (*The Sun* and *The Times*), in Australia (*The Daily Telegraph*, *Herald Sun* and *The Australian*), in the US (*The Wall Street Journal* and the *New York Post*), book publisher HarperCollins, and the television broadcasting channels Sky News Australia and Fox News (through the Fox Corporation). He was also the owner of Sky (until 2018), 21st Century Fox (until 2019), and the now-defunct *News of the World*.

6   Fred West, a Gloucestershire builder, was accused of committing 12 murders between 1971 and 1994. The remains of nine victims were found at the family home. West committed suicide before his trial, but his wife, Rose, was convicted of ten murders and sentenced to life imprisonment.

Chapter 3

1   The miners' strike of 1984–5 in Britain was a major industrial action that aimed to prevent colliery closures proposed by the Conservative government.

2   The poll tax riots were a series of riots in British towns and cities during protests against the Community Charge (commonly known as the 'poll tax') introduced by the Conservative government.

3   The 'Guildford Four' and the 'Birmingham Six' refer to two groups who were wrongly convicted of bombings attributed to the Provisional Irish Republican Army. The 'Tottenham Three' refers to three individuals whose convictions for the murder of PC Keith Henry Blakelock during rioting at the Broadwater Farm housing estate were subsequently quashed.

Chapter 4

1   German Gorbuntsov is a Russian businessman, banker and philanthropist. In 2012, he survived an attempt on his life in Central London which, according to *The Guardian*, originated from the Solntsevskaya Bratva organised crime syndicate in Moscow.

2 Government Communications Headquarters, commonly known as GCHQ, is an intelligence and security organisation responsible for providing signals intelligence and information assurance to the government and armed forces of the United Kingdom.

Chapter 5

1 In October 2010, three G4S guards restrained and held down 46-year-old Angolan deportee Jimmy Mubenga on departing British Airways flight 77, at Heathrow Airport. Security guards kept him restrained in his seat as he began shouting and seeking to resist his deportation. Police and paramedics were called when Mubenga lost consciousness. Mubenga was pronounced dead later that evening at Hillingdon hospital. Passengers reported hearing cries of "don't do this" and "they are trying to kill me".

2 In his (2021) work, Ellis explains that he uses the LGBTQI (lesbian, gay, bisexual, transgender, queer and intersex) initialism to encompass sexual orientation and gender identity communities. He notes that this initialism 'is intended to be inclusive of the range of perspectives and lived experience across these communities and at the same time reflects the limitations of such intitialisms in capturing all of those lived experiences' (Ellis, 2021, p 1).

3 Black Lives Matter is a decentralised political and social movement protesting against incidents of police brutality and all racially motivated violence against Black people.

4 The Independent Police Complaints Commission was a non-departmental public body in England and Wales responsible for overseeing the system for handling complaints made against police forces in England and Wales. On 8 January 2018, the IPCC was replaced by the Independent Office for Police Conduct (IOPC).

5 The IOPC oversees the police complaints system in England and Wales.

Chapter 6

1 *Mother Jones* is an American magazine that focuses on news, commentary and investigative reporting on topics including politics, the environment, human rights, health and culture. Its political inclination is variously described as either liberal or progressive.

2 *The Center for Investigative Reporting* is an American non-profit news organisation. It is known for reporting that reveals inequities, abuse and corruption, and holds those responsible accountable.

3 *ProPublica*, legally Pro Publica, Inc., is a non-profit organisation based in New York City. It is a newsroom that aims to produce investigative journalism in the public interest.

4 The *International Consortium of Investigative Journalists*, legally International Consortium of Investigative Journalists, Inc., is an independent global network of 280 investigative journalists and over 100 media organisations spanning more than 100 countries.

References

Albeanu, C. (2016) 'Inside the organisations plugging the gap', in J. Mair, T. Clark, N. Fowler, R. Snoddy and R. Tait (eds) *Last Words? How Can Journalism Survive the Decline of Print?*, Bury St Edmunds: Abramis, pp 327–32

Alejandro, J. (2010) *Journalism in the Age of Social Media*, Oxford: Reuters Institute for the Study of Journalism

Alfter, B. (2016) 'Cross-border collaborative journalism: Why journalists and scholars should talk about an emerging method', *Journal of Applied Journalism & Media Studies*, 5(2): 297–311

Alibhai-Brown, Y. (1998) 'The media and race relations', in T. Blackstone, B. Parekh and P. Sanders (eds) *Race Relations in Britain: A Developing Agenda*, London: Routledge, pp 111–27

Allen, H. (1987) *Justice Unbalanced*, Milton Keynes: Open University Press

Anderson, C.W. (2013) *Rebuilding the News: Metropolitan Journalism in the Digital Age*, Philadelphia: Temple University Press

Atkin, C.K., Burgoon, J.K. and Burgoon, M. (1983) 'How journalists perceive the reading audience', *Newspaper Research Journal*, 4(2): 51–63

Baack, S. (2018) *Knowing what Counts: How Journalists and Civic Technologists Use and Imagine Data*, Groningen: RUG

Bakir, V., Feilzer, M. and McStay, A. (2017) 'Veillance and transparency: A critical examination of mutual watching in the post-Snowden, Big Data era', *Big Data & Society*, March 2017, DOI: 10.1177/2053951717698996

Ball-Rokeach, S.J., Kim, Y.-C. and Matei, S. (2001) 'Storytelling neighborhood: Paths to belonging in diverse urban environments', *Communication Research*, 28(4): 392–428

BBC (2012) 'Filkin report: Police warned over press links', *BBC News website*, 4 January

Beck, U. (1992) *Risk Society: Towards a New Modernity*, London: Sage

Becker, H.S. (1967) 'Whose side are we on?', *Social Problems*, 14(3): 239–47

Becker, H.S. (2007) *Telling About Society*, Chicago: Chicago University Press

Beckett, C. (2016) *Fanning the Flames: Reporting Terror in a Networked World*, New York: Tow Center for Digital Journalism, Columbia Journalism School

Beckett, C. (2018) 'The power of journalism: Back to the future of news', in C. Foster-Gilbert (ed) *The Power of Journalists*, London: Haus Publishing, pp 51–60

Beetham, D. (1991/2013) *The Legitimation of Power*, Basingstoke: Palgrave Macmillan

Benson, R. (2018) 'Can foundations solve the journalism crisis?', *Journalism*, 19(8): 1059–77

Berger, P. and Luckmann, T. (1967) *The Social Construction of Reality*, London: Allen Lane

Birnbauer, B. (2019) *The Rise of Nonprofit Investigative Journalism in the United States*, New York: Routledge

Bivens, R.K. (2008) 'The internet, mobile phones and blogging: How new media are transforming traditional journalism', *Journalism Practice*, 2(1): 113–29

Bizzi, L. (2013) 'The dark side of structural holes: A multilevel investigation', *Journal of Management*, 39(6): 1554–78

Bock, M.A. (2016) 'Film the police! Cop-watching and its embodied narratives', *Journal of Communication*, 66(1): 13–34

Boczkowski, P.J. and Mitchelstein, E. (2017) 'Scholarship on online journalism: Roads traveled and pathways ahead', in P.J. Boczkowski and C.W. Anderson (eds) *Remaking the News: Essays on the Future of Journalism Scholarship in the Digital Age*, Cambridge, MA: MIT Press, pp 15–26

Booth, A. (1989) *Raising the Roof on Housing Myths*, Leeds: Shelter

Bowling, B., Reiner, R. and Sheptycki, J. (2019) *The Politics of the Police* (5th edn), Oxford: Oxford University Press

Bradford, B., Jackson, J. and Stanko, E. (2009) 'Contact and confidence: Revisiting the impact of public encounters with the police', *Policing and Society*, 19(1): 20–46

Brainard, L.A. and McNutt, J.G. (2010) 'Virtual government and citizen relations', *Administration and Society*, 42(7): 836–58

Bullock, K. (2018) 'The police use of social media: Transformation or normalisation?', *Social Policy & Society*, 17(2): 245–58

Burt, R.S. (1992) *Structural Holes: The Social Structure of Competition*, Cambridge, MA: Harvard University Press

Burt, R.S. (1997) 'The contingent value of social capital', *Administrative Science Quarterly*, 42(2): 339–65

Burt, R.S. (2002) 'Bridge decay', *Social Networks*, 24(4): 333–63

Burt, R.S. (2004) 'Structural holes and good ideas', *American Journal of Sociology*, 110(2): 349–99

Burt, R.S. (2007) 'Secondhand brokerage: Evidence of the importance of local structure for managers, bankers, and analysts', *Academy of Management Journal*, 50(1): 119–48

Busby, M. (2021) 'Families of citizens dying after contact with police still await justice', *The Guardian*, 18 January

Callison, C. and Young, M.L. (2020) *Reckoning: Journalism's Limits and Possibilities*, New York: Oxford University Press

Campbell, D. (2013) 'Cops and hacks: Is Leveson the end of a beautiful friendship?', in J. Mair (ed) *After Leveson? The Future for British Journalism*, Bury St Edmunds: Abramis, pp 195–200

Campbell, D. (2016) *We'll All Be Murdered in Our Beds! The Shocking History of Crime Reporting in Britain*, London: Elliott and Thompson

Canella, G. (2021) 'Journalistic power: Constructing the "truth" and the economics of objectivity', *Journalism Practice*, DOI: 10.1080/17512786.2021.1914708

Cantwell-Corn, A. and Aviram, A. (2019) 'Finally exposed: How Lopresti ice cream boss kept men in slave-like conditions, tenants and families in squalor. But people spoke out', *The Bristol Cable*, 23 May

Carlen, P. (1988) *Women, Crime and Poverty*, Milton Keynes: Open University Press

Carvajal, M., García-Avilés, J.A. and González, J.L. (2012) 'Crowdfunding and non-profit media: The emergence of new models for public interest journalism', *Journalism Practice*, 6(5–6): 638–47

Casciani, D. (2021) 'What is the police, crime, sentencing and courts bill and how will it change protests?', *BBC News website*, 22 March

Chappell, T. and Rispoli, M. (2020) 'Defund the crime beat', *NiemanLab*, December

Chibnall, S. (1977) *Law-and-Order News: An Analysis of Crime Reporting in the British Press* (2003 edn), London: Routledge

Chibnall, S. (1979) 'The Metropolitan Police and the news media', in S. Holdaway (ed) *The British Police*, London: Edward Arnold, pp 135–49

Christmas, L. (1997) *Chaps of Both Sexes*, Devizes: BT Forum

Clifford, K. and White, R.D. (2017) *Media and Crime: Content, Context and Consequence*, South Melbourne: Oxford University Press

Colbran, M.P. (2017) 'Leveson five years on: The effect of the Leveson and Filkin Reports on relations between the Metropolitan Police and the national news media', *The British Journal of Criminology*, 57(6): 1502–19.

Colbran, M.P. (2020) 'Policing, social media and the new media landscape: Can the police and the traditional media ever successfully bypass each other?', *Policing and Society*, 30(3): 295–309

Coogans, H. (2021) 'How journalists tracked down missing data to change the conversation on homelessness', *Global Investigative Journalism Network*, 21 April

Cooke, L. and Sturges, P. (2009) 'Police and media relations in an era of freedom of information', *Policing and Society*, 19(4): 406–24

Costera Meijer, I. (2001) 'The public quality of popular journalism: Developing a normative framework', *Journalism Studies*, 2(2): 189–205

Crump, J. (2011) 'What are the police doing on Twitter? Social media, the police and the public', *Policy & Internet*, 3(4): 1–27

Davies, G. (2015) 'Public interest stories are going unreported after launch of Met's own news website and "good news" PR teams', *Press Gazette*, 6 May

Davies, N. (1999) 'The decline of the court reporter', *The Guardian*, 11 January

Davies, N. (2008) *Flat Earth News*, London: Vintage

Davies, N. (2014) *Hack Attack: How the Truth Caught Up with Rupert Murdoch*, London: Vintage

De Certeau, M. (1984) *The Practice of Everyday Life*, Berkeley and Los Angeles: University of California Press

Dean, M. (2012) *Democracy Under Attack: How the Media Distort Policy and Politics*, Bristol: Policy Press

Delanty, G. (2003) *Community*, London: Routledge

Denef, S., Bayerl, P.S. and Kaptein, N. (2013) *Social Media and the Police: Tweeting Practices of British Police Forces during the August 2011 Riots*, Fraunhofer Institute for Applied Information Technology, DOI: 10.1145/2470654.2466477

Deuze, M. and Witschge, T. (2020) *Beyond Journalism*, Cambridge: Polity Press

Doyle, A. (2011) 'Revisiting the synopticon: Reconsidering Mathiesen's "The Viewer Society" in the age of Web 2.0', *Theoretical Criminology*, 15(3): 283–99

Edwards, M. (2021) 'The police have their version of the Bristol protests: Locals tell a different story', *The Guardian*, 28 March

Elliott-Cooper, A. (2021) *Black Resistance to British Policing*, Manchester: Manchester University Press

Ellis, J. and McGovern, A. (2016) 'The end of symbiosis? Australia police-media relations in the digital age', *Policing and Society*, 26(8): 944–62

Ellis, J.R. (2020) 'More than a trivial pursuit: Public order policing narratives and the "social media test"', *Crime Media Culture*, 17(2): 185–207

Ellis, J.R. (2021) *Policing Legitimacy: Social Media, Scandal and Sexual Citizenship*, Cham: Springer

Emsley, C. (1996) *The English Police: A Political and Social History* (2nd edn), London: Longman

Ericson, R.V. (1995) 'The news media and account ability in criminal justice', in P. Stenning (ed) *Accountability for Criminal Justice*, Toronto: University of Toronto Press, pp 135–61

Ericson, R.V., Baranek, P.M. and Chan, J.B.L. (1987) *Visualising Deviance: A Study of News Organization*, Milton Keynes: Open University Press

Ericson, R.V., Baranek, P.M. and Chan, J.B.L. (1989) *Negotiating Control: A Study of News Sources*, Toronto: University of Toronto Press

Ericson, R.V., Baranek, P.M. and Chan, J.B.L. (1991) *Representing Order: Crime, Law and Justice in the News Media*, Milton Keynes: Open University Press

Erikson, K.T. (1966) *Wayward Puritans: A Study in the Sociology of Deviance*, New York: John Wiley and Sons

Evans-Pritchard, E.E. (1940) *The Nuer*, New York: Oxford University Press

Faludi, S. (1992) *Backlash: The Undeclared War Against Women*, London: Chatto & Windus

Fedorcio, R. (2012) 'Metropolitan Police Service Media Relations Standard Operating Procedure, 5 July 2006', included within Exhibit DF/2, provided to Leveson Inquiry by Dick Fedorcio

Fenton, N. (2009) *New Media, Old News: Journalism and Democracy in the Digital Age*, London: Sage

Filkin, E. (2012) *The Ethical Issues Arising from the Relationship Between Police and Media: Advice to the Commissioner of Police of the Metropolis and his Management Board*, London: MPS

Fleming, L., Mingo, S. and Chen, D. (2007) 'Collaborative brokerage, generative creativity, and creative success', *Administrative Science Quarterly*, 52(3): 443–75

Freckelton, I. (1988) 'Sensation and symbiosis' in I. Freckelton and H. Selby (eds) *Police in Our Society*, Sydney: Butterworths, pp 57–84

Galtung, J. (1986) 'On the role of the media in worldwide security and peace', in T. Varis (ed) *Peace and Communication*, San Jose, Costa Rica: Universidad para La Paz, pp 249–66

Gelsthorpe, L. and Morris, A. (eds) (1990) *Feminist Perspectives in Criminology*, Milton Keynes: Open University Press

Gilley, B. (2009) *The Right to Rule: How States Win and Lose Legitimacy*, New York: Columbia University Press

Goffman, E. (1959) *The Presentation of Self in Everyday Life*, New York: Doubleday

Goldsmith, A.J. (2010) 'Policing's new visibility', *The British Journal of Criminology*, 50(5): 914–34

Granovetter, M.S. (1973) 'The strength of weak ties', *American Journal of Sociology*, 78(6): 1360–80

Greer, C. (2010a) 'Introduction' and chapter commentaries in C. Greer (ed) *Crime and Media: A Reader*, Abingdon: Routledge, pp 1–8, 201–2, 264–5

Greer, C. (2010b) 'News media criminology', in E. McLaughlin and T. Newburn (eds) *The SAGE Handbook of Criminological Theory*, London: Sage Publications, pp 490–513

Greer, C. and Jewkes, Y. (2005) 'Extremes of otherness: Media images of social exclusion', *Social Justice*, 32(1): 20–31

Greer, C. and McLaughlin, E. (2010) 'We predict a riot? Public order policing, new media environments and the rise of the citizen journalist', *The British Journal of Criminology*, 50(6): 1041–59

Greer, C. and McLaughlin, E. (2011a) '"Trial by media": Policing, the 24–7 news mediasphere, and the "politics of outrage"', *Theoretical Criminology*, 15(1): 23–46

Greer, C. and McLaughlin, E. (2011b) 'Trial by media: Riots, looting, gangs and mediatised police chiefs', in T. Newburn and J. Peay (eds) *Policing: Politics, Culture and Control*, Oxford: Hart Publishing, pp 135–53

Greer, C. and McLaughlin, E. (2012) 'Media justice: Madeleine McCann, intermediatization and "trial by media" in the British press', *Theoretical Criminology*, 16(4): 395–416

Greer, C. and McLaughlin, E. (2013) 'The Sir Jimmy Savile scandal: Child sexual abuse and institutional denial at the BBC', *Crime, Media, Culture*, 9(3): 243–63

Greer, C. and McLaughlin, E. (2015) 'The return of the repressed: Secrets, lies, denial and "historical" institutional child sexual abuse scandals', in D. Whyte (ed) *How Corrupt is Britain?*, London: Pluto, pp 113–23

Greer, C. and McLaughlin, E. (2016) 'Theorizing institutional scandal and the regulatory state', *Theoretical Criminology*, DOI: 10.1177/1362480616645648

Greer, C. and McLaughlin, E. (2017) 'News power, crime and media justice', in A. Liebling, S. Maruna and L. McAra (eds) *The Oxford Handbook of Criminology* (6th edn), Oxford: Oxford University Press, pp 260–83

Groot Kormelink, T. and Costera Meijer, I. (2018) 'What clicks actually mean: Exploring digital news user practices', *Journalism*, 19(5): 668–83

The Guardian (2015) 'Hacking investigations cost Met police £41.3m', 11 December

Hall, S., Critcher, C., Jefferson, T., Clarke, J. and Roberts, B. (1978) *Policing the Crisis: Mugging, the State, and Law and Order*, London: Macmillan

Halliday, J. (2011) 'Tory MP Louise Mensch backs social network blackouts during civil unrest', *The Guardian*, 12 August

Hamada, R. (2021) 'Grassroots operations', in H. De Burgh and P. Lashmar (eds) *Investigative Journalism* (3rd edn), Abingdon: Routledge, pp 111–22

Heidensohn, F. (1985) *Women and Crime*, New York: New York University Press

Heidensohn, F. (2000) *Sexual Politics and Social Control*, Milton Keynes: Open University Press

Hillyard, P. and Tombs, S. (2005) 'Beyond criminology?', in W. McMahon (ed) *Criminal Obsessions: Why Harm Matters More Than Crime* (2nd edn), London: Centre for Crime and Justice Studies, pp 6–23

Hillyard, P. and Tombs, S. (2017) 'Social harm and zemiology', in A. Liebling, S. Maruna and L. McAra (eds) *The Oxford Handbook of Criminology* (6th edn), Oxford: Oxford University Press, pp 284–305

HMIC (2011) *Without Fear or Favour: A Review of Police Relationships*, London: HMIC

Hockin, S.M. and Brunson, R.K. (2018) 'The revolution might not be televised (but it will be lived streamed): Future directions for research on police-minority relations', *Race and Justice*, 8(3): 199–215

Home Office (2004) *Building Communities, Beating Crime: A Better Police Service for the 21st Century*, Norwich: The Stationery Office

Hough, M., Jackson, J., Bradford, B., Myhill, A. and Quinton, P. (2010) 'Procedural justice, trust and institutional legitimacy', *Policing: A Journal of Policy and Practice*, 4(3): 203–10

Hu, X. and Lovrich, N.P. (2019) 'Small police agency use of social media: Positive and negative outcomes noted in a case study', *Policing: A Journal of Policy and Practice*, DOI:10.1093/police/paz077

Innes, M. (1999) 'The media as an investigative resource in murder enquiries', *The British Journal of Criminology*, 39(2): 269–86

IPCC (2007) *Independent Police Complaints Commission Stockwell 2 Report: An Investigation into Complaints About the Metropolitan Police's Handling of Public Statements Following the Shooting of Jean Charles de Menezes on 22 July 2005*, London: IPCC

Jamieson, S. (2016) 'Social media is the "new neighbourhood policing" says prize-winning tweeting officer', *Daily Telegraph*, 5 January

Jewkes, Y. (2004) *Media & Crime*, London: Sage

Jewkes, Y. (2011) *Media & Crime* (2nd edn), London: Sage

Kahn, G. (2017) 'Transparency is the new objectivity', *MediaShift*, 27 September

Kalish, L. (2019) 'Social media as image management: How cops are using TikTok to distract from police brutality', *Bitch Media*, 26 July

Kaniss, P. (1991) *Making Local News*, Chicago: Chicago University Press

Karlsson, M. (2010) 'Rituals of transparency', *Journalism Studies*, 11(4): 535–45

Karlsson, M. (2011) 'The immediacy of online news, the visibility of journalistic processes and a structuring of journalistic authority', *Journalism*, 12(3): 279–95

Keane, J. (2013) *Democracy and Media Decadence*, Cambridge: Cambridge University Press

Kim, Y.-C. and Ball-Rokeach, S.J. (2006) 'Civic engagement from a communication infrastructure perspective', *Communication Theory*, 16(2): 173–97

Kleinig, J. (1996) *The Ethics of Policing*, Cambridge: Cambridge University Press

Konieczna, M. (2018) *Journalism Without Profit: Making News When the Market Fails*, New York: Oxford University Press

Kovach, B. and Rosenstiel, T. (2001) *The Elements of Journalism*, New York: Three Rivers Press

Laurie, P. (1970) *Scotland Yard: A Personal Inquiry*, London: The Bodley Head

Laville, S. (2012a) 'Police are using phone-hacking scandal to claw back control of information', *The Guardian*, 22 July

Laville, S. (2012b) 'Witness statement of Sandra Laville', provided to Leveson Inquiry, February

Lawrence, R. (2000) *The Politics of Force: Media and the Construction of Police Brutality*, Berkeley: University of California Press

Lee, M. and McGovern, A. (2014) *Policing and Media: Public Relations, Simulations and Communications*, Abingdon: Routledge

Leishman, F. and Mason, P.J. (2003) *Policing and The Media: Facts, Fictions and Factions*, Cullompton: Willan Publishing

Leveson, Lord Justice (2012a) *An Inquiry into the Culture, Practices and Ethics of the Press*, London: The Stationery Office

Leveson, Lord Justice (2012b) *An Inquiry into the Culture, Practices and Ethics of the Press, Executive Summary*, London: The Stationery Office

Lewis, P., Newburn, T., Taylor, M., Mcgillivray, C., Greenhill, A., Frayman, H. and Proctor, R. (2011) *Reading the Riots: Investigating England's Summer of Disorder*, London: The London School of Economics and Political Science and *The Guardian*

Lewis, S.C. and Usher, N. (2014) 'Code, collaboration, and the future of journalism: A case study of the hacks/hackers global network', *Digital Journalism*, 2(3): 383–93

Liebermann, J.D., Koetzle, D. and Sakiyama, M. (2013) 'Police departments' use of Facebook: Patterns and policy issues', *Policy Quarterly*, 16(4): 438–62

Loader, I. (1997) 'Policing and the social: Questions of symbolic power', *British Journal of Sociology*, 48(1): 1–18

Loader, I. and Mulcahy, A. (2003) *Policing and the Condition of England*, Oxford: Oxford University Press

Loftus, B. (2009) *Police Culture in a Changing World*, Oxford: Oxford University Press

Mann, S. and Ferenbok, J. (2013) 'New media and the power politics of sousveillance in a surveillance-dominated world', *Surveillance & Society*, 11(1/2): 18–34

Manning, P. (1997) *Police Work* (2nd edn), Prospect Heights: Waveland Press

Manning, P. (2001) 'Theorising policing: The drama and myth of crime control in the NYPD', *Theoretical Criminology*, 5(3): 315–44

Manning, P. (2003) *Policing Contingencies*, Chicago: Chicago University Press

Mark, R. (1978) *In the Office of Constable*, London: Collins and Son

Matharu, H. (2021) '"Uncomfortable conversations" need to be had about why murder of two black sisters "hardly made the news" says MP', *Byline Times*, 22 March

Mawby, R.C. (1999) 'Visibility, transparency and police-media relations', *Policing and Society*, 9(3): 263–86

Mawby, R.C. (2002a) *Policing Images: Policing, Communication and Legitimacy*, Cullompton: Willan Publishing

Mawby, R.C. (2002b) 'Continuity and change, convergence and divergence: The policy and practice of police-media relations', *Criminal Justice*, 2(3): 303–24

Mawby, R.C. (2010) 'Chibnall revisited: Crime reporters, the police and "law-and-order news"', *The British Journal of Criminology*, 50(6): 1060–76

Mawby, R.C. (2012) 'Crisis? What crisis? Some research-based reflections on police-press relations', *Policing: A Journal of Policy and Practice*, 6(3): 272–80

Mawby, R.C. (2014) 'The presentation of police in everyday life: Police-press relations, impression management and the Leveson Inquiry', *Crime, Media and Culture*, 10(3): 239–57

Mawby, R.C. (2016) 'A question of scandal? The police and the phone-hacking business', *Criminology & Criminal Justice*, 17(4): 485–502

McLaughlin, E. (2005) 'Recovering blackness/repudiating whiteness: The *Daily Mail*'s construction of the five white suspects accused of the racist murder of Stephen Lawrence', in K. Murji and J. Solomos (eds) *Racialization: Studies in Theory and Practice*, Oxford: Oxford University Press, pp 163–83

Mediatique (2018) 'Overview of recent dynamics in the UK press market', *DCMS*, April, https://secure.toolkitfiles.co.uk/clients/19826/sitedata/Reports/Press-report-for-DCMS.pdf

Meijer, A. and Thaens, M. (2013) 'Social media strategies: Understanding the differences', *Government Information Quarterly*, 30(4): 343–50

Meyers, C. (2020) 'Partisan news, the myth of objectivity, and the standards of responsible journalism', *Journal of Media Ethics*, 35(3): 180–94

Mizruchi, M.S. and Stearns, L.B. (2001) 'Getting deals done: The use of social networks in bank decision-making', *American Sociological Review*, 66(5): 647–71

Molina, M.D., Sundar, S.S., Le, T. and Lee, D. (2021) '"Fake news" is not simply false information: A concept explication and taxonomy of online content', *American Behavioral Scientist*, 65(2): 180–212

Morris, R. (2000) 'Gypsies, Travellers and the media: Press regulation and racism in the UK', *Communications Law*, 5(6): 213–19

Morrisey, B. (2003) *When Women Kill: Questions of Agency and Subjectivity*, London: Routledge

Mulligan, M. (2015) 'On ambivalence and hope in the restless search for community: How to work with the idea of community in the global age', *Sociology*, 49(2): 340–55

Muncie, J. (2001) 'The construction and deconstruction of crime', in J. Muncie and E. McLaughlin (eds) *The Problem of Crime* (2nd edn), London: Sage, pp 7–70

Myhill, A. and Bradford, B. (2012) 'Can police enhance public confidence by improving quality of service? Results from two surveys in England and Wales', *Policing and Society*, 22(4): 397–425

Napoli, P.M., Stonbely, S., McCollough, K. and Renninger, B. (2015) *Assessing the Health of Local Government Ecosystems: A Comparative Analysis of Three New Jersey Communities*, New Brunswick: Rutgers University, http://mpii.rutgers.edu/wp-content/uploads/sites/129/2015/06/Assessing-Local-Journalism_Final-Draft-6.23.15.pdf

Newburn, T. (1999) *Understanding and Preventing Police Corruption: Lessons from the Literature*, London: Home Office Policing and Reducing Crime Unit

Newburn, T. (2007) *Criminology*, Cullompton, UK: Willan Publishing

Newman, N., Fletcher, R., Kalogeropoulos, A., Levy, D.A.L. and Nielsen, R.K. (2017) *Reuters Institute Digital News Report 2017*, Oxford: Reuters Institute, University of Oxford

Obstfeld, D. (2005) 'Social networks, the *tertius iungens* orientation, and involvement in innovation', *Administrative Science Quarterly*, 50(1): 100–30

O'Connor, C.D. (2017) 'The police on Twitter: Image management, community building, and implications for policing in Canada', *Policing and Society*, 27(8): 899–912

Oldroyd, R. (2016) 'Foundations and the foundation of a new way of funding journalism', in J. Mair, T. Clark, N. Fowler, R. Snoddy and R. Tait (eds) *Last Words? How Can Journalism Survive the Decline of Print?*, Bury St Edmunds: Abramis, pp 316–20

Oldroyd, R. (2021) 'Mission-driven journalism', in H. De Burgh and P. Lashmar (eds) *Investigative Journalism* (3rd edn), Abingdon: Routledge, pp 100–10

O'Malley, P. (2009) 'Responsibilisation', in A. Wakefield and J. Fleming (eds) *The SAGE Dictionary of Policing*, London: Sage, pp 277–9

O'Neill, S. (2013) 'MP criticises Scotland Yard for failing to involve public in fight against terrorism', *The Times*, 25 May

Peplow, S. and West, E.J. (2019) 'Race, immigration, and the British media since 1945', *Immigrants & Minorities*, 37(3): 131–5

Pfohl, S. (1985) *Images of Deviance and Social Control*, New York: McGraw-Hill

Phillips, A. (2010) 'Transparency and the new ethics of journalism', *Journalism Practice*, 4(3): 373–82

Porlezza, C. and Splendore, S. (2016) 'Accountability and transparency of entrepreneurial journalism: Unresolved ethical issues in crowdfunded journalism projects', *Journalism Practice*, 10(2): 196–216

Price, J. (2017) 'Can The Ferret be a watchdog? Understanding the launch, growth and prospects of a digital, investigative journalism start-up', *Digital Journalism*, 5(10): 1336–50

Procter, R., Crump, J., Karstedt, S., Voss, A. and Cantijoch, M. (2013) 'Reading the riots: What were the police doing on Twitter?', *Policing and Society*, 23(4): 413–36

Punch, K.F. (1998) *Introduction to Social Research: Quantitative & Qualitative Approaches*, London: Sage Publications

Punch, M. (ed) (1983) *Control in the Police Organization*, Cambridge, MA: MIT Press

Punch, M. (1985) *Conduct Unbecoming: The Social Construction of Police Deviance and Control*, London: Tavistock

Ralph, L. (2021) 'The dynamic nature of police legitimacy on social media', *Policing and Society*, DOI: 10.1080/10439463.2021.1956493

Raymond, M. (2018) 'Why the police started doing "banter" on Twitter', *Vice*, 9 February

Reiner, R. (2000) *The Politics of the Police* (3rd edn), Oxford: Oxford University Press

Reiner, R. (2003) 'Policing and the media', in T. Newburn (ed) *Handbook of Policing*, Cullompton: Willan Publishing, pp 259–81

Reiner, R. (2010) *The Politics of the Police* (4th edn), New York: Oxford University Press

Reuters (2009) 'Three top economists agree 2009 worst financial crisis since Great Depression; risks increase if right steps are not taken', *Reuters*, 27 February

Richardson, A.V. (2020) *Bearing Witness While Black: African Americans, Smartphones, & the New Protest #Journalism*, New York: Oxford University Press

Richardson, J. and O'Neill, R. (2012) '"Stamp on the camps": The social construction of Gypsies and Travellers in media and political debate', in J. Richardson and A. Ryder (eds) *Gypsies and Travellers: Empowerment and Inclusion in British Society*, Bristol: Policy Press, pp 169–86

Robinson, J.G. (2019) 'The audience in the mind's eye: How journalists imagine their readers', *Columbia Journalism Review*, 26 June

Robinson, S. (2018) *Networked News, Racial Divides: How Power and Privilege Shape Public Discourse in Progressive Communities*, Cambridge: Cambridge University Press

Rock, A. (2014) '"We must go about it in our own way and have complete control": The British film industry and the Metropolitan Police Press Bureau, 1919–1938', in L. Mee and J. Walker (eds) *Cinema, Television and History: New Approaches*, Newcastle upon Tyne: Cambridge Scholars Publishing, pp 26–46

Rodan, S. and Galunic, C. (2004) 'More than network structure: How knowledge heterogeneity influences managerial performance and innovativeness', *Strategic Management Journal*, 25(6): 541–62

Rosen, J. (1999) 'The challenge of public journalism', in T.L. Glasser (ed) *The Idea of Public Journalism*, New York: Guilford Press, pp 20–48

Ross, K. (1998) 'Making race matter: An overview', in B. Franklin and D. Murphy (eds) *Making the Local News: Local Journalism in Context*, London: Routledge, pp 228–40

Rowbotham, J., Stevenson, K. and Pegg, S. (2013) *Crime News in Modern Britain: Press Reporting and Responsibility, 1820–2010*, Basingstoke: Palgrave Macmillan

Ryall, M.D. and Sorenson, O. (2007) 'Brokers and competitive advantage', *Management Science*, 53(4): 566–83

Saeed, A. (2007) 'Media, racism and Islamophobia: The representation of Islam and Muslims in the media', *Sociology Compass*, 1(2): 443–62

Sandhu, A. and Haggerty, K.D. (2017) 'Policing on camera', *Theoretical Criminology*, 21(1): 78–95

Schlesinger, P. and Tumber, H. (1994) *Reporting Crime: The Media Politics of Criminal Justice*, Oxford: Oxford University Press.

Schneider, C.J. (2016) *Policing and Social Media: Social Control in an Era of New Media*, Lanham, MD: Lexington Books

Schudson, M. (2008) *Why Democracies Need an Unlovable Press*, Cambridge: Polity

Schwendinger, H. and Schwendinger, J. (1970) 'Defenders of order or guardians of human rights?', *Issues in Criminology*, 5(2): 123–57

Seibert, S.R., Kraimer, M.L. and Liden, R.C. (2001) 'A social capital theory of career success', *Academy of Management Journal*, 44(2): 219–37

Siapera, E. and Papadopoulou, L. (2016) 'Entrepreneurialism or cooperativism? An exploration of cooperative journalism enterprises', *Journalism Practice*, 10(2): 178–95

Silverman, C. (2016) 'This analysis shows how viral fake election news stories outperformed real news on Facebook', *BuzzFeed News*, 16 November

Silverman, J. (2012) *Crime, Policy and the Media: The Shaping of Criminal Justice, 1989–2010*, Abingdon: Routledge.

Simmel, G. (1950) *The Sociology of Georg Simmel*, New York: Simon & Schuster

Simonson, J. (2016) 'Copwatching', *California Law Review*, 104(2): 391–446

Singer, J.B. (2007) 'Contested autonomy: Professional and popular claims on journalistic norms', *Journalism Studies*, 8(1): 79–95

Skogan, W.G. (2006) 'Asymmetry in the impact of encounters with police', *Policing and Society*, 16(2): 99–126

Smith, A. and Anderson, M. (2018) *Social Media Use in 2018*, Washington, DC: Pew Research Center

Soda, G. and Bizzi, L. (2012) 'Think different? An examination of network antecedents and performance consequences of creativity as deviation', *Strategic Organization*, 10(2): 99–127

Spilsbury, M. (2021) *Diversity in Journalism: An Update on the Characteristics of Journalists*, Saffron Walden: National Council for the Training of Journalists

Stearns, E. (2017a) 'MPS social media policy', *Freedom of Information Request*, 2 January

Stearns, E. (2017b) 'Media policy toolkit – Q&A's', *Freedom of Information Request*, 2 January

Stoddard, E.R. (1968) 'The informal "code" of police deviancy: A group approach to "blue-coat crime"', *The Journal of Criminal Law, Criminology, and Police Science*, 59(2): 201–13

Stonbely, S. (2017) *Comparing Models of Collaborative Journalism*, Montclair: Center for Cooperative Media, Montclair State University

Stovel, K. and Shaw, L. (2012) 'Brokerage', *Annual Review of Sociology*, 38: 139–58

Strauss, A. and Corbin, J.M. (1998) *Basics of Qualitative Research: Techniques and Procedures for Developing Grounded Theory* (2nd edn), London: Sage Publications

Sunshine, J. and Tyler T.R. (2003) 'The role of procedural justice and legitimacy in shaping public support for policing', *Law & Society Review*, 37(3): 513–48

Sutherland, E. (1949) *White Collar Crime*, New York: Dryden Press

Tifft, L. and Sullivan, D.C. (2001) 'A needs based social harm definition of crime', in S. Henry and M. Lanier (eds) *What is Crime? Controversies over the Nature of Crime and What to Do About It*, Lanham, MD: Rowman & Littlefield, pp 179–206

Turvill, W. (2015) ' "It takes two to tango": Met's PR bosses on RIPA, hacking and rebuilding "trust" with journalists', *Press Gazette*, 2 December

Tyler, T.R. (1997) 'The psychology of legitimacy: A relational perspective on voluntary deference to authorities', *Personality and Social Psychology Review*, 1(4): 323–45

Usher, N. (2016) *Interactive Journalism: Hackers, Data, and Code*, Urbana, IL: University of Illinois Press

Usher, N. (2021) *News for the Rich, White and Blue: How Place and Power Distort American Journalism*, New York: Columbia University Press

Vickers, H. (2019) 'Tory MP wants to get rid of sites and move Travellers into houses', *The Bristol Cable*, 25 February

Vickers, H. (2020) 'Why we must challenge media narratives of Travellers', *The Bristol Cable*, 20 August

Walker, M. (2021) 'U.S. newsroom employment has fallen 26% since 2008', *Pew Research Center*, 13 July

Walker, N. (1996) 'Defining core police tasks: The neglect of the symbolic dimension', *Policing and Society*, 6(1): 53–71

Ward, S.J.A. (2010) 'Inventing objectivity: New philosophical foundations', in C. Meyers (ed) *Journalism Ethics: A Philosophical Approach*, New York: Oxford University Press, pp 137–52

Wardle, C. and Derakhshan, H. (2017) *Information Disorder: Toward an Interdisciplinary Framework for Research and Policymaking*, Strasbourg: Council of Europe

Webber, E. (2019) 'Police will get powers to arrest travellers and seize caravans if they set up illegal campsites on private or public land', *MailOnline*, 3 November

Wenzel, A. (2020) *Community-Centered Journalism: Engaging People, Exploring Solutions and Building Trust*, Urbana, IL: University of Illinois Press

Westley, W. (1970) *Violence and the Police*, Cambridge, MA: MIT Press

Williams, M.L., Edwards, A., Housley, W., Burnap, P., Rana, O., Avis, N., Morgan, J. and Sloan, L. (2013) 'Policing cyber-neighbourhoods: Tension monitoring and social media networks', *Policing and Society*, 23(4): 461–81

Wilson, C.P. (2000) *Cop Knowledge: Police Power and Cultural Narrative in Twentieth Century America*, Chicago: Chicago University Press

Wolff Olins (1988) *A Force for Change: A Report on the Corporate Identity of the Metropolitan Police*, London: Wolff Olins Corporate Identity

Wood, M.A. (2019) 'Policing's "meme strategy": Understanding the rise of police social media engagement work', *Current Issues in Criminal Justice*, 32(1): 40–58

Wood, M.A. and McGovern, A. (2020) 'Memetic copaganda: Understanding the humorous turn in police image work', *Crime Media Culture*, 17(3): 305–26

Wykes, M. (2001) *News, Crime and Culture*, London: Pluto Press

Young, A. (1988) '"Wild women": The censure of the suffragette movement', *International Journal of the Sociology of Law*, 16(3): 279–93

Young, A. (1990) *Femininity in Dissent*, London: Routledge

Zedner, L. (2004) *Criminal Justice*, Oxford: Oxford University Press

Zhou, N. (2019) '"We've also addressed puppies": NZ police chided over social media posts', *The Guardian*, 13 June

Index

References to figures appear in *italic* type.
References to endnotes show both the
page number and the note number (186n1).